DATE DUE

ACTING FOR ENDANGERED SPECIES

DEVELOPMENT OF WESTERN RESOURCES

The Development of Western Resources is an interdisciplinary series focusing on the use and misuse of resources in the American West. Written for a broad readership of humanists, social scientists, and resource specialists, the books in this series emphasize both historical and contemporary perspectives as they explore the interplay between resource exploitation and economic, social, and political experiences.

John G. Clark, University of Kansas, Founding Editor
Hal K. Rothman, University of Nevada, Las Vegas, Series Editor

ACTING FOR ENDANGERED SPECIES
The Statutory Ark

Shannon Petersen

 University Press of Kansas

3-20-2003
WW
+ 29.95

Published by the University Press of Kansas (Lawrence, Kansas 66049), which was
organized by the Kansas Board of Regents and is operated and funded by Emporia State
University, Fort Hays State University, Kansas State University, Pittsburg State University,
the University of Kansas, and Wichita State University.

Library of Congress Cataloging-in-Publication Data

Petersen, Shannon C.
    Acting for endangered species : the statutory ark / Shannon C. Petersen.
        p. cm. — (Development of western resources)
    Includes index.
        ISBN 0-7006-1172-X (hbk. : alk. paper)
    1. Endangered species—Law and legislation—United States.
I. Title.
II. Series.
    KF5640.P48 2002
    346.7304'69522—dc21
                        2001007417

British Library Cataloguing in Publication Data is available.

Printed in the United States of America
10 9 8 7 6 5 4 3 2 1

The paper used in this publication meets the minimum requirements of the American
National Standard for Permanence of Paper for Printed Library Materials Z39.48-1984.

For Zanette,
with whom I wish to spend the remainder of my days.

Contents

Introduction

Today, the Endangered Species Act of 1973 (ESA) stands among the strongest of environmental laws.[1] Former Secretary of the Interior Bruce Babbitt has described it as "undeniably the most innovative, wide-reaching, and successful environmental law" in recent U.S. history.[2] The U.S. Supreme Court has called it "the most comprehensive legislation for the preservation of endangered species ever enacted by any nation."[3] Because its link to the protection of human health and quality of life is the most tenuous among environmental laws, historian Roderick Nash has called the ESA the strongest American legal expression to date of environmental ethics.[4] Although the ESA may be the "crown jewel of the nation's environmental laws," it has also been the "pit bull of environmental laws."[5]

The power of the ESA rests primarily in three of its sections: Section 4, Section 7, and Section 9. Together, these sections form the substantive foundation of the act and the source of most of its controversy today. The ESA also includes a citizen suit provision that has served as a powerful tool for environmental groups to enforce and expand the powers of Sections 4, 7, and 9.[6] Indeed, litigation has played a crucial role in broadening the scope of the act and provoking controversy. Although many other sections of the ESA provide significant protection for species, these three are the most important.

Section 4 instructs the secretaries of the interior and commerce to list species as either threatened or endangered based solely on the best scientific data available.[7] The secretary of the interior, responsible for avian, terrestrial, and freshwater species, has delegated this power to the Fish and Wildlife Service (FWS), while the secretary of commerce, responsible for marine and anadromous species, has delegated this power to the National Marine Fisheries Service (NMFS). The ESA defines "species" to include subspecies of fish, wildlife, and plants and distinct population segments of vertebrate fish and wildlife that interbreed when mature.[8] Endangered species are those in danger of extinction throughout all or a significant portion of their range, while threatened species are those likely to become endangered in the near future.[9] Species eligible for listing include all plants, mammals, fish, birds, amphibians, reptiles, mollusks, crustaceans, arthropods, or other invertebrates.[10] Most important, Section 4 prohibits any consideration of economic factors when determining whether or not to list a species.

Labeled "Interagency Cooperation," Section 7 commands federal agencies to consult with FWS or NMFS before taking any action that might jeopardize a listed species. Specifically, it directs all federal agencies to consult with the secretary to ensure that "any action authorized, funded, or carried out by such agency . . . is not likely to jeopardize the continued existence of any endangered species or threatened species."[11] Originally only a couple of lines long, this section has since expanded to several pages beginning with a series of amendments in the late 1970s. In a landmark decision in 1978, the U.S. Supreme Court interpreted Section 7 as an absolute bar on any federal action that FWS or NMFS determines would jeopardize a listed species. This decision transformed Section 7 into a powerful substantive limit on all development projects authorized, funded, or carried out by the federal government.

Section 9 prohibits the taking of endangered species.[12] As defined in the ESA, the term "take" means "to harass, harm, pursue, hunt, shoot, wound, kill, trap, capture, or collect, or to attempt to engage in any such conduct."[13] In 1975, the secretary of the interior issued a regulation interpreting "harm" to include any activity resulting in environmental modification or degradation of a listed species' habitat that would kill or injure the species.[14] Theoretically, under this definition the ESA may limit land use activities on private property that might indirectly harm a listed species, making Section 9 of the ESA "perhaps the most powerful regulatory provision in all of environmental law."[15] Federal courts have consistently upheld this broad interpretation of Section 9.[16]

The ESA's very strength, however, threatens its future. In particular, two great controversies have eroded political support for the law—the snail darter controversy during the late 1970s and the northern spotted owl controversy during the early 1990s. In the wake of the spotted owl crisis, the nation elected a conservative Congress that pledged to "rethink, not repair," environmental laws. This Congress targeted the ESA especially, with House Speaker Newt Gingrich stating that it made little sense to spend money on species protection because extinction is "the way life is."[17] Attempts to repeal or weaken the ESA during the 1990s did not succeed, but Congress deadlocked over the legislation during that decade, failing to amend or reauthorize appropriations for the act.[18]

When Congress passed the ESA in 1973, it did so nearly unanimously, without significant discussion or debate. *Acting for Endangered Species* explains how and why the act eventually became so controversial. It describes the early history of wildlife protection in this country, followed by an examination of what Congress intended when it passed the ESA and what President Nixon intended when he signed it into law. Most important, *Acting for Endangered Species* analyzes how environmentalists aggressively used the ESA in court not only to expand the scope and power of the act itself but also as a tool to achieve other environmental goals. After the passage of the legislation, the history of the ESA is largely one of environmental and judicial activism followed by congressional and administrative reaction designed primarily to limit the scope of legal decisions regarding the law.

Such has been the case not only with the ESA but also with most of the nation's environmental laws. Since the late 1970s, litigation and judicial decisionmaking have driven environmental policy in this country more than legislation and administrative rulemaking. The history of the ESA provides just one example of how environmentalists, their lawyers, and the judiciary have shaped the environmental movement in recent decades. Although others have written about the emergence of modern environmentalism, most have overlooked or underemphasized the role of the courts in that movement.

The courts, of course, have not played an all-important role in shaping the modern environmental movement. Their policymaking ability is constrained by the Constitution, by the literal language of the law, and by the parties who choose, or choose not, to bring cases to court. Nevertheless, as the history of the ESA reveals, the courts can and do make policy; they have profoundly shaped endangered species (and environmental) policy during the last decades of the twentieth century. In doing so, the courts have also created great controversy by fueling legislative and administrative backlash and by contributing to organized opposition to the ESA and other environmental laws. At a minimum, the courts deserve more attention from historians than they have received.

This book is divided into three parts and six chapters. The first part, "Legislating Salvation," traces federal legislative efforts to protect endangered species from the late nineteenth century to 1973. Chapter 1, "Bison to Bald Eagles," begins with the failed congressional attempts to protect the American bison during the late nineteenth century and concludes with efforts to protect the bald eagle in the 1950s. Aside from providing a mere chronology of federal wildlife law, Chapter 1 attempts to describe the larger scientific and political contexts of endangered species preservation. Specifically, it traces the influence of changes in scientific understanding on the politics of species preservation. Chapter 1 also describes emerging federal wildlife law as part of the general growth of the federal government in the first half of the twentieth century. In particular, it tracks a series of expansive judicial interpretations of the U.S. Constitution justifying the federal government's usurpation of traditional state power to regulate wildlife. In these ways, Chapter 1 provides the necessary background for understanding the ESA itself.

Chapter 2, "Congress and Charismatic Megafauna," begins with the emergence of the environmental movement during the 1960s and concludes with the passage of the ESA in 1973. Aside from positioning the ESA within the environmental movement, Chapter 2 attempts to explain what Congress and President Nixon intended when they enacted the law. Most individuals in Congress and the Nixon administration believed the ESA to be a largely symbolic effort to protect charismatic megafauna representative of our national heritage, like bald eagles, bison, and grizzly bears. Congress thought it could protect such species simply by prohibiting their direct killing and by halting the international trade of the species themselves and of their products. Few if any believed at the time that the ESA would protect seemingly insignificant species irrespective of economic considerations, halt federal development projects, and regulate private property.

Parts two and three of the book track the two most important controversies over the ESA—the snail darter and spotted owl disputes. Generally, this portion of the book shows how environmentalists used the courts to enforce the ESA, expand the act's scope, and achieve other environmental goals. These parts also examine how Congress and the administration responded to judicial decisions. Both controversies are situated within their larger political and social contexts; in particular, both are analyzed within the changing landscape of scientific understanding.

Part two traces the snail darter controversy. Chapter 3, "The Fish That Stopped a Dam," culminates in the decision of *Tennessee Valley Authority v. Hill*. In that case, the Supreme Court halted the completion of Tellico Dam on the Little Tennessee River to protect the endangered snail darter, a small fish, and by doing so dramatically expanded the meaning of Section 7 of the ESA.[19] Chapter 4, "Dammed Fish," describes congressional and administrative reaction to the Court's decision. Congress amended the ESA to create an exemption process from the requirements of Section 7 and granted Tellico Dam a direct legislative exemption from the law. The snail darter controversy also made the administration more reluctant to list obscure species when such a listing might potentially affect economic development.

Over a decade later, this administrative hesitancy contributed to the spotted owl crisis, which is examined in part three. Chapter 5, "Spotty Wisdom," depicts the emergence of the controversy as environmentalists sued to force a hostile administration to protect the spotted owl. It concludes with the federal court decision ordering the listing of the owl as threatened under the ESA. Chapter 6, "Giving a Hoot," describes the administrative and legislative responses to this ruling and to a series of other court decisions enjoining virtually all timber sales on old-growth forests in the Pacific Northwest pending an acceptable administrative plan to protect the owl. Eventually, the newly elected Clinton administration drafted and implemented such a plan. The owl controversy, however, died slowly. It created many enemies for the ESA, threatening the act's future at the turn of the twenty-first century.

Without the assistance and guidance of the following scholars, this book would not have been possible: Arthur McEvoy, William Cronon, Stanley Kutler, Lawrence Friedman, Barton Thompson, Daniel Flores, and Meg Caldwell. Without the love and support of my parents, James and Cathering Petersen, nothing would have been possible, including this book. Finally, I am indebted to the staff of the University Press of Kansas.

PART I: LEGISLATING SALVATION

CHAPTER ONE

Bison to Bald Eagles

In 1859, Charles Darwin described extinction as the unavoidable consequence of the struggle among the species. Eventually, "rare species will be . . . beaten in the race for life" by stronger species.[1] Darwin was writing about evolution generally, not about the human-caused extirpation of many of the world's plants and wildlife. Many Americans in the late nineteenth century, however, interpreted his work as scientific justification for human-caused extinction. For them, the loss of wildlife was a tragic but inevitable cost of progress.

Nevertheless, there were some who sought to protect certain species from the fate of the dinosaur and giant sloth. Mostly they did this for self-serving reasons. Prior to the Endangered Species Act of 1973, Americans deemed three kinds of species worthy of legislative protection: game species, "industrial" species (like commercial fish and furbearers that provided the raw materials for certain American industries), and a few species of charismatic megafauna representative of the national heritage (these included bison, bald eagles, and blue whales).

Before the ESA, the federal government played a minor role in the protection of wildlife. Indeed, the federal government did not pass wildlife legislation until the second half of the nineteenth century. Throughout the twentieth century, however, the federal government gradually asserted its power to regulate wildlife, often at the expense of state authority. Thus, wildlife law up to and including deliberation over the ESA became a battleground between those who believed species required national protection and those who wished to preserve states' rights. This battle was fought largely in courtrooms.

The story of species protection prior to the ESA also reflects broader trends in science and politics from the nineteenth century through the twentieth century. To begin with, wildlife law stemmed from a new awareness that certain species were in danger of going extinct without some form of protection. Eventually, the emergence of ecology provided further justification for protecting all species, not just those with obvious value. In addition, wildlife policy developed within the larger contexts of the conservation and environmental movements. The history of wildlife law up to the ESA, therefore, encapsulates a complex interaction of science, politics, and the law.

The United States inherited a legacy of wildlife regulation from colonial government. As early as 1694, the Massachusetts Bay Colony imposed the first closed hunting season in North America. It applied to all deer within the colony. In 1708, certain New York counties established closed seasons on the heath hen, grouse, quail, and turkey.[2] In the seventeenth and eighteenth centuries especially, the colonists hunted not only for sport but for subsistence. In many regions along the eastern seaboard, hunting rapidly depleted the most popular game species.

Following colonial rule, the various states continued to promulgate wildlife laws, primarily to protect game species. In 1842, the U.S. Supreme Court authorized such state regulation in the case of *Martin v. Waddell,* where it held that the states inherited the "prerogatives and regalities" of the Crown and Parliament.[3] Specifically, the Court referred to the power of the king, and now the states, to regulate lands, waters, and presumably wildlife held within the "public trust."[4] Initially, this holding applied only to the original thirteen states. Three years later, however, in *Pollard v. Hagan,* the Supreme Court extended the public trust doctrine to all states admitted into the nation.[5]

During the nineteenth century, conflict between state and federal wildlife law was minimal because little federal wildlife law existed. Mostly, the federal government avoided intruding on state prerogatives by regulating only those species of wildlife living within federal lands outside of state jurisdiction. The federal government did this under the authority of the property clause of the Constitution: "Congress shall have Power to dispose of and make all needful Rules and Regulations respecting the Territory or other Property belonging to the United States."[6] In 1868, Congress passed a law prohibiting the killing of certain fur-bearing animals in the territory of Alaska.[7] Three years later, it created the Office of the U.S. Commissioner of Fish and Fisheries to conserve fisheries along the coasts and navigable waterways.[8] Congress also took indirect steps to secure wildlife habitat when it passed the Forest Reserve Act of 1891, which authorized the president to establish national forests out of the public domain to protect timber, water, and wildlife resources from overexploitation.[9] By the end of the nineteenth century, the federal government had begun to regulate wildlife living within the vast federal lands of the American West.

On the few occasions that federal actions or claims conflicted with state wildlife regulations during the nineteenth century, the courts generally favored the states. For example, in 1855 the Supreme Court examined a Maryland law that regulated the taking of oysters from the state's waters in *Smith v. Maryland.* The defendant shipowner violated the state law but argued in his defense that because he was licensed by the United States to engage in coastal trade, he was protected from state regulation by the interstate commerce clause of the U.S. Constitution.[10] In this way, the facts of the case resembled those of the landmark case *Gibbons v. Og-den*, where the Supreme Court held that the interstate commerce clause preempted state regulation.[11] In *Smith v. Maryland*, however, the Court held that state regulation of wildlife, even on navigable waterways, did not interfere with the exclusive federal power to regulate interstate commerce.[12]

The Court's judgment protected the exclusive right of the states to regulate fish and wildlife even as it relied generally on the commerce clause to support the rapid growth of federal regulatory power during the nineteenth century.[13] The Court justified its ruling in *Smith v. Maryland* by analogizing Maryland's oyster regulation with state quarantine and health laws, which were traditional exceptions to the dormant commerce clause recognized by the Court in *Gibbons v. Ogden*.[14] The Court found state wildlife laws immune from dormant commerce clause claims because of the states' traditional power to protect the resources of state land and water held in public trust.[15] In 1876, the Court went even further by declaring that the states actually owned the fish and wildlife resources of public trust lands and waters. Accordingly, a state could regulate its fish and wildlife as it would regulate any other "common property."[16]

Supported by these rulings, during the late nineteenth century the states continued to promulgate fish and game laws to protect the food supply and the interests of sport hunters. Yet, the states either could not or would not do anything about the rapid disappearance of the bison from the Great Plains during the 1870s, primarily because most of the region remained territories of the United States not yet organized and admitted as states. Those states that did support bison populations during the 1870s—Kansas, Nebraska, Texas, and Colorado—did nothing to protect the bison until it was too late. Indeed, the Texas Legislature rejected outright a bill to impose a closed hunting season because of the belief that eradicating the bison would facilitate the pacification and removal of hostile Indian tribes. Colorado and Kansas adopted closed seasons on buffalo hunting in 1875, but not until there were only a few bison remaining within their borders.[17] In the absence of state action, many Americans began to call on the U.S. Congress to protect the American bison.

The story of the bison is significant to the history of endangered species protection for several reasons. First, the bison's fate illustrates how quickly one species could be driven to the brink of extinction by the forces of modernization, including westward expansion and settlement, the introduction of competing species like cattle, and the gruesome efficiency of market hunting. Second, the bison's plight provoked the first federal effort to protect a particular species. Finally, efforts to protect the bison were motivated more by a desire to preserve a symbol of the nation's heritage than to conserve a resource for sport or market hunters. In these ways, congressional attempts to protect the bison during the 1870s foreshadowed the growing role of the federal government in wildlife law during the twentieth century.

Bison once numbered about twenty-five million on the Great Plains.[18] As late as 1871, observers described the bison as ranging in "countless herds."[19] At about this same time, however, market hunting for buffalo hides began in earnest, facilitated by the expansion of the railroad. These hides were used primarily to make leather machine belts crucial to the factories of the east. Bison were also killed for sport and, to a lesser degree, for meat. In 1871, a *New York Times* reporter asked a buffalo hunter, "Will you not in time exterminate these animals?" He replied, "It is impossible; they are as countless as the blades of grass on the plains, and though thousands are slaughtered, there seems to be no dimmution [sic] of numbers. . . . It will take a hundred years, almost, to make them scarce, for their range of country is so immense."[20]

Yet, just a year later, the *New York Times* reported that the "enormous slaughter" of the American bison was rapidly leading to that animal's disappearance on the Great Plains.[21] With the disappearance of the bison came a reassessment of the bison hunter. In 1871, the newspaper had described the buffalo hunter as a "brave, wild set, true frontiersmen, making their money easily, and spending it freely."[22] In 1872, however, the *Times* wrote: "There is as much honor and danger in killing a Texas steer as there is in killing a buffalo. . . . It would be equally as good sport, and equally as dangerous, to ride into a herd of tame cattle and commence shooting indiscriminately."[23] The newspaper described the killing of the bison as "wanton" and as a "wholesale butchery" that was as "needless as it is cruel,"[24] concluding by urging its readers to lobby Congress to protect the animal.

In 1874, Congress passed a bill to save the bison from extermination. The bill made it unlawful for any non-Indian to kill or wound any female buffalo found within the territories of the United States. A second provision of the bill prohibited any person from killing or wounding any greater number of male buffalo than was needed for food or that could be used, cured, or preserved for food or for the market.[25] Violators were subject to a one hundred dollar fine for each buffalo killed or injured. Second-time offenders could also face up to thirty days in jail.

Although the Senate passed the bill without debate, the House split over several points. Those who supported the bill argued that the bison required conservation because it was a vital food source for both Indians and white settlers. They also emphasized that buffalo hides and other body parts provided raw materials necessary for industrial expansion. Some simply argued that the bison was "noble game" worthy of protection from "reckless slaughter."[26] One congressman concluded that national legislation was required because the bison was a migratory animal, moving from state to state and through the territories so that no one state could regulate its protection.[27]

Many in the House, however, opposed the bill. Some argued that the buffalo should not be protected because it roamed about wild, competing with domestic livestock for pasture. One congressman complained that bison were "as uncivilized as the Indian."[28] Most opponents objected to the bill because protecting bison would mean protecting the seminomadic, hunting lifestyles of the Plains Indians, thus interfering with their pacification and "civilization."[29] Finally, some in Congress believed that the law would be useless because the eradication of the buffalo was the inevitable price of westward expansion and settlement.

Nevertheless, the bill passed the House and proceeded to President Grant for his signature. Grant, however, refused to sign the bill into law, and it died as a result of his pocket veto. It is difficult to determine exactly why President Grant opposed protecting the bison, as no record exists giving his reasons. It is probable that he agreed with his secretary of the interior, Columbus Delano, and with the members of Congress who spoke out against the bill during congressional deliberations. In his annual report for 1872, Delano wrote that the destruction of bison and other game on the Great Plains forced the Indians "toward industrial pursuits and peaceful habits" on the reservations.[30] For President Grant, protecting the bison would likely exacerbate the Indian problem.

In 1876, Congress again considered legislation to protect the bison; it was identical to the bill considered four years earlier. The only difference was that in the intervening years the number of bison left on the plains had plummeted even further to where only "hundreds" remained.[31] To many in Congress, this decline provided all the more reason to protect the few remaining herds. To others, it merely indicated that the annihilation of the buffalo was "predestinated [sic] . . . a necessity to the successful cultivation of the soil of the western Territories."[32] Despite the rapidly dwindling numbers of bison, the essential arguments for and against protecting the animal remained similar to what they had been in 1872. In February 1876, the House passed the bill 104 votes to 36.

The Senate version of the bill, however, never made it through committee. Again, it is difficult to ascertain why, with any certainty, because of the lack of record, but it is probable that the Indian question again played an important role. During the House deliberations, many agreed with the opinion of Congressman Throckmorton that "for the civilization of the Indian and the preservation of peace on our borders the more buffaloes are exterminated the better it will be for our country."[33] Senate support for the bill probably died on June 25, 1876, along with General

George Armstrong Custer and 264 soldiers from the 7th Cavalry. The Battle of the Little Bighorn shocked the nation, reminding it that Indian resistance to westward expansion was not yet a thing of the past. As a result, Congress and the administration never enacted a prohibition on the killing of bison.

In any case, protection for free-roaming herds of bison on the Great Plains soon became moot. In 1883, the *New York Times* reported that the appearance of a single buffalo in the northern plains was an exceedingly rare occurrence, when just ten years earlier the buffalo were as numerous as cattle.[34] Just one year later, the *Times* reported that the "noble bison" was on the "eve of final extinction."[35] At the end of the century, William T. Hornaday, superintendent for the National Zoological Park in New York, lamented the "wanton destruction of a valuable beast, purely and distinctly American in its character."[36] He estimated that only eighty-six bison remained in the United States.

Eventually, federal protection for the bison came not from laws prohibiting their taking, but from the creation of preserves and parks. The establishment of Yellowstone National Park in 1894, for example, provided crucial habitat for the few remaining bison, preventing their complete extinction in the United States.[37] In 1907, Hornaday called for the expansion of federal and state reserves where bison could range unmolested and free. He argued that the federal government should take measures to rehabilitate bison populations for two reasons. First, he wrote that the extinction of the "grandest bovine animal of our time," whose history is "interwoven with the history of our westward course of empire, would be a National disgrace and calamity."[38] He also argued that crossbreeding healthy bison populations with cattle would result in superior meats and hides. The next year, in 1908, Congress created a National Bison Range in Montana.[39]

In 1896, the same year Hornaday observed that only eighty-six bison remained in the United States, nineteenth-century wildlife law jurisprudence culminated in the Supreme Court case of *Geer v. Connecticut*.[40] In that case, the defendant Geer appealed his conviction under a Connecticut law, which forbade the out-of-state transport of game birds taken within the state. Again the Court considered whether a state law improperly interfered with the interstate commerce clause, and again the Court found that it did not. In reaching this decision, the Court held that states have the "undoubted authority to control the taking and use of that which belonged to no one in particular but was common to all."[41] In effect, the Court held that states "own" the wildlife, which they hold in public trust.[42] The Court concluded that because this "common ownership imports the right to keep the property . . . always within its jurisdiction for every purpose," state fish and game laws do not interfere with the interstate commerce clause.[43]

Almost as soon as the courts articulated this state ownership doctrine, however, it began to erode. The first significant direct step toward national wildlife regulation came when Congress passed the Lacey Act of 1900. The act's sponsor, Representative John Lacey (R-IA), believed that the states alone could not prevent species extinction, but that national action was required.[44] The legislation relied on the commerce clause to make it a federal crime to transport in interstate commerce wild animals, birds, or their products killed in violation of state law.[45] The Supreme Court never addressed the constitutionality of the Lacey Act, but the few lower courts that did confront the issue upheld the law as a permissible exercise of the commerce power.[46] The law did not preempt state wildlife regulation, but it did mark the first significant foray of the federal government into wildlife protection.[47]

The Lacey Act can best be understood as part of a package of federal legislation embraced by progressive conservationists around the turn of the twentieth century. Progressive conservationists were utilitarian; they believed that the nation's natural resources, including wildlife, needed to be managed to achieve the greatest good for the greatest number of Americans. Progressive conservationists had faith in science, efficiency, and expert management through government agencies.[48] Eventually, many came to believe that federal management would produce better science and be more efficient than state management. In contrast to preservationists, progressive conservationists advocated the efficient development of the nation's resources. They wanted to conserve wildlife for use by sport hunters and market interests, not merely preserve wildlife from extinction.

No one better represented national progressive conservationism than Theodore Roosevelt, who became president in 1901 after an assassin's bullet ended the presidency of William McKinley. A founding member of the Boone and Crockett Club, an exclusive hunting club with powerful members, Roosevelt cared deeply and vigorously about the fate of wildlife. In 1903, he created the first national refuge explicitly for the protection of wildlife on Florida's Pelican Island. Sport hunters also began to call for the expansion of forest reserves to protect the habitat of game mammals, birds, and fishes.[49] For this and other reasons, Roosevelt more than doubled the acreage of national forest reserves, renamed national forests in 1907, before Congress withdrew his power to do so.[50] He contributed greatly to wildlife conservation through the preservation of habitat.

Progressive conservationists also took more direct steps to protect endangered wildlife. In particular, they believed that federal law would best defend the dwindling populations of migratory birds, which fell prey not only to sport hunters but also to market hunters harvesting feathers to appease Victorian fashion. In 1905, for example, a *New York*

Times article blamed the extermination of the snowy heron and the American egret on the feathered hats favored by women.[51] Gender, it seemed— whether manly sport hunting or feminine fashion—affected how and why species became depleted. New York State attempted to halt the feather trade by passing a law in 1906 prohibiting the possession of plumage of certain wild birds with the intent to sell them.[52] Scattered state and local laws, however, did little to protect migratory species of birds, which ranged thousands of miles in the course of a year.

Moreover, state action often came too little and too late. In Massachusetts, the chairman of the Fisheries and Game Commission approached the state legislature for emergency funds to protect the heath hen from "total extinction." By that time, the few hens remaining in the state were confined solely to the island of Martha's Vineyard. Their numbers were so reduced that the commissioner wanted the money so that he could buy artificial incubators.[53] The states eventually recognized the necessity of federal legislation to protect migratory birds from extinction.[54]

Scientists also argued for a national law. William Hornaday, for example, expanded his crusade for the bison to include other species that might benefit from federal protection. In 1911, he wrote to a *New York Times* audience, lamenting the extinction of the Carolina parakeet. He warned that unless drastic national measures were taken, the whooping crane, the trumpeter swan, the great sage grouse, and the prairie sharp-tailed grouse would all become extinct.

In making such arguments, conservationists like Hornaday often appealed to the darker side of progressivism by blaming America's wildlife problems on immigrants. The conservationists believed that market hunters were primarily poor immigrants who did not respect or honor the sport hunter's ethic. For example, Hornaday blamed the decimation of songbirds in New York on Italians. He warned that unless the federal government did something now, America's great-grandchildren "will find the United States as barren of wild life as Italy is to-day."[55]

Proponents supported a federal law to protect migratory birds for several reasons. First, scientists like Hornaday seemed to agree that a national law was necessary to protect species that migrate as far and wide as bird species do. Second, progressive conservationists had faith in the power of the federal government to enforce game laws where states could not. For example, one conservationist wrote to the *New York Times* that "those who have made a joke of local game laws may think twice before they try their jokes on the Federal Government, with its unequaled power of detection and apprehension and its inexorable justice for wanton offenders."[56] Others, like William Haskell, counsel for the American Game Protective Association, wrote that not only was a national law necessary to protect birds, but it also would be a legitimate function of the federal government under the interstate commerce clause. He noted how courts had increasingly recognized the prerogative of the federal government to regulate all matters related to interstate commerce, even if doing so imposed on traditional state concerns like the regulation of wildlife.[57]

The fate of the passenger pigeon provided another argument for the enactment of a national law protecting migratory birds. In 1914, the last passenger pigeon died in a zoo in Cincinnati. At one time, flocks of these birds covered American skies in the hundreds of thousands. Indeed, scientists believe that no other species of bird ever approached the passenger pigeon in numbers. Estimates of their peak population range to three billion, at one time constituting 25 to 40 percent of the total bird population of the United States. Yet, within a relatively short period, human hunting and habitat modification caused the passenger pigeon population to crash to a point where it could no longer recover. Various state laws passed during the late nineteenth century to protect the bird proved woefully ineffective.[58]

For all of these reasons, in 1916 the federal government stepped in to protect migratory birds. It did so first by making a treaty with Canada, known as the Convention for the Protection of Migratory Birds. In signing this treaty, the federal government recognized the national and international scope of the species extinction crisis.[59] Two years later, Congress ratified this treaty with the Migratory Bird Treaty Act of 1918.[60] The act made it a federal offense to capture, kill, possess, purchase, sell, barter, or transport any bird protected by the treaty except as permitted by regulation of the secretary of the interior.[61] While earlier federal action had relied on the commerce clause or the power to regulate the public domain, the effort to protect migratory birds from extinction rested on the treaty-making power of the Constitution.[62]

The state of Missouri promptly challenged the constitutionality of the new law, claiming that the Tenth Amendment, which reserved for the states powers not specifically delegated to the federal government, prevented federal regulation of wildlife. Missouri also argued that the state ownership doctrine granted states the exclusive right to regulate in this area.[63] In the landmark decision of *Missouri v. Holland,* however, the Supreme Court upheld the act as a valid exercise of the federal treaty-making power. Moreover, it rejected outright the contention that the state ownership doctrine precluded federal regulation.[64] This decision paved the way for further federal action. In 1929, the Migratory Bird Conservation Act supplemented the "take" prohibition of the Migratory Bird Treaty Act by authorizing the secretary of the interior to acquire and establish bird refuges within the public domain.[65]

During the first two decades of the twentieth century, progressive conservationists remained remarkably united in blaming market hunters for species depletion and praising sport hunters for species conservation. Beginning noticeably in the 1920s, though, certain organizations and prominent conservationists began to criticize sport hunters. In 1920, for example, the Long Island Fish and Game Protective Association formed to protest game laws that they believed were interpreted for the benefit of clubs of wealthy sportsmen rather than for residents of Long Island.[66] As game laws became more restrictive, especially those regarding migratory birds, many sport hunters and their organizations began to chafe.[67] In 1925, Hornaday argued that the growing number of extinct and endangered species proved that America's six million sport hunters could not regulate themselves.[68] A *New York Times* article that same year admonished that "wise sportsmen" should support federal laws like the Migratory Bird Treaty Act.[69]

The onset of the Great Depression in 1929 posed even more serious problems for species conservation. The New York State Conservation Department reported that poaching had increased in the state due to the economic hardship brought about by the Depression.[70] In addition, the drought that turned much of the American West into a dust bowl also significantly reduced waterfowl habitat throughout the country, requiring emergency regulations to shorten the hunting season to avoid the "calamity of extermination."[71] At the Seventeenth Annual American Game Conference, President Hoover declared that "along with the industrial and farming crisis, this country was also facing a fish and game crisis." He said that the duress of the Depression should not hinder greater efforts to protect and propagate "useful" wildlife.[72] Despite the rhetoric, the Hoover administration did little to expand the scope of federal wildlife law.

As in many other areas, New Dealers significantly extended federal involvement in species protection. In 1932, Congress created a Special Committee on Conservation of Wildlife Resources to investigate and coordinate all federal efforts to conserve wildlife. During the hearings of this committee in 1934, Jay Darling, chief of the Bureau of Biological Survey, reported that the most pressing problem in wildlife conservation remained the restoration of migratory waterfowl. He testified that despite the Migratory Bird Treaty Act, the migratory waterfowl population in the United States had plummeted more than 75 percent since 1910.[73] He argued that the federal government needed to do more to protect wildlife and assured the chairman of the committee that federal efforts would not necessarily usurp states' rights.[74]

Darling also informed Congress about the history and role of the Bureau of Biological Survey in species protection. The bureau was first organized in 1885 within the Department of Agriculture as the Division of Economic Ornithology and Mammalogy. In 1896, the name changed to the

Division of Biological Survey and in 1905 to the Bureau of Biological Survey. Darling described how at first it was purely a scientific, investigatory agency, but that in recent decades it had become the lead federal agency for wildlife conservation (and for the extermination of predatory and "other undesirable species").[75] In 1934, the Biological Survey administered 2.6 million acres of wildlife sanctuary, not including lands in Alaska.

Representatives from other federal natural resource agencies also testified at the hearing. Arno Cammerer, the director of the National Park Service, urged Congress to protect several species of furbearers, including the wolf, wolverine, badger, otter, and fisher, to prevent their otherwise likely extermination.[76] Ironically, at the same time the Bureau of Biological Survey was actively engaged in the destruction of several of these species as part of its mission to control predators for the sake of the livestock industry. A representative of the U.S. Forest Service also urged Congress to extend federal protection for wildlife. According to the Forest Service, wildlife should be protected because of its growing recreational value and for economic reasons associated with outdoor recreation.[77]

During the same month of these hearings, Congress passed the Fish and Wildlife Coordination Act.[78] For the first time ever, this law recognized that industrialization threatened habitat and directed the secretary of the interior to investigate the effects of domestic sewage, trade wastes, and other polluting substances on wildlife. The act, foreshadowing Section 7 of the ESA, encouraged dam-building agencies to consult with the Bureau of Fisheries about the potential impact on fish before a dam would be built.[79] The strictly procedural and voluntary nature of these two provisions, however, made them weak. Nevertheless, the law at least acknowledged the connection between indirect habitat degradation and wildlife health.

The Fish and Wildlife Coordination Act also proposed that federal lands be set aside to protect wildlife habitat.[80] This third provision realized some success through the expansion of national forest reserves, national wildlife refuges, and the national park system during the 1930s. In particular, the passage of the Migratory Bird Hunt Stamp Act in 1934, popularly known as the Duck Stamp Act, led to the dramatic expansion of the national wildlife refuge system. The Stamp Act required waterfowl hunters to purchase stamps from the federal government as licenses to hunt. The money generated from stamps went directly toward the acquisition of waterfowl habitat, which the federal government then protected as a wildlife refuge.

At the beginning of his second term in office, President Franklin Roosevelt renewed his administration's commitment to fish and game conservation by pledging new legislative efforts to protect wildlife.[81] To this end, in 1936 President Roosevelt convened the North American Wildlife

Conference, attended by state and federal agencies, private interest groups, and representatives from Canada and Mexico. The chairman of the conference and the chief of the U.S. Forest Service, F. A. Silcox, argued that wildlife should be protected for scientific, aesthetic, spiritual, and recreational reasons.[82] Even more significant, Ben Thompson from the National Park Service led a session on the "Problem of Vanishing Species."[83] The session revealed the increasing interest of the federal government in taking measures to prevent the ultimate extinction of species, even when these species were already so depleted that they no longer provided a sport or industrial resource. Moreover, the session provided further evidence that the National Park Service took an early leadership role in trying to prevent species extinction.

The North American Wildlife Conference inspired further congressional action. Early in 1937, the Special Committee on the Conservation of Wildlife Resources requested that the Bureau of Biological Survey prepare a report on its past, current, and future plans to protect wildlife. The committee thought the report would provide them with information upon which to base further wildlife conservation legislation.

The report itself revealed how the Bureau of Biological Survey in the late 1930s perceived the extinction crisis and what it thought its role should be in addressing the problem. First, the bureau believed that game species should be managed like a crop, "for game is a crop—a product of the land that can be grown like wheat, corn, or tobacco."[84] Second, it blamed the depletion of waterfowl, bison, elk, wild turkeys, bear, beaver, and other species primarily on "the white man's gun" rather than habitat degradation or other indirect causes.[85] Finally, the bureau envisioned a minor role for itself in preventing species extinction because it believed that it had jurisdiction only over those species found on federal lands. It saw its primary role as managing federal bird and wildlife refuges and providing states with scientific information about the status of endangered species.

In 1938, Jay Darling, the former chief of the Bureau of Biological Survey and then president of the General Wildlife Federation, testified before Congress about what it could do to protect wildlife. Specifically, he described several areas where the federal government had not taken action to conserve wildlife, lamenting the absence of any agency of the U.S. government empowered to protect wildlife species against "total extermination."[86] He recommended that the Bureau of Biological Survey be given adequate authority to take such action as may be necessary to prevent the extinction of all "valuable" wildlife species.[87] For Darling and most conservationists at the time, "valuable" species included migratory birds, game species, furbearers, and game and commercial species of fish. Nevertheless, explicit concern for species extinction, rather than just general fish and game conservation, eventually led to greater federal involvement in national wildlife law.

Change came slowly. In 1939, the Bureau of Biological Survey reported modest new initiatives in providing aid to the states, acquiring additional land and establishing more wildlife refuges, and implementing more intensive game management.[88] The bureau also testified on its use of the Civilian Conservation Corps to create suitable habitat for waterfowl by building dikes, dams, and other water control structures.[89] In 1940, Congress transferred the Bureau of Biological Survey from the Department of Agriculture to the Department of the Interior, where the agency was renamed the U.S. Fish and Wildlife Service. The transfer represented a reevaluation of the idea that wildlife species should be treated as crops. In addition, the change in names revealed that the agency would no longer be simply a scientific agency, but that it would be a management agency in charge of conserving the nation's fish and wildlife resources.

FWS expanded its role in species conservation in a number of ways. It began to track extinction rates of threatened species, to manage those species to prevent their extinction, and to advocate legislation for additional administrative authority over endangered wildlife. Initially, FWS was most interested in protecting endangered species that had sport or industrial value or that were of historic or symbolic worth to the nation. Of course, concern for these kinds of species predated FWS, extending back at least to the bison. During the mid–twentieth century, however, efforts to protect endangered wildlife again centered on individual species.

Beginning in the 1930s, conservationists recommended legislative protection for the grizzly and brown bear.[90] In 1932, John Holzworth, the chairman of the Alaska Bear Committee for the New York Zoological Society and American Society of Mammalogists, testified before Congress that Alaskan brown bears were "certainly of such character and fame" that they should be sufficiently protected to prevent their extermination.[91] The National Park Service also argued that the grizzly bear deserved protection because it was "a fine American animal."[92] In 1934, scientists reported that only 1,013 grizzly bears remained in the United States, not counting those in the territory of Alaska. Congress, however, failed to pass legislation to protect the grizzly or brown bears.

In another example of the nation's focus on charismatic, individual species, during the 1930s Congress considered protection for the bald eagle. One bill introduced in 1930 would have made it illegal for any person to kill or capture any bald eagle except when the eagle was in the act of destroying wild or tame lambs or fawns or foxes on fox farms. During congressional deliberations over the bill, the National Audubon Society presented evidence that the bald eagle was in danger of extinction.[93] Representative August Andresen (R-MN), the sponsor of the bill, argued that the bald eagle should be protected because it "is the emblem of our national independence. . . . We protect the American flag and it seems to me logical that we might protect the emblem."[94] Although the bill received the support of all the major conservation organizations, it failed to pass the House because of opposition from the livestock industry, which viewed the eagle as a dangerous predator.[95]

In part due to the support of the newly reorganized FWS, however, in 1940 Congress succeeded in passing a law to protect the bald eagle. In doing so, Congress noted that the United States had adopted the bald eagle as its national symbol in 1782, and that since then it had become a "symbolic representation of a new nation under a new government in a new world."[96] As a result, the bald eagle was "no longer a mere bird of biological interest but a symbol of the American ideals of freedom."[97] The act made it a federal crime to take, possess, sell, purchase, or trade in any bald eagle or its products except within the territory of Alaska and provided for a maximum penalty of five hundred dollars and six months in jail per violation. Perhaps knowing they would lose, the states did not challenge the constitutionality of the new federal law.[98]

Nevertheless, the states resented the growing involvement of the federal government in wildlife conservation. They found themselves in a difficult situation. On the one hand, they appreciated federal aid in the form of money and scientific information about wildlife health, yet they also viewed wildlife regulation as the exclusive province of state power protected by the Tenth Amendment. For example, Seth Gordon, the vice president of the International Association of Game, Fish, and Conservation Commissioners and the executive director of the Pennsylvania Game Commission, praised the "long strides" the federal government had taken in recent years to assist the states in wildlife conservation.[99] But he also argued that states had the "exclusive right" to regulate and control the taking of wildlife and criticized federal agencies for usurping state powers.[100] Generally, the states appreciated federal aid and advice, but they wanted to preserve their autonomy and traditional rights to regulate wildlife.

World War II temporarily interrupted further progress in federal wildlife law, despite war rhetoric to the contrary. Just two weeks before the bombing of Pearl Harbor, FWS Director Ira Gabrielson testified before Congress that wildlife conservation was crucial to the war effort. He argued that sport hunting and other outdoor recreational activities involving wildlife guarded against "subversive tendencies" and preserved the "national morale."[101] Apparently, hunting represented and preserved the American way of life. The next year, however, Gabrielson reported that because of the war many FWS programs had been discontinued or greatly reduced in scope despite growing evidence of a global species extinction crisis.[102] He noted that the war had changed the agency's mission. During the national crisis, FWS managed wildlife so as to increase the food supply from game animals and to protect domestic livestock and crops through the control of predators, pests, and disease.[103]

In the long term, though, the war contributed indirectly to even greater federal management of wildlife. To begin with, pollution from wartime industries threatened fish and wildlife populations, generating federal efforts to minimize the impacts of that pollution.[104] Moreover, wartime innovation and postwar prosperity led to a dramatic increase in outdoor recreation nationwide. Albert M. Day, the new director of FWS, worried that this development would further tax already scarce wildlife resources, requiring yet more management by the agency.[105] Meanwhile, FWS assured the states that federal efforts to protect wildlife following the war would not interfere or infringe on state management.[106] Initially, this appeared to be the case.[107]

Soon, however, the federal government began new initiatives to protect endangered wildlife, even at the expense of state prerogative. In 1950, Congress considered an amendment to the Bald Eagle Protection Act of 1940 that would have extended that law's prohibition against taking bald eagles to include those found in the new state of Alaska. Proponents of the amendment argued that the "bald eagle should be protected as a symbol of independence and freedom."[108] They also argued that protection in Alaska was crucial, as it was the only place where healthy, stable populations of bald eagles remained.[109] Opponents of the amendment, however, believed that the bald eagle could be adequately protected under state law and regulation.[110] Because of state opposition, the amendment failed.

In 1962, however, Congress successfully enhanced protection for the bald eagle and extended protection to the golden eagle.[111] In part, Congress wanted to protect the golden eagle because it could easily be confused with the bald eagle, "the national symbol of the United States," especially when immature.[112] In addition, Congress sought to protect the golden eagle because it was endangered and because it was "one of the most spectacular and beautiful birds in America."[113] Most of the major conservation organizations supported the amendment, while several states and the livestock industry opposed it. Unlike the 1950 amendment, this amendment to the Bald Eagle Protection Act passed easily. By the early 1960s, changes in scientific understanding, the emergence of the modern environmental movement, and decreased deference to state authority had prepared the federal government to take over the protection of all the nation's endangered wildlife.

The emergence of the science of ecology provided the rationale for the expansion of federal power. Like federal wildlife law itself, ecology—

the branch of science concerned with the interrelationship between organisms and their environment—had its birth near the turn of the twentieth century. The German biologist Ernst Haeckel first coined the term *oekologie* in 1873 from the Greek work *oikos*, or home. In 1892, chemist Ellen Swallow publicized the word in America, changing it to *oekology*, and in 1910 applied the term to human ecology.[114] In 1916, botanist Frederic Clements posited an influential ecological principle when he described organisms, if undisturbed by human activity or environmental catastrophy, as developing in succession until they reached a climax state of equilibrium.[115] In 1935, biologist Arthur Tansley introduced the concept of the ecosystem, in which organisms and environmental factors interact and develop in a way that tended toward the creation of an equilibrated system.[116] According to Eugene Odum, writing in the 1950s and 1960s, biological diversity helped maintain the natural balance, or equilibrium, of the climax state.[117]

For Congress and the administration, these ecological principles had several implications. First, they implied that if left undisturbed by humans, nature tended toward harmony and balance, something that environmental policies should encourage. Second, maintaining maximum wildlife diversity was an essential ingredient of this Edenic ideal, and species extinction was a cardinal sin. Because of the complex interaction and interrelationship of organisms and environmental processes, the loss of biological diversity through species extinction would have an incalculable but undoubtedly harmful effect on human society. Many began to believe that the federal government should therefore do its utmost to prevent species from going extinct, even those species whose value was not apparent.

It is difficult, of course, to gauge how well policymakers understood these developments in ecological understanding. Certainly, no one popularized ecological principles better than Aldo Leopold, now known as the father of modern wildlife management. In his classic *A Sand County Almanac*, published posthumously in 1949, Leopold merged science, ethics, and nature writing into a best-seller that became an almost sacred guide for many environmentalists and natural resource managers. Most significant, he translated the ecological principles of Clements, Tansley, and others into what he called the "land ethic." According to this ethic, "a thing is right when it tends to preserve the integrity, stability, and beauty of the biotic community. It is wrong when it tends otherwise."[118] As Leopold's essay "On a Monument to the Pigeon" indicated, human-caused extinction violated this ethic in the most egregious way.[119]

In some ways, however, the science of ecology began to clash with the economy-based policies of FWS and the Department of the Interior. For example, in 1953 FWS proposed a plan to hire hunters and assign them to airplanes where they could systematically purge Alaska of predators like the wolf in order "to make the territory completely safe for reindeer, caribou, and moose."[120] FWS planned to supplement this aerial assault on predators by scattering poison pellets on animal carcasses across the Alaskan tundra. Scientists at the American Society of Mammalogists Conference opposed the plan. In particular, they stressed the important role that wolves and other predators played in the Alaskan ecology by maintaining healthy and stable populations of ungulates and other species.

Such sentiments could have come directly from Leopold's essay, "Thinking Like a Mountain." In that essay, he drew from his experience as a young ranger for the U.S. Forest Service, when he and his fellows "never heard of passing up a chance to kill a wolf."[121] Back then, like many conservationists, Leopold believed that fewer wolves meant more deer and that "no wolves would mean a hunters' paradise."[122] But after shooting a wolf on one occasion and seeing the "fierce green fire dying in her eyes," he realized that "neither the wolf nor the mountain agreed with such a view."[123] For Leopold, the "mountain" was a metaphor for an ecosystem, the complex interaction of organisms and environmental factors that required the wolf as much as the deer in order to maintain equilibrium.

FWS and the Department of the Interior felt pressured, both internally and externally, to practice sound science in their conservation programs. Nevertheless, politics demanded that they also adhere to the interests of sport hunters and the western livestock industry. Throughout the 1950s and 1960s, agencies within the Department of the Interior worked both to conserve certain species and to eradicate others. By the late 1960s and early 1970s, however, the department's predator control program came under increasing public criticism.[124] Finally, in 1972, President Nixon promulgated an executive order barring the use of poisons to control predators on all public lands.[125]

During the 1950s, few federal efforts, other than additional protections for the bald and golden eagles, emerged to protect species. Indeed, on some fronts Eisenhower's administration appeared to backslide. For example, the Department of the Interior became more permissive in allowing extractive industries onto the national wildlife refuges, especially through oil and gas leasing. Representative Lee Metcalf (D-MT) described the problem as "a continued and growing attack upon the wildlife refuges of the Nation" and proposed a bill to prevent the secretary of the interior from disposing of the national wildlife refuges without the permission of Congress.[126] Overall, although Congress considered minor fish and wildlife legislation during the 1950s, it proposed no significant new protection for endangered species.[127]

In many ways, efforts to protect endangered species during the nineteenth and the first half of the twentieth centuries reflected changes in scientific understanding from Charles Darwin to Eugene Odum. Yet despite growing awareness of the scope of the extinction crisis and progress in the field of ecology, endangered species laws during this time reflected a profound bias in favor of "useful" game species or charismatic megafauna representative of the national heritage. As a result, Congress chose to protect individual species like bison, migratory birds, and bald eagles. By the 1960s, however, the popularization of ecology joined with a burgeoning environmental movement to create significant change in endangered species policy. Most significant, Congress moved from protecting individual species to comprehensive species protection.

Legislative, judicial, and administrative efforts from the nineteenth to the mid-twentieth centuries laid the foundation for the endangered species legislation of the 1960s and 1970s. Most important, throughout the earlier time period Congress slowly extended federal authority over the regulation of the nation's wildlife. By doing so, it created and empowered a federal administration of wildlife experts. In turn, the judiciary consistently upheld this usurpation of state authority based on expansive interpretations of the U.S. Constitution's property clause, the treatymaking power, and the commerce clause. Changes in scientific understanding—a slow realization of the scope and magnitude of the extinction crisis—motivated much of this change in constitutional doctrine. From Darwin to Odum, scientists helped dictate the course of endangered species law.

CHAPTER TWO

Congress and Charismatic Megafauna

During the 1960s, the political climate for wildlife protection changed dramatically from what it had been during the 1950s. This change originated from grassroots environmental activists working at local levels. A growing public awareness of environmental problems, including species extinction, fostered a national environmental movement, which pushed for legislative action. If the environmental movement had a beginning, it was in 1962 when Rachel Carson, a former biologist with the Fish and Wildlife Service, published *Silent Spring*. In her book, Carson described how the nation's growing addiction to pesticides, herbicides, and insecticides poisoned wildlife and threatened human health.[1] Songbirds falling dead from suburban trees provided a graphic image of environmental destruction with which people could identify and empathize. More than any other single factor, Carson's book acted as a catalyst for the modern environmental movement.[2]

People and organizations concerned about wildlife extinction played a central role in the environmental movement of the 1960s. Late in 1961, for example, the World Wildlife Fund (WWF) was formed to raise money to save the world's most endangered species from extinction. Scientists with the WWF believed that "since the time of Jesus" about two hundred species of mammals and birds had become extinct, almost 70 percent of those within the last century and 38 percent within the last fifty years.[3] WWF blamed the most current extinctions on the pollution of the sea, drought, poaching, poison, and inundation from dams. Somewhat naively, WWF also believed that $1.5 million would be sufficient to save the species most seriously threatened with extinction, including the giant tortoise, the Ceylon elephant, the African mountain lion, the California condor, the whooping crane, and more than a dozen other species.[4] Such was the state of popular scientific understanding of the scope, cause, and remedy of the extinction crisis in 1961.

The same year WWF organized, Congress considered a bill to protect marine mammals on the high seas. If it had passed, the bill would have prohibited the taking of polar bears, sea otters, and walruses on the nation's seas and along its coastlines. The sponsor of the bill, Representative John Saylor (R-PA), blamed the near extinction of these marine mammals on sport hunting. He claimed that Congress had the power to enact such a law because the takings prohibition applied to the coasts of the United

States, where federal jurisdiction extended.[5] All of the major conservation organizations supported the bill, including the National Audubon Society, the Wildlife Institute, and the Izaak Walton League of America.

Although Congress failed to pass comprehensive endangered species legislation early in the 1960s, the administration began to act toward this end under existing authority. In 1964, FWS created the Committee on Rare and Endangered Species, composed of nine biologists. According to the committee, thirty-five to forty species of North American animals had gone extinct within the span of U.S. history.[6] The committee compiled the first list of species known to be threatened with extinction, which included a total of sixty types: thirty-five kinds of birds, sixteen of mammals, six of fish, and three of reptiles. The committee identified overhunting, habitat destruction, and pollution as the primary causes of species extinction. As the administration began to closely study and track the extinction crisis, Congress indirectly protected endangered species by passing the Wilderness Act of 1964, thus preserving crucial habitat for many.[7]

Just a year later, Congress considered legislation to protect endangered species directly. Although the bills failed to pass Congress in 1965, they were significant for a number of reasons. First, hearings on these bills raised awareness in Congress about the scope of the extinction crisis. For example, the secretary of the interior, Stewart Udall, testified that since the founding of the nation twenty-four birds and twelve mammals native to the United States had disappeared from the face of the earth. He warned that unless something was done soon some thirty-five mammals and thirty to forty species of birds would follow them into extinction.[8] The legislation also drew the support of an increasingly coordinated and powerful environmental lobby, including older conservation organizations like the National Audubon Society and newer groups like the Defenders of Wildlife. The hearings revealed, moreover, that these organizations were becoming increasingly critical of the administration's overemphasis on the protection of game species.[9]

The bills, if passed, would have been more comprehensive than any endangered species legislation to date. Yet, they would have extended protection only to those species listed by FWS, which were overwhelmingly mammals or birds. Rhetoric on the floor of Congress also emphasized charismatic megafauna. In the Senate, Secretary Udall urged the passage of the bill to protect species like "the whooping crane, trumpeter swan, prairie chicken, California condor, Kenai moose, Kodiak bear, Key deer, fur seal, and American bison."[10] Support for extending protection to such species was strong, and although the 89th Congress failed to pass an endangered species law during its first session in 1965, it seemed poised to do so during the second session.

Early in 1966, articles and editorials from the *New York Times* and other national papers advocated the passage of the endangered species legislation being considered by Congress. The *Times* reported that the whooping crane, California condor, and American bald eagle were among the seventy-eight species that the Department of the Interior then considered endangered. According to scientists, only forty-four whooping cranes and thirty-eight condors remained alive. The newspaper quoted Secretary Udall as advocating a law that, among other things, would require federal agencies to consider the impact on endangered species before building dams, draining swamps, or harvesting timber.[11] News coverage of pending endangered species legislation helped raise public support for and awareness of endangered species protection.

The news media also served to popularize ecological principles. For example, one *New York Times* editorial argued that even seemingly value-less species should be protected for ecological reasons. Such species would benefit humans through the advancement of scientific research on their place in the food chain and on their part of the "vast web of life."[12] The editorial warned that "unless man, the giant predator, becomes the farsighted conservator of this planet, he may join the whooping crane, the great blue whale and the golden eagle as a threatened species."[13] In this way, the *Times* both reflected and perpetuated the popular understanding of ecology, as that branch of science became the philosophical force behind the environmental movement.

Finally, in the fall of 1966, Congress passed the Endangered Species Preservation Act (the 1966 Act).[14] It was the first comprehensive legislative response to the modern extinction crisis and marked a significant departure from the individual species protection laws of the past. The 1966 Act had several significant provisions. First, it required the Department of the Interior to continue compiling lists of endangered species.[15] It then directed the Departments of Interior, Agriculture, and Defense to protect those listed species "insofar as is practicable and consistent" with the primary purposes of the services, bureaus, and agencies within their departments.[16] Moreover, it charged the Department of the Interior to consult with and "encourage" all other federal agencies to conform to the purposes of the act "where practicable."[17]

In addition, the 1966 Act created the National Wildlife Refuge System out of a hodgepodge of wildlife refuges and other federal preserves and authorized funds for the maintenance and expansion of that system.[18] Traditionally, the wildlife refuges had been managed primarily for waterfowl, but the 1966 Act directed FWS to manage those lands for other endangered species as well. Finally, it prohibited the "taking" of a species or its products within wildlife refuges without a permit.[19]

The 1966 Act represented a great step forward in federal wildlife law, but its scope and power were limited. First, it applied only to domestic vertebrate species of fish and wildlife and did not extend to plants, sub-species, or population segments. Moreover, because it protected only species listed by FWS and because the agency's list consisted over-whelmingly of charismatic mammals and birds, in reality the 1966 Act applied only to a small number of species actually threatened with ex-tinction. Second, the language of the law made agency cooperation with its purposes explicitly voluntary. Ideally, under the 1966 Act the various federal agencies were supposed to consult with FWS before beginning or authorizing development projects to ascertain if those activities would further jeopardize listed species. But because of the voluntary and flexi-ble language of the statute, such consultation rarely happened and even more rarely halted a proposed federal action.

Most important, the restriction against the taking of a species ap-plied only within the National Wildlife Refuges. The 1966 Act, therefore, did nothing to protect endangered species on private, state, or even other federal lands. Moreover, the law's taking prohibition did not extend to authorized activities on a National Wildlife Refuge that might indirectly harm a listed species. Despite these weaknesses, the 1966 Act announced that the federal government, not the states, would be responsible for ad-dressing the extinction crisis. Unlike the regulation of fish and game for sport hunters, endangered species required national protection through federal law.

In 1967, Congress considered bills to supplement the Endangered Species Preservation Act of 1966. In particular, many in Congress began to recognize the international scope of the extinction crisis and hoped to ex-tend legislative protection in this direction. Senator Ralph Yarborough (D-TX) argued that while much had been done to protect endangered American species "such as the western bison, whooping crane, and bald eagle," as yet the United States had done nothing to protect the "distinc-tive" species of other nations.[20] Dillon Ripley, the secretary of the Smith-sonian Institution, testified that the large international market in animal skins and plumage posed a major threat to many of these endangered species.[21] The bills' supporters in Congress hoped to prevent the extinction of such species by prohibiting the importation of them or their products. The 90th Congress, however, failed to pass such legislation in 1967 or 1968.

During those years, public support for stronger endangered species legislation grew as more Americans became aware of the scope and con-sequences of the extinction crisis. In 1967, the *New York Times* reported that FWS's list of endangered species had expanded to include 78 species: 36 birds, 22 fishes, 14 mammals, and 6 reptiles and amphibians.[22] An ed-itorial that same year warned that 250 species faced extinction, including the "blue whale, the polar bear and the leopard, the fearsome tiger and the humble alligator." The editorial blamed "man, the giant predator," who preyed upon these animals for fashion and money.[23] Another editorial, printed a few weeks later, was more specific. It argued that the fur trade hastened the extinction of some of the rarest and most beautiful mammals on the planet.[24]

In 1969, Congress again considered several bills to prevent the importation of endangered species and their products. During congressional hearings, Senator Yarborough referred to the International Union for the Conservation of Nature and Natural Resources Red Data Book that listed six hundred species of fish and wildlife as endangered worldwide. He argued that the rapid disappearance of many of the world's "most exotic and beautiful species" could be blamed on the fur and skin trade.[25] A study in 1972, for example, found that between 1968 and 1970, the U.S. market in skins and furs resulted in the importation of 18,456 leopard skins, 31,105 jaguar skins, and 249,680 ocelot skins.[26] In the United States, the primary victim of this trade was the alligator.

During congressional hearings, Congress heard from a variety of interest groups concerned about the bills. Once again, most major environmental organizations testified in support of the proposed law, including the National Audubon Society, the Defenders of Wildlife, the National Wildlife Federation, and the Sierra Club. Certain industries opposed the bills considered in 1969. These included the organizations representing the fur and skin industries: the American Fur Merchants' Association, the Fur Brokers' Association of America, the General Hide and Skin Corporation, and the Tanners' Council of America.[27] Unlike the 1966 Act, the bills considered in 1969 had a direct impact on certain clearly identified economic interests and for this reason provoked opposition where the earlier law had not.

After much deliberation, the 91st Congress passed the Endangered Species Conservation Act of 1969 (the 1969 Act).[28] The 1969 Act included several provisions designed to address the international extent of the extinction crisis. First, it directed FWS to expand the endangered species lists to include species not found in the United States and called for an international convention to discuss how to protect them.[29] The 1969 Act then banned the importation of any such species or its product.[30] In addition, it extended the Lacey Act by prohibiting the interstate selling or transportation of endangered species of reptiles, amphibians, mollusks, and crustaceans.[31]

Finally, the 1969 Act expanded the definition of "fish or wildlife" beyond fish, mammals, and birds. Under the new definition, the 1966 and 1969 Acts extended protection to endangered species of amphibians, reptiles, and invertebrates as well.[32] In these ways, the 1969 Act broadened the kinds of species deemed worthy of legislative protection and recognized the global sweep of the extinction crisis. Signing the bill into law, President Nixon called it "the most significant action this nation has ever taken in an international effort to preserve the world's wildlife."[33] In one of the few issues ever litigated under the 1969 Act, a federal court held that the law did not preempt a New York statute prohibiting the importation of certain species not included on the federal endangered species list. In effect, federal endangered species law did not preempt stronger state laws.[34]

Over the next few years, the American public became even more informed about the scope and consequences of the extinction crisis. In 1969, James Fisher and others wrote a book entitled *Wildlife in Danger* in which Fisher observed that people had never been more concerned about the disappearance of wildlife.[35] He noted that since 1600, a hundredth of the "higher" animals (mammals and birds) had become extinct, while nearly half were currently threatened with extinction, mostly due to overhunting.[36] A year later, the *New York Times* publicized anthropologist Paul Martin's thesis that prehistoric human overhunting was primarily responsible for the extinction of dozens of large mammals, like the mastodon, during the Pleistocene era.[37] For many, Martin's overkill thesis served as a warning to modern human society.

As a result of this increasing scientific knowledge, during the early 1970s environmentalists, scientists, and wildlife managers began to consider the plight of endangered species of plants. In 1971, the *Times* reported that for the first time FWS would include plants on its list of endangered species, joining some eight hundred species of wildlife already cited. According to the article, most endangered species currently listed were large appealing animals like the eagle, the tiger, the giant otter, the crocodile, the condor, the whale, and the rhinoceros. Scientists quoted in the article said that of the twenty thousand plant species in the world, about 10 percent were threatened with extinction. These plants, scientists argued, should be protected because of their potential as sources for food and medicine.[38]

Despite a growing appreciation for plants and other species of less obvious value, congressional preservation efforts continued to focus on charismatic megafauna representative of the national heritage. In 1971, Congress passed the Wild Free-Roaming Horses and Burros Act to preserve what Congress called "living symbols of the historic and pioneering spirit of the West."[39] The act prohibited the taking of wild horses and burros on all federal lands managed by the Forest Service and the Bureau of Land Management. This taking prohibition applied to far more land than the 1966 Act's prohibition, which pertained only to National Wildlife Refuges, although it did refer to all listed species and not just to wild horses and burros. In 1976, the Supreme Court defended the act against a constitutional attack by New Mexico when it held that the property clause of the U.S. Constitution "necessarily includes the power to regulate and protect wildlife" living on federal land.[40]

In 1972, Congress enacted the Marine Mammal Protection Act. Congress chose to protect marine mammals, like blue whales, largely because of their intelligence and their highly developed social systems—in short, because they seemed so human.[41] The central provision of that law placed a moratorium on the taking or importation of certain marine mammals threatened with extinction.[42] The act itself, however, was far more complex than a mere prohibition on taking. It established a detailed, comprehensive program for the protection of marine mammals, and in doing so it replaced many existing state programs and completely preempted the states from any authority over marine mammals. Once again, the courts later upheld this federal preemption of state action.[43]

Despite these laws, scientists, environmentalists, and many policy analysts began to recognize the inadequacy of existing federal protections for endangered species. Ledyard Stebbins, a professor of genetics at the University of California, Davis, argued before Congress that stronger federal legislation was needed to protect endangered species, especially plants, from extinction.[44] The *New York Times* quoted the president of the National Wildlife Federation, who said that despite existing laws, the "world today stands in grave danger of losing many animals and plants which have given joy to countless generations."[45] Writing to an audience of lawyers and lawmakers, William S. Boyd argued that the Constitution would permit the federal government to pass much stronger and more comprehensive endangered species legislation than the 1966 and 1969 Acts.[46] He and many others believed that such a law would be needed to save endangered species.

In 1972, President Nixon himself called for the adoption of "a stronger law to protect endangered species of wildlife."[47] Nixon claimed that "even the most recent act to protect endangered species, which dates only from 1969, simply does not provide the kind of management tools needed to act early enough to save a vanishing species."[48] On the same day as the president's address, Representative John Dingell (D-MI) introduced in the House endangered species legislation endorsed by the Nixon administration.[49] Ten days later, Senator Mark Hatfield (R-OR) submitted identical legislation to the Senate.[50] The 92d Congress, however, failed to pass new endangered species legislation in 1972.

Early in 1973, the 93d Congress, which was dominated by Democrats, reconsidered four new endangered species bills. On January 3, Representative Dingell introduced House Resolution 37, cosponsored by seventy members of the House.[51] On June 12, Senator Harrison Williams (D-NJ) introduced Senate Bill 1983.[52] The newly reelected Nixon administration also supported a stronger endangered species law and had its own bills introduced in both the House and the Senate, where they found bipartisan support.[53] Congress eventually approved the Democrat-sponsored bills, House Resolution 37 and Senate Bill 1983, which differed only modestly from the administration's proposal.[54]

Congress debated little over the various provisions of these bills. Moreover, the few congressional concerns did not center on Sections 4, 7, or the application of the Section 9 prohibition to habitat modification, but on issues relatively inconsequential to later developments. To the extent that Congress debated at all about these bills, it argued about the potential preemption of traditional state authority to manage wildlife. Senator Stevens (R-AK), in particular, worried about this and proposed an unsuccessful amendment to bolster state authority under the ESA.[55] Moreover, the only conservation organization to oppose the ESA, the Wildlife Management Institute, did so because it believed that the act would usurp state power.[56]

Debate over the preemption of state authority also arose from Section 9, although this discussion had nothing to do with whether or not habitat modification fell within the definition of the take prohibition. Under the 1966 and 1969 Acts, the federal prohibition against taking a listed species extended only to those taken within the National Wildlife Refuge System and, through the Lacey Act, to any taking or trade in listed species contrary to existing state law. There was no independent federal prohibition against killing or otherwise directly harming listed species outside of the National Wildlife Refuge System. Section 9 of the ESA changed this requirement, making it a federal crime to take any listed species anywhere within the United States. By doing so, the act necessarily intruded on state prerogative.

Proponents of the ESA successfully assuaged concerns over federal preemption. Representative James Grover (R-NY) assured his colleagues that the bill adequately protected legitimate state interests because it permitted the states to enact their own, more restrictive laws if desired.[57] Representative Dingell also stressed that the ESA would not preempt the states from enacting their own endangered species legislation.[58] Senator Williams stated simply that the law "in no way limits the power of any State to enact legislation or regulations more restrictive than the provisions of the act."[59] However, the act did not permit states to adopt less restrictive means to protect listed species. Outside of Congress, environmentalists and others argued that the ultimate authority for species protection should rest with the federal government rather than with the states because it could do a better job of addressing what was a national, even international, extinction crisis.[60]

Despite this and other minor concerns, congressional support for the bills soon became widespread and enthusiastic. In the Senate, especially, debate over the ESA was almost nonexistent. Even Senator Stevens, who initially expressed concern over the potential impact on state authority, rose to speak in support of Senate Bill 1983, stating that while "the bill is not perfect, I believe it takes a major step in the protection of American endangered and threatened species."[61] The bill's supporters also included those who would later regret their decisions, including Bob Dole (R-KS), Jesse Helms (R-NC), Howard Baker (R-TN), Bob Packwood (R-OR), and Mark Hatfield (R-OR). On July 24, 1973, the Senate approved Senate Bill 1983 unanimously, 92 to 0, with eight not voting.[62]

The House was almost as united behind House Resolution 37. Representative Grover observed, "I know of no opposition to H.R. 37 and urge its immediate passage."[63] Representative Dingell remarked that in the month since the committee report on the House bill had been available for review, he had "yet to hear a whisper of opposition to its passage at the earliest opportunity."[64] On September 18, 1973, the House of Representatives passed H.R. 37 by a vote of 390 to 12, with thirty-two not voting.[65] None of the twelve who voted against the bill voiced his opposition during congressional deliberations just prior to the vote.

The House and Senate bills then proceeded to the conference committee, which essentially adopted the Senate version of the bill, although it incorporated a few elements from the House bill. The conference report explained what it believed to be the significant differences between the Senate and House bills, but it failed to mention at least one major difference.[66] Regarding the Section 9 prohibition against taking a listed species, Senate Bill 1983 defined "take" to include actions that might "harm" a listed species, while House Resolution 37 only included actions that would directly injure or kill a listed species.[67] This difference, despite its importance to later developments, went unnoticed, or at least it provoked no comment or debate at the time. For the most part, the House and Senate bills were remarkably similar, including the parts of Section 4 and Section 7 relevant to subsequent controversies over the ESA. The topic most discussed during the conference concerned the division of administrative duties between the secretaries of the interior and commerce, a relatively minor point.[68]

The ESA emerged from the conference committee even more popular than it had been before. On December 19, the Senate agreed to the conference report, again unanimously.[69] The next day, the House considered the conference report, and Representative Dingell observed, "It would be no exaggeration to say that scarcely a voice has been heard in dissent."[70] The House agreed to the conference report by a vote of 345 to 4, with seventy-three representatives not voting.[71] Those four who voted against the act included Robin Beard (R-IN), Harold Gross (R-IA), Earl Landgrebe

(R-IN), and Robert Price (R-TX).[72] But none of them articulated opposition to the conference bill on the floor of Congress.

The bill then proceeded to the desk of the president. Even though it was not precisely the initiative introduced by his administration, President Nixon supported the bill enthusiastically. During the signing ceremony, he concluded, "Nothing is more priceless and more worthy of preservation than the rich array of animal life with which our country has been blessed."[73] On December 28, 1973, President Nixon signed the ESA into law.

The ESA received such overwhelming support for a variety of reasons. When Congress considered new endangered species legislation, environmentalism enjoyed a level of popularity unknown today. Indeed, the ESA arrived on the "peak of the environmental wave" and represented the "quintessential environmental issue."[74] The year before its passage, Tom Garrett, wildlife conservation director for Friends of the Earth, noted that environmental legislation, particularly wildlife protection, was "a richly rewarded political issue."[75] The *Washington Post* editorialized that public sentiment "clearly" supported increased protection for endangered species.[76]

Many politicians sought to capitalize on this popularity. Some hoped that by doing so they could unite a country deeply divided by civil rights, women's liberation, and the Vietnam War.[77] Nixon himself declared that "the quality of life on this good land is a cause to unite all Americans."[78] Sinking ever deeper into the morass of Watergate, he probably yearned for a little unity by the end of 1973, while the Republicans in Congress may have hoped to rehabilitate their party.[79] Nixon, and perhaps conservatives in general, supported the ESA not so much out of a sincere commitment to species preservation but for self-serving reasons.[80]

To many politicians, the ESA must have appeared to be a win-win situation, which seemed especially true because no significant special interest group came forward to oppose it. During the Senate hearings in June 1973, numerous administrative agency experts and every major environmental organization testified in support of the ESA. Even the National Rifle Association urged the passage of a stronger wildlife law.[81] The only opposition came from a couple of groups representing the fur industry and state fish and game agencies, which worried about the preemption of state authority.[82] Nor did significant special interest opposition materialize during the House hearings.[83] With "little open opposition to the bills," there appeared to be no reason, "except congressional inertia," for inaction.[84]

Few at the time opposed the ESA because no one anticipated how it might interfere significantly with economic development or personal property interests.[85] One leading advocate of the act observed, "Because someone does not necessarily have to combat vested economic interests, some politicians use the issue to parade themselves as environmentalists knowing they will not seriously offend corporate interests."[86] The ESA was such an issue. The timber industry, other natural resource industries, and private property groups declined to fight the law in 1973 because they failed to see how it might affect them. In addition, unlike today, no organized antienvironmental coalition existed to probe and protest environmental legislation like the ESA.

Members of Congress also failed to anticipate many of the act's consequences. In particular, they overlooked or underestimated the potential powers of Sections 4, 7, and 9 and debated instead about relatively minor provisions of the law. Representative Dingell, for example, listed the nine "principal" changes that would be affected by the bill's passage. None of these included any mention that Section 4 would cause a wide diversity of species to be listed regardless of economic considerations, that Section 7 would halt federal projects that might jeopardize species, or that Section 9 might result in the regulation of land use or private property.[87] For Representative Dingell at least, the most significant aspects of the ESA included its distinction between threatened and endangered species and its ban on the export of listed species.[88]

Others believed that Section 6, which provided for federal cooperation with the states, was the most significant provision of the act. Senator John Tunney (D-CA), the Senate manager of the bill, called Section 6 "perhaps the most important section" of the ESA.[89] Senator Stevens called Section 6 "the major backbone" of the law.[90] The Senate Report stated that the primary purpose of the act was to promote cooperative management between the states and the federal government.[91] Of course, it is difficult to ascertain whether the legislators actually believed this supposition, or if they were just trying to assuage concerns over federal preemption. Nevertheless, Congress either found the inherent powers of Sections 4, 7, and 9 unworthy of debate, or it grossly underestimated them.[92]

To begin with, Congress failed to recognize the diversity of species protected under Section 4. Instead, congressional rhetoric about the act displayed a profound bias toward charismatic megafauna. In the House, Representative Dingell claimed that his bill would protect American species like the eastern timber wolf, the wolverine, and the eastern cougar as well as the kangaroo and the elephant.[93] Representative Leonor Sullivan (D-MO), the chair of the committee that oversaw House Resolution 37, urged the passage of the ESA to protect blue whales and "spotted cats."[94] No one in the House mentioned mollusks or anthropods, and only a few mentioned plants.

Senators, too, referred almost exclusively to the need to protect charismatic wildlife. Senator Leonor Roth (R-DE) urged the passage of the ESA because her constituents in Delaware "admire the graceful and inspiring flight of the few American bald eagles remaining in the state."[95] Senator Williams, the sponsor of the Senate bill, exclaimed, "Most animals are worth very little in terms of dollars and cents. However, their esthetic value is great indeed. The pleasure of simply observing them . . . is unmeasurable."[96] These sentiments applied poorly to species like the snail darter and furbish lousewort that later aroused such controversy.

Congress's failure to recognize that the ESA would protect plants almost as much as wildlife can perhaps be explained by other reasons, too. When it considered the act in 1973, the status of plant species was poorly understood. To remedy this problem, Congress included a provision in the law, Section 12, directing the Smithsonian Institution to study and report on endangered and threatened plant species in the United States. Congress indicated that the results of the study would provide a basis for amending the ESA or writing new legislation. In the meantime, plants would continue to be listed under Section 4 according to the same criteria as wildlife.[97] When finally completed in 1974, the report did not lead to any amendments to the ESA or to additional legislation.[98] Instead, plants continued to be listed according to Section 4. In this way, the strongest provisions of the act, originally intended for wildlife, applied almost equally to plants.

The Nixon administration shared congressional sentiment regarding the kinds of species the ESA would, or should, protect. Although the administration's bills were in other ways remarkably similar to the bills introduced by the Democrats in Congress, they explicitly did not extend protection to threatened or endangered plants.[99] During the signing ceremony, Nixon's comments seemed oblivious to the change: "This legislation provides the Federal Government with the needed authority to protect an irreplaceable part of our national heritage—threatened wildlife."[100] Not only did Nixon ignore plants, but his comments reflected the widespread perception of the act as an attempt to preserve only those wildlife representative of the nation's heritage.

Congress and the administration's focus on charismatic megafauna reflected the emphasis of the news media, special interests, and, presumably, the public at the time. For example, in June 1973, the *Washington Post* included an editorial supporting the passage of the ESA. Of the "some 900" animal species threatened with extinction, the editorial specifically mentioned only the cheetah, the Puerto Rican parrot, and the red wolf.[101] A couple of months later, the *Post* published another editorial in support of the ESA, in which it focused on the plight of endangered wolves.[102] In September, the newspaper published an article about the law that featured a picture of a timber wolf and indicated that aside from the wolf, the ESA would also protect "the bald eagle, mountain lion, grizzly bear, black footed ferret, cheetah, and other endangered animals."[103] The Defenders of Wildlife urged the passage of the ESA to protect the endangered eastern timber wolf, American alligator, and grizzly bear.[104]

Even scientific literature from the time emphasized charismatic megafauna. One treatise on extinct and vanishing animals began with a summary of the disappearance of the bison from the American Great Plains and proceeded from there to focus exclusively on large appealing animals.[105] A pictorial work entitled *Endangered Species,* published in 1972, advocated the role of zoos in species conservation. Of the seventy-five species featured, every one was either an animal or a bird, and most were big animals like the "maned" wolf, the polar bear, and the Rocky Mountain goat.[106] In 1973, the International Union for the Conservation of Nature and Natural Resources published a list of species that had become extinct since 1600; the entire list consisted only of mammals.[107]

Aside from overlooking the implications of Section 4, Congress almost completely ignored Section 7's requirement of interagency cooperation, presumably because they found that section relatively unimportant or uncontroversial.[108] There was, however, at least one instance during deliberations over the ESA in which Congress discussed Section 7. Senator Tunney, the Senate manager of the bill, responded to a concern that the section might stop the Army Corps of Engineers from building a road in Kentucky. He described what he thought Section 7 meant:

> As I understand it after the consultation process took place . . . the Corps of Engineers, would not be prohibited from building the road if they deemed it necessary to do so. . . . they would have the final decision after consultation. . . . So, as I read the language, there has to be consultation. However, the Bureau of Public Roads or any other agency would have the final decision as to whether such a road should be built.[109]

According to Tunney, Section 7 meant that agencies proposing development projects that might jeopardize listed species must consult the Department of the Interior, but that the ultimate decision to continue with a project rested with the development agency. This explanation would have rendered Section 7 largely procedural rather than substantive, much like the requirements for an Environmental Impact Statement found in the National Environmental Policy Act of 1969.[110] Of course, this view differed entirely from the Supreme Court's interpretation of Section 7 five years later.[111]

As for Section 9, no one in Congress contemplated that the prohibition against taking a listed species might lead to the regulation of land use activities on private property or seemed to make the connection between habitat degradation and the taking of a species. At least, no such recognition could be gleaned from the committee reports, the floor debates, or the congressional hearings. Furthermore, there is little evidence that even the environmental organizations believed that Section 9 extended to land use regulation. Only one reference could be found supporting the position that Section 9 applied to habitat degradation, and that opinion came from a member of an environmental organization.[112] No member of Congress questioned the environmental representative on this point or raised the issue elsewhere.

Despite the emergence of ecology earlier in the century and the rise of the modern environmental movement, congressional ignorance largely reflected the state of scientific understanding at the time. Not until the early 1980s did an appreciation for biological diversity become widespread.[113] Indeed, the word "biodiversity" was not known prior to the 1980s. The very idea of biodiversity "represented a distinct advance in conceptualization" because it stressed the importance of all species and because of its emphasis on habitat protection.[114] During the 1990s, scientists began to speak of the need to protect ecosystem health as well as biodiversity. Some even criticized the ESA, with its emphasis on identifying and protecting individual species, as scientifically anachronistic.[115]

Few scientists critical of the act today, however, argue that it should be scrapped altogether. Instead, most propose that the ESA merely be reinterpreted and implemented in such a way as to better conform with current scientific understanding.[116] To a certain extent, such has been the case with Sections 7 and 9. What it means to "jeopardize" or "harm" a species today differs significantly from what it meant in 1973.

Congressional inability to predict the potential scope of Sections 4, 7, and 9 also reflected an inaccurate assessment of the nature of the modern extinction crisis. For example, Senator Williams, the Senate sponsor of the ESA, stated that overhunting was "undoubtedly" the "major reason" for species extinction.[117] Such a view supports the argument that Congress was concerned primarily with protecting game species rather than plants and relatively unknown species of fish and wildlife. Moreover, if overhunting was the primary cause for species extinctions, all that was required to solve the problem was to prohibit hunting and other activities that directly harmed species. Provisions, like Sections 7 and 9, that extended to habitat modification would not be necessary. Of course, scientists today believe that the modern extinction crisis stems primarily from adverse habitat modification associated with human activities in general and not just overhunting.[118]

Congressional scientific knowledge in 1973 also mirrored the popular understanding of the day. An editorial in the *Washington Post* blamed the extinction crisis largely on the international trade in endangered species: "Big money is at stake for many nations that trade in wild animal skins, in whale oil for cosmetics, in supplying wildlife for zoos, pets and medical research."[119] In urging the passage of a stronger ESA, the *Post* criticized the weaknesses of the 1969 Act, but for the wrong reasons. Specifically, it criticized the absence of protection for species merely threatened with becoming endangered.[120] Although the distinction drawn by the ESA between threatened and endangered species was significant, it was not nearly as crucial to species survival as Sections 4, 7, and 9.

Finally, despite the rhetoric over the ESA, most in and outside of Congress thought the act relatively insignificant. With the exception of the *Washington Post*, the national press all but ignored congressional consideration of the legislation during 1973. Moreover, the press barely even mentioned the law's enactment. The day after the ESA became law, the *New York Times* noted its passage as an afterthought in an unrelated article on an act transferring federal job-training funds to the states.[121] The *Times* sandwiched the one-sentence announcement about the passage of the ESA between descriptions of an act to build a Lyndon Baines Johnson Memorial grove of trees on the banks of the Potomac and an act to insure mortgage insurance for fire safety equipment in nursing homes. Despite earlier editorials about protecting endangered species, the *Washington Post* gave no more coverage to the passage of the ESA than the *New York Times* did.[122] The *Los Angeles Times* also covered the signing of the bill in one sentence, while the *Chicago Tribune* ignored it altogether.[123] It seemed that few at the time appreciated the significance of the ESA.

PART II: THE SNAIL DARTER

CHAPTER THREE

The Fish That Stopped a Dam

For several years following its passage, the Endangered Species Act of 1973 remained relatively uncontroversial. In part, this was because the Department of the Interior and the Department of Commerce implemented the act conservatively.[1] To begin with, the U.S. Fish and Wildlife Service, the agency primarily responsible for implementing the act, listed species slowly. With the law's passage in 1973, 126 species were automatically named; in 1974, however, FWS added no species, and in 1975 it only listed 8. No plant species were included at all, and by February 1977, the agency had identified only six critical habitats and approved only eight recovery plans for these species.[2]

Administrative foot-dragging over the ESA also manifested itself in other ways during the mid-1970s. For example, FWS declined to pursue ESA enforcement actions in court against federal development projects that jeopardized listed species; instead, the agency attempted less aggressive and less effective means. In July 1975, for example, FWS implemented an emergency determination of critical habitat to protect the endangered Mississippi sandhill crane. The agency had listed this subspecies as endangered in 1973, and only forty of the cranes were believed to survive in the wild.[3] FWS pursued this administrative action in lieu of filing suit.

The action temporarily halted further construction on a 5.7-mile segment of Interstate 10. Once completed, Interstate 10 would stretch from Los Angeles, California, to Jacksonville, Florida. FWS believed that if built as planned, the highway segment would destroy at least seven known nesting sites of the cranes as well as other areas designated as critical habitat. The weakness in the agency's "emergency" action, however, was that it only would have delayed the construction for 120 days. FWS hoped that during that time it could successfully negotiate with the Department of Transportation to come to a compromise solution, despite the fact that extensive negotiation prior to the emergency action had failed.[4]

While FWS negotiated, environmental organizations resorted to the ESA's citizen suit provision and sued the Department of Transportation.[5] In the first such case of its kind, the National Wildlife Federation and the Mississippi Wildlife Federation sought to permanently enjoin the Department of Transportation from completing the highway as planned. They argued that the highway would jeopardize the continued existence of the crane, thus violating Section 7 of the ESA, which instructs all federal agencies to "consult" with the secretary of the interior to "insure that any action authorized, funded, or carried out by such agency . . . is not likely to jeopardize the continued existence of any endangered species and threatened species" or result in the destruction or modification of critical habitat.[6] In August 1975, the federal district court dismissed the case, holding that the plaintiffs had failed to prove that the highway would jeopardize the continued existence of the cranes.[7]

The National Wildlife Federation, however, appealed and, pending that appeal, secured a temporary injunction on the completion of the highway. In March 1976, the Fifth Circuit Court of Appeals in *National Wildlife Federation v. Coleman* reversed the decision of the district court, holding that the secretary of transportation had failed to meet the requirements of Section 7.[8] Specifically, the court held that Section 7 imposed a "mandatory obligation" on federal agencies to consider all the ways in which projects authorized, funded, or carried out by them might jeopardize listed species. In addition, federal agencies must also "take the necessary steps" to ensure that their actions do not jeopardize listed species.[9]

Reviewing the record, the Fifth Circuit concluded that the district court had erred when it held that the secretary of transportation had "adequately considered" the effects of the highway on the crane.[10] Although the Fifth Circuit agreed with the district court that the Mississippi sandhill crane could probably survive the direct loss of three hundred acres of habitat resulting from the construction, it held that the secretary of transportation must also consider the indirect effects of the highway on the crane. In particular, the Fifth Circuit found sufficient evidence in the record to conclude that residential and commercial development would accompany the completion of the highway. This development would most likely occur near a planned interchange located within the cranes' critical habitat.[11] In sum, the Fifth Circuit held that Section 7 required federal agencies to consider both the direct and indirect effects of their actions.

The Fifth Circuit, however, did not order a permanent injunction on the construction of the highway through the cranes' critical habitat. Instead, it enjoined the completion of the project until the secretary of transportation modified the construction plan to ensure that the highway would not jeopardize the Mississippi sandhill crane. According to the National Wildlife Federation, the actions necessary to bring the highway into compliance with Section 7 included the elimination of the highway interchange, the exclusion of borrow pits within the cranes' critical habitat, and the acquisition and protection of land by the Department of Transportation to mitigate the loss of critical habitat taken by the highway. Although the court noted the National Wildlife Federation's opinion, it held that the Department of the Interior must make the final decision about what modifications to the plan would be necessary to protect the crane. According to the court, the Department of the Interior, not the plaintiffs bringing the suit, would have the ultimate authority over whether the injunction should be lifted.[12]

In the course of its decision, the Fifth Circuit attempted to explain Section 7's meaning. To begin with, the court found that Section 7 imposed on federal agencies the "mandatory duty" to ensure that their actions would not jeopardize endangered species or destroy or modify critical habitat.[13] To meet this obligation, agencies would be required to consult with the secretary of the interior before taking any actions that might affect endangered species or their critical habitats. The court also observed that

> once an agency has had meaningful consultation with the Secretary of Interior concerning actions which may affect an endangered species the final decision of whether or not to proceed with the action lies with the agency itself. Section 7 does not give the Department of Interior a veto over the actions of other federal agencies, provided that the required consultation has occurred.[14]

In effect, this part of the Fifth Circuit's decision interpreted Section 7 as a purely procedural requirement.

The court in *National Wildlife Federation v. Coleman* gave contradictory interpretations of Section 7. On the one hand, it defined Section 7 as a substantive requirement that all federal agencies ensure that their actions do not jeopardize endangered species. According to this view, Section 7 was an absolute prohibition on agency actions that directly or indirectly jeopardized protected species. Ultimately, this was the interpretation best reflected in the court's decision, which essentially granted the secretary of the interior "veto" power over the highway project. By order of the court, the Department of Transportation could not complete its highway unless the Department of the Interior approved its plan.[15] Yet, the court clearly stated that the final decision on whether to proceed with an agency action rested with the agency itself and that Section 7 merely required consultation.[16] Two years after the Fifth Circuit's decision, the Supreme Court would resolve the internal contradiction of this case.

In the meantime, the Fifth Circuit's decision roused little controversy. There were several reasons for this. First, Mississippi sandhill cranes were the kind of charismatic megafauna that Congress and the American public most expected and wanted the ESA to protect. More important, following the court order the Departments of Transportation and Interior worked out a compromise solution, and Interstate 10 was completed with minimal impact on the Mississippi sandhill crane. Finally, the contradictory language found in the Fifth Circuit's decision allowed both sides of a nascent ESA debate to claim victory.

The case was significant, however, for other reasons. First, it demonstrated the administration's reluctance to enforce the ESA during the 1970s, at least when doing so meant challenging the development projects of other federal agencies. Second, it revealed that environmental organizations could and would use the citizen suit provision of the ESA to enforce the act themselves, and in doing so they would argue for expansive interpretations of its substantive provisions. Finally, the case suggested the potential of Section 7 to halt major development projects if those projects jeopardized protected species. By the end of the 1970s, aggressive lawsuits brought by environmentalists, coupled with expansive judicial interpretations of Section 7 of the ESA, would threaten the future of the act itself.

In the meantime, the ESA continued to enjoy almost unqualified support in Congress in the months following the Fifth Circuit's decision in *National Wildlife Federation v. Coleman*. In May 1976, Congress held hearings to consider extending appropriations for implementing the law, which were due to expire in June of that year. During these hearings, environmental organizations, scientific foundations, and government agencies united in strong support of the ESA and of bills to extend appropriations for it.[17] Although some business interests, like Ringling Brothers Barnum and Bailey Circus, testified in support of minor amendments to the act that might protect their particular concerns, no organized or general opposition to the legislation materialized during the hearings.[18] Moreover, no group mentioned the recently decided Mississippi sandhill crane case.

Following the hearings, Congress spent little time debating the ESA and its appropriation reauthorization. The Department of the Interior and the Department of Commerce requested appropriations of $24.5 million for fiscal years 1977 and 1978, an amount that significantly exceeded earlier annual appropriations for the act.[19] The departments explained that the increase was necessary to meet unanticipated costs associated with the acquisition of critical habitat for listed species. Congress not only met their request but exceeded it, appropriating $31.8 million for fiscal years 1977 and 1978.[20] The bill passed both houses of Congress without debate, and the president signed it into law on June 30, 1976.[21] This was the last time that Congress or the president would consider the ESA in the absence of controversy.

The continued popularity of the ESA during the mid-1970s can be attributed not just to the lack of controversy surrounding it but also to growing concern over the extinction crisis. Responding to this crisis, in

1976 eight hundred people from thirty-five nations assembled in San Francisco for a World Wildlife Fund conference to discuss the plight of endangered species. According to the *New York Times*, the dominant theme at the conference was how the loss of any species, no matter how seemingly insignificant, might imperil human society.[22] Nevertheless, despite some desire of environmentalists and scientists to use the ESA to protect less notable species, FWS continued to implement the act with a focus on charismatic megafauna.[23] In doing so, FWS merely reflected public sentiment of the day, sentiment roused by the plight of endangered whales but largely apathetic to the fate of more obscure species.

It was not whales or wolves or bears that first provoked significant controversy over the ESA. Instead, it was a virtually unknown, three-inch fish called a snail darter. The darter was a tan-colored member of the perch family. Its name derived from the fact that it fed primarily on snails along the bottom of the Little Tennessee River, the only place on Earth where scientists could locate the species. Scientists had determined that the snail darter needed free-flowing water to provide the high levels of oxygen required for survival.[24]

Unfortunately for the darter, the Tennessee Valley Authority (TVA) threatened to destroy its habitat by completing Tellico Dam on the Little Tennessee River. TVA began construction of Tellico Dam in 1966, and almost immediately environmentalists attacked the project. Eventually, these attacks became lawsuits, and in 1972, a federal district court temporarily enjoined the completion of the dam pending a trial on the merits of a case brought by the Environmental Defense Fund (EDF).[25] In that case, EDF argued that TVA had not complied with the National Environmental Policy Act because it had failed to adequately address the significant environmental impacts from the project or discuss all the reasonable alternatives. The federal district court ultimately disagreed with the environmentalists, however, and lifted the temporary injunction on the dam.[26] The Sixth Circuit Court of Appeals affirmed the trial court's decision, holding that the district court correctly applied the proper balancing test to a project that would admittedly entail considerable ecological damage but would also have many offsetting economic and social benefits.[27]

Environmentalists soon found new grounds upon which to base a suit to halt the dam. In 1973, freed from its injunction, TVA resumed the construction of Tellico Dam. Anticipating the inundation of the valley, David Etnier, an ichthyologist and assistant professor of zoology at the University of Tennessee, began a biological census of the Little Tennessee River. During that census, he discovered the snail darter, a species of perch heretofore unknown to the world. A number of students assisted Professor Etnier in this study, including one law student, Hiram Hill. After Etnier discovered the fish, Hill approached his environmental law professor, Zygmunt Plater, with the idea of writing about the potential impact on Tellico Dam if the snail darter were listed as an endangered species.[28]

An environmentalist as well as a lawyer and a scholar, Plater thought the idea had far more potential than just serving as an academic paper. On January 20, 1975, Plater, joined by local groups of environmentalists, petitioned the secretary of the interior to list the snail darter as an endangered species.[29] TVA objected to the proposal, but FWS, considering solely the best scientific information available as required by Section 4, concluded that the snail darter was an endangered species and listed it as such effective on November 10, 1975. In its listing decision, FWS noted that the impoundment of water behind the proposed Tellico Dam would result in the total destruction of the snail darter's habitat.[30] Soon after the listing, FWS identified a seventeen-mile stretch of the Little Tennessee River located in Loudon County, Tennessee, as critical habitat.[31] Despite these findings, the Department of the Interior refused to pursue an enforcement action against TVA to halt construction of the dam.

Instead, on February 18, 1976, Plater led the Association of Southeastern Biologists, the Audubon Council of Tennessee, and others in a citizen suit to enjoin the completion of the dam. Eventually, parties to the suit consisted not only of environmentalists but also biologists, local farmers, and members of the Cherokee nation. They united primarily to stop a dam, to save an ecosystem, to prevent their farms from being inundated, and to protect sacred sites. To these ends, the snail darter and the ESA were mostly tools, yet these plaintiffs did not believe they were misusing the law. For them, the snail darter, the river valley, the fertile soil, and the cultural heritage of the region were all connected and all worth saving by any legal means available.[32]

Initially, these plaintiffs complained that TVA had violated both Sections 7 and 9 of the ESA. Specifically, they argued that TVA failed under Section 7 to "take such actions necessary to insure" that it would not jeopardize the continued existence of the darter.[33] They also argued under Section 9 that TVA's dam-building had resulted in the illegal taking of the endangered darter.[34] The federal district court, however, concluded that although the completion of Tellico Dam would jeopardize the continued existence of the snail darter, the ESA did not require an injunction. In light of this conclusion, the court deemed it unnecessary to consider the Section 9 complaint.[35]

The district court reasoned that to hold otherwise and enjoin the completion of the dam would be unreasonable. The court explained that congressional appropriations for Tellico Dam began in 1966 and continued up through 1976, even after Congress was made aware of the dam's potential to destroy the snail darter. Over $78 million had been invested in the dam so far, and as of the end of March 1976, it was about 80 percent complete. The court observed that "at some point in time a federal project becomes so near completion and so incapable of modification that a court of equity should not apply a statute enacted long after inception of the project to produce an unreasonable result."[36] The court concluded that although the ESA did not require construction to be halted on this particular project, the situation would be different if the project were capable of reasonable modifications that would ensure compliance with the act or if the project had not been under way for nearly a decade.[37] The district court, therefore, believed Section 7 analysis required a balancing of equities, and that in this case the equities favored completion of the dam.

The environmentalists, of course, appealed the decision to the Sixth Circuit, which agreed to hear the case. That court began its decision with some impatience, noting that this was the third time in five years it had to resolve a dispute between environmentalists and the TVA over the legality of Tellico Dam.[38] Nevertheless, the Sixth Circuit held in favor of the environmentalists, reversing the district court's decision as an abuse of discretion and enjoining the completion of Tellico Dam. First, the court reasoned that current project status could not be translated into a workable standard of judicial review. "Whether a dam is 50% or 90% completed is irrelevant in calculating the social and scientific costs attributable to the disappearance of a unique form of life."[39] According to the Sixth Circuit, just because TVA had begun construction on Tellico Dam in 1966 and by 1976 had completed over 80 percent of the project, it did not warrant an exemption from Section 7.

Moreover, the Sixth Circuit held that continued congressional appropriation for the dam, even upon disclosure of the plight of the darter, did not provide a legitimate exemption from the requirements of the ESA: "Advisory opinions by Congress concerning the 'proper' application of an existing statute cannot influence our review because they lack the force of law."[40] To hold otherwise, the court wrote, would allow the legislature to intrude on the exclusive power of the judiciary, thus trampling on the doctrine of separation of powers. Instead, congressional intent must be gleaned from the language and legislative history of the ESA itself and could only be legitimately interpreted by the courts. By dismissing these two factors considered by the district court, the court of appeals could find no justification within the act itself for exempting TVA from the requirements of Section 7. It therefore reversed the holding of the district court and ordered that Tellico Dam be permanently enjoined until either Congress explicitly exempted the dam or the snail darter was removed from the endangered species list.[41]

A few months later, TVA appealed to the U.S. Supreme Court. Between the Sixth Circuit's decision in January 1977 and the Supreme

Court's holding in June 1978, the ESA descended into a maelstrom of controversy. In an attempt to limit this controversy and perhaps save the act from legislative evisceration, FWS acted to administratively weaken the power of Section 7. It began by proposing a rule stating that it was ultimately the responsibility of the "action agency"—an agency taking some development action, like authorizing the construction of a highway or building a dam—to decide whether or not it was in compliance with Section 7. Under the proposed rule, the action agency would make the initial determination about whether consultation with FWS or the National Marine Fisheries Service (NMFS) was even necessary. Upon a written request for consultation by the action agency, FWS or NMFS would take sixty days for a threshold examination of the potential effects of the proposed action. Once the action agency received the final biological opinion from either FWS or NMFS, it would have the final responsibility for determining how or whether to proceed with the action. In the proposed rule, the services asserted that their role under Section 7 was "limited to providing biological advice and assistance, not in determining if a project may continue."[42] That decision, the services believed, should rest with the action agencies themselves.

The services, however, eventually adopted a stance slightly more in keeping with the Sixth Circuit's decision. In their final rule, Section 7 consultation was mandatory if the federal action agency found that its activities or programs might affect a listed species. The action agency must still initiate consultation by a written request to one of the services, but the services could also contact the agencies and require consultation if they failed to make the necessary request. Most important, the final rule still left it to the agencies themselves, after consultation, to decide how to proceed with the proposed action in light of its biological impacts on listed species. In drafting the final rule, the services hoped to keep the Section 7 requirements procedural rather than substantive, in this way limiting the impact of the Sixth Circuit's decision and minimizing controversy.[43]

Despite these efforts by the administration to dilute the court's holding, the Sixth Circuit's decision provoked Congress into considering amendments to weaken the ESA. First, in the spring of 1977, Representative Robin Beard (R-TN) introduced a bill in the House that would have prevented Section 7 from applying to projects begun prior to 1973. This bill, if it had been passed into law, would have voided the Sixth Circuit's decision and allowed the completion of Tellico Dam. Several other representatives and senators submitted bills in 1977 designed to weaken the ESA. Even Representative Al Gore (D-TN) introduced a bill to exempt Tellico Dam, as well as another TVA dam, from the requirements of the act.[44] None of the ESA-related bills introduced in 1977, however, became law.

ESA oversight hearings held in July 1977 provided another forum for debate over the Sixth Circuit's interpretation of Section 7. Senator Howard Baker (R-TN) reflected the belief of many legislators when he argued that the Sixth Circuit decision contradicted the original intent of Congress when it adopted Section 7.[45] Representative John Duncan (R-TN) joined Baker in these criticisms, claiming that the Sixth Circuit's interpretation of the ESA "does not promote balanced decision-making."[46] Duncan believed that when Congress passed the act in 1973 it did not intend for Section 7 to serve as a potential veto over virtually every federally funded or authorized project. Of course, during these hearings many in Congress also rose to speak in defense of the ESA. Representative John Culver (D-IA), for example, stressed the successes of the act in saving such species as the whooping crane, the alligator, and the leopard. He claimed that the publicity generated by the media over the snail darter and Tellico Dam obscured these successes.[47]

The Carter administration also revealed its split over the ESA during these hearings. FWS, representing the Department of the Interior, dodged the question of whether the administration agreed or disagreed with the Sixth Circuit's interpretation of Section 7. Instead, it argued that because of the intransigence of the TVA in this particular case, the dam should not be completed at the expense of the darter.[48] Joining FWS, Charles Warren, the chairman of the Council of Environmental Quality, testified that the "vast majority" of conflicts between endangered species and federal projects had been resolved through the consultation process. He claimed that Tellico Dam was merely an aberration not representative of any fundamental weakness in the act.[49] TVA, however, responded that the Sixth Circuit's interpretation of Section 7 was incorrect because it established an absolute standard rather than a balancing test. TVA also argued that environmentalists were misusing the ESA because their primary goal was to halt the dam, not to protect the darter.[50] In this way, at least two separate agencies within the federal government disagreed over the interpretation of Section 7 and how that section should be applied in this case.

During these hearings, economic and environmental interests also faced off over Tellico Dam and proposed amendments to the ESA. Charles Hall, the mayor of Tellico Plains, Tennessee, testified that the dam would create six thousand new jobs and indirectly thousands more in his community, and that millions of dollars of damage would be saved through flood control.[51] Lynn Seeber, the general manager of the TVA, testified that $105 million had already been spent on the dam and that this money would be wasted should the Sixth Circuit's injunction stand. He also testified that the completed dam would provide enough hydroelectric energy to heat twenty thousand homes annually, generating power equivalent to $3.5 million a year.[52] To many, it seemed that the economic health of this particular region of Tennessee was at stake.

In addition to these specific concerns, a number of organized business interests also argued that the act should be weakened or repealed. The ESA's new enemies included groups like the National Cattlemen's Association, the American Mining Congress, and the Federal Timber Purchaser's Association.[53] None of these interest groups had a direct stake in the outcome of the snail darter controversy. Nonetheless, they spoke out against the act because they began to realize how a broad interpretation of the ESA might eventually affect their own economic interests by requiring potential FWS Section 7 oversight and veto power over the issuance of grazing permits, mining claims, and timber sales. This was the first time in its history that the ESA faced such organized and powerful opposition.

For their part, the environmental lobby supported the holding of the Sixth Circuit and strongly opposed any amendments that might weaken the act. Representatives of the Friends of the Earth, the Environmental Defense Fund, the Sierra Club, the World Wildlife Fund, the National Wildlife Federation, the National Audubon Society, the Environmental Defense Fund, the Nature Conservancy, the American Rivers Conservation Council, and others testified in support of the act. These organizations claimed to represent millions of American environmentalists eager to keep the ESA strong. They stressed its successes, warned of the ongoing extinction crises, and pointed out the flexibility of the act in almost all cases except for the fight over Tellico Dam.[54]

To resolve some of the contentions between economic interests and environmentalists, Congress instructed the General Accounting Office (GAO) to prepare a report on the costs, alternatives, and benefits of the Tellico Dam project. The GAO completed that report in October 1977 and concluded that, irrespective of the endangered species issue, Tellico Dam should not be completed for economic reasons. According to the GAO, cost-benefit analysis did not support the completion of the dam or the proposed alternatives. Based on this conclusion, it recommended that Congress at least temporarily prohibit TVA from completing the project and urged Congress not to pass proposed legislation to exempt TVA from the requirements of the ESA. The GAO, however, also recommended further economic and biological study of the project before Congress reached a final and permanent decision about the dam and the snail darter.[55]

Supporters of the dam, however, ignored the GAO report. In November 1977, during floor debate over extending appropriations for the ESA, Congressman Jamie Whitten (D-MS) inelegantly summed up his assessment of the situation:

> In the Tellico Dam they had to seek out the so-called snail darter, not to save the species, but to find one whereby they could stop a dam within five percent of being completed and which would have fur-

nished energy to 30,000 homes. . . . Down in Tennessee they went to
the bottom of the stream and found a darter, where the citizens who
filed an injunction could not identify or separate them from two
other darters. The only thing we could see as Members of Congress
was a little slight dot for two of them, what you would call a minnow. Nobody heard of them until they set out to stop a dam.[56]

Whitten then wondered whether the environmentalists that brought the
suit intended "to put the country back as it was at the time of the Indians." He concluded, "Things that are dear to us and valuable to us we are
in favor of, but where this is being used to stop the development of this
country, we cannot afford it."[57] Although Whitten seemed most concerned about the economic impacts of the ESA, he overlooked the economic shortcomings of the Tellico Dam project itself.

Others in Congress echoed Whitten, raising serious concern over the
way in which the ESA might be applied in the wake of the Sixth Circuit's
decision. Representative Wesley Watkins (D-OK), for example, worried
that the power of the ESA had grown to the point that there was now "a
serious possibility that a mutation or long-distant cousin of the snail
darter or something in my district will prevent any type of economic
growth for our people."[58] Supporters of the law attempted to assure their
colleagues that the intent of the ESA was not to impede public works
projects but to protect endangered species, and that in all cases but this
one the act worked flexibly and reasonably. Despite growing opposition
to the ESA, in December 1977, Congress reauthorized appropriations
through 1980, agreeing to reconsider amending the act during the next
session.[59]

Early in 1978, Congress considered another House bill to extend appropriations for the ESA through 1981.[60] The bill proposed a significant
increase in appropriations, nearly all of which would have been allocated
to the implementation of Section 7. As a result of the holding of the Sixth
Circuit, the secretary of the interior planned to create twenty Section 7
consultation teams to provide technical assistance to other federal agencies on endangered species conflicts. During hearings over this bill held
in February 1978, the chair of the Subcommittee on Fisheries and Wildlife
Conservation and the Environment noted that these consultation teams
would be vital to avoid future conflicts like Tellico Dam.[61] The chair indicated that the subcommittee would only consider the question of extending appropriations and would not consider testimony regarding the
scope and possible amendment of Section 7 until oversight hearings were
held later in the spring. Environmental organizations and representatives
of natural resource industries, however, ignored this condition, making
arguments for and against amendments to Section 7.

Meanwhile, in April 1978, the Senate Subcommittee on Resource Protection met to consider a bill that would have amended the ESA by creating a cabinet-level committee empowered to exempt certain federal actions from the requirements of Section 7.[62] Lynn Greenwalt, director of FWS and the administration's key representative, opposed the bill, arguing that Section 7 conflicts could be resolved through the current administrative process. He pointed out that, of the thousands of Section 7 consultations since the passage of the act, only three federal projects were impacted by court decisions, and only one of those, Tellico Dam, seemed to have reached an impasse.[63] Interestingly, Greenwalt characterized the consultation process as "discretionary" prior to the Sixth Circuit's decision and reported that during fiscal year 1977, FWS conducted forty-five hundred such discretionary consultations.[64] As a result of the Sixth Circuit's decision, however, FWS expected to engage in over twenty thousand Section 7 consultations during 1979. Greenwalt also compared the Section 7 requirement to the procedural requirements of the National Environmental Policy Act, suggesting that, according to the administration's interpretation, Section 7 lacked substantive bite.[65] In other words, the administration believed that the Sixth Circuit's decision now required Section 7 consultations in all cases of potential jeopardy, but the ultimate decision to continue with a project would remain with the development agency.

Although environmentalists disagreed with the administration's narrow interpretation of Section 7, they too opposed the amendment. Zygmunt Plater, representing the Environmental Policy Center and the Little Tennessee River Alliance, argued that the amendment would decrease the incentive that action agencies had to act in good faith when consulting FWS or NMFS to determine whether their actions might jeopardize a species. He also noted that the amendment would, for the first time ever, permit a conscious, government-sanctioned decision to exterminate a species, and that this decision would be made by "nonelected bureaucrats."[66] Finally, Plater warned that the amendment would not require action agencies to consider reasonable and prudent alternatives to their proposed actions during the consultation process. Representatives from the major environmental organizations joined him in criticizing the proposed amendment.[67]

Others, of course, spoke in favor of the amendment to weaken the ESA. Representing investor-owned electric companies nationwide, the Edison Electric Institute criticized the inflexibility of the act and said that it hoped its testimony would remedy the "common misconception" that the law only impacted public works or federal actions.[68] The Colorado River Conservation District also criticized the "total inflexibility" of the ESA and explicitly blamed this inflexibility on the Sixth Circuit's recent interpretation of the act.[69] A number of senators and representatives joined these and other economic interests in attacking the court's interpretation of Section 7. As a result of the Sixth Circuit's decision, by the spring of 1978, the ESA had made many enemies.

Those responsible for administering the ESA paid close attention to these hearings, primarily because they opposed amendments that might weaken the act.[70] As mentioned earlier, FWS resisted the Sixth Circuit's holding and attempted to limit it through administrative rules that allowed for more flexibility in the Section 7 consultation process. FWS also tried to defuse the Tellico Dam situation in other ways. For example, it attempted to relocate some snail darters in the hope of establishing healthy populations elsewhere and thus allowing the completion of Tellico Dam. These efforts, however, were plagued with difficulties, including one "accident" that resulted in the death of ninety-eight darters.[71] Ultimately, additional administrative actions on Section 7, and Tellico Dam specifically, awaited resolution by the U.S. Supreme Court.

As a result of the lower court cases, congressional hearings, and administrative actions, the snail darter controversy captured a national audience. Press coverage intensified as the U.S. Supreme Court prepared to hear oral arguments on the case. Just two weeks prior to those arguments, the *New York Times* reported that the Sixth Circuit's decision had provoked some in Congress to introduce amendments to weaken the ESA by creating a new administrative body authorized to exempt federal actions from Section 7 requirements.[72] On April 14, the *Times* wrote that the ESA had become "the object of antienvironmentalist backlash," quoting Senator Jake Garn (R-UT) as saying that "I frankly don't give a damn if a 14-legged bug or a woundfin minnow live or die."[73] According to the newspaper, Garn warned that the entire act was in danger of repeal if not weakened by the Supreme Court or amended to create more flexibility.

On April 18, 1978, the Supreme Court heard oral arguments from both sides of the case. The next day, the *New York Times* wrote that "laughter swept the courtroom" when the attorney general, arguing on behalf of the TVA, displayed a vial containing the small fish that had caused all the fuss.[74] The newspaper also described the unusual split in the administration over the interpretation of Section 7. According to the attorney general, Section 7 did not require TVA to abandon its dam, primarily because construction began before the passage of the ESA and appropriations for the dam continued well after its passage. The secretary of the interior, however, attached an appendix to the attorney general's brief, arguing that such circumstances did not exempt Tellico Dam from the requirements of Section 7. The *Times* reported that the justices seemed particularly interested in whether snail darters transplanted to other rivers had survived and thrived, leading the newspaper to speculate that the Court might remand the case to resolve this point, thus prolonging the controversy.

Soon after these oral arguments but before the Supreme Court's final decision, the House of Representatives began oversight hearings on the ESA. Once again, these hearings focused on the Sixth Circuit's interpretation of Section 7 and how Tellico-type impasses might be avoided in the future.[75] Several in Congress, including John Duncan (R-TN), believed that FWS had successfully relocated snail darters to the Hiwassee River, thus resolving the conflict, allowing the completion of Tellico Dam, and mooting the case still pending before the Supreme Court.[76] Others simply ignored the Supreme Court, either supporting or opposing amendments to Section 7 of the ESA regardless of the outcome of the pending case. What differentiated these hearings from earlier ones, however, was their length and scope—they included over one hundred oral testimonies and statements and nearly fifty other communications. Perhaps most remarkable of all was the number of senators and representatives who testified, an indication that Congress was serious about amending the act. The Court attempted to reach its final decision during these hearings and must have been keenly aware of the political ramifications of that decision.

Politics aside, the Court faced lengthy legal arguments, posed not just by the petitioners and respondents in this case but also by organizations filing amicus curiae, or "friend-of-the-court," briefs. The first arguments came to the Court in May 1977, when TVA wrote its petition for a writ of certiorari, asking the Court to hear its appeal from the Sixth Circuit.[77] Soon after, the respondents in this case, Hiram Hill, Zygmunt Plater, Donald Cohen, the Audubon Council of Tennessee, and the Association of Southeastern Biologists, filed a brief in opposition to TVA's petition. In this brief, respondents argued that the Supreme Court should deny certiorari primarily for two reasons: the Sixth Circuit had reached its unanimous decision correctly under the law, and Congress was considering a political resolution of the conflict between the act and Tellico Dam.[78] The Natural Resources Defense Council made similar arguments in its friend-of-the-court brief filed in opposition to TVA's petition for certiorari.[79] On November 14, 1977, however, the U.S. Supreme Court agreed to hear the case, granting TVA's petition.[80]

Two months later, TVA filed its brief with the Court, focusing not on the larger question of whether Section 7 acted as a substantive bar against agency action following a finding of jeopardy, but on narrower issues. Essentially, TVA argued that Section 7 could not apply to Tellico Dam because construction began before the ESA was passed, because the dam was about 75 percent complete when the snail darter was listed, and because Congress granted the dam an implied exemption from the act by continuing to authorize appropriations for it after the snail darter was listed.[81] The environmentalists responded that Section 7 of the ESA made no allowances for projects begun before the passage of the act or nearly complete at the time of listing. They also argued that the only exemptions that applied to Section 7 were those explicitly provided for in the statute, and to recognize implied exemptions would be contrary to established legal precedent. The environmentalists also peppered their brief with nongermane arguments, praising the near pristine quality of the Little Tennessee River, attacking Tellico Dam for economic reasons, and pointing to widespread political opposition to the dam.[82]

To counter the respondents, TVA filed a lengthy reply brief. In it, TVA argued that many of the environmentalists' arguments had nothing to do with the issues before the Court in this case and stated that it was up to Congress, not the Court, to evaluate the costs and benefits of the project. Nevertheless, TVA also responded directly and at length to the environmentalists' policy arguments, in particular disagreeing with respondents' claims that the economic costs and adverse effects of Tellico Dam outweighed its benefits.[83] TVA also disagreed with the respondents' argument that it failed to consult with the secretary of the interior in a good-faith effort to protect the snail darter by finding alternatives to impoundment of the reservoir. It concluded that despite its good-faith efforts to consider alternatives during the consultation process, there was no way to both build the dam and protect the darter.[84] Finally, TVA argued that Section 7 was a purely procedural requirement without substantive force to halt projects even after a finding of jeopardy, an argument it had not emphasized in its original brief.[85]

In addition to the arguments of the petitioners and the respondents, the Court received amicus curiae briefs from six other interested parties. Of these, only the Southeastern Legal Foundation's brief declined to formally endorse either position. The foundation claimed to be a nonprofit organization dedicated to advancing the public interest in adversary proceedings involving significant issues affecting the American Southeast. According to its brief, recent evidence indicated that the Tellico Dam structure as it then stood, even without the closing of the sluice gates, prevented young snail darters from swimming upstream to spawn. Therefore, the darter was doomed to extinction in the Little Tennessee River regardless of whether the dam was completed, and its only hope of survival was successful relocation.[86] The foundation concluded that continuing to enjoin the completion of Tellico Dam would be both futile and wasteful.[87] Despite this position, the solicitor general on behalf of TVA refused to consent to the filing of the Southeastern Legal Foundation's brief.[88]

Two amicus briefs, however, did directly support TVA's position. In the first brief, a number of local government and civic organizations within Monroe County (where Tellico Dam was located) argued that the dam should be completed because of its vital economic benefits to the region. According to their brief, Tellico Dam would enhance the standard of living in a three-county area of east Tennessee and "contribute to the general welfare of the Nation," and to continue to enjoin the dam would destroy their "hopes and plans for a better way of life."[89] These local governments and organizations contended that the respondents in the case were misusing the ESA and thwarting the intent of Congress. They failed, however, to back up this contention with much legal argument, relying instead on economic and public policy arguments.[90]

The Pacific Legal Foundation also filed a brief in support of the petitioners. This foundation purported to be a nonprofit organization operating from California for the purpose of engaging in litigation affecting the broad public interest and claimed over twenty thousand contributors and supporters nationwide. In contrast to the Monroe County brief in support of the petitioners, the Pacific Legal Foundation focused on traditional legal arguments. Primarily, its brief attempted to persuade the Supreme Court that Congress intended the ESA to be implemented in a manner sensitive not only to biological factors but also to economic and social concerns. The foundation, therefore, supported the district court's decision, which had concluded that the economic and social benefits of the dam outweighed the value of the snail darters in this case.[91]

Countering these briefs in favor of the petitioners, three amicus briefs supported the respondents. Predictably, the nation's major environmental organizations joined Hiram Hill, Zygmunt Plater, and their local environmental organizations in arguing to uphold the Sixth Circuit's decision. The Environmental Defense Fund, the National Audubon Society, the National Wildlife Federation, the Natural Resources Defense Council, the Sierra Club, and the Defenders of Wildlife filed a brief opposing the completion of Tellico Dam. The organizations maintained that there was no disagreement among the parties that a violation of Section 7 took place. Instead, their arguments focused on why TVA could not legitimately claim implied exemptions to Section 7. These environmental organizations also warned the Court that this case had implications far beyond the fate of the snail darter and one dam. According to them, the Court's decision would affect "the future of the endangered species preservation program."[92]

The East Tennessee Valley Landowners Association also filed an amicus brief in support of halting the dam. This association consisted of farmers, landowners, and businesspeople in East Tennessee, some of whom owned land in areas to be inundated by the Tellico Dam project. Their brief directly countered the one filed by Monroe County. According to the association, the dam project would "eliminate a major bloc of the area's prime class agricultural land," thus contributing to a national trend that threatened the role of the United States in the world economy.[93] Like the Monroe County brief, this brief relied little on legal arguments and instead appealed to the Court based on economic, social, and policy concerns. It demonstrated to the Court and to Congress that economic interests were not unified in support of the dam.

Adding to an already diverse mix, the Eastern Band of Cherokee Indians also filed an amicus brief in support of the environmentalists. The Cherokee claimed "unique" historical and cultural interests in the lands to be impounded by TVA.[94] Specifically, they believed that the area to be inundated by the dam included the site of the sacred Cherokee town of Echota, a capitol of the Cherokee Nation as early as the sixteenth century; the Cherokee town of Tennase, from which the state of Tennessee derived its name; and the Cherokee villages of Citico, Toqua, Tommotley, and Toskeegee, the birthplace of Sequoya, inventor of the Cherokee alphabet. According to the Cherokee, to allow the completion of Tellico Dam and the inundation of the Little Tennessee River Valley would forever bury an important part of their culture.[95] In their brief, the Cherokee also translated these cultural issues into economic arguments in support of halting the Dam, claiming that the Indian heritage of the Little Tennessee River Valley attracted tourists to the area.[96]

Finally, on June 15, 1978, in the landmark case of *Tennessee Valley Authority v. Hill*, the Supreme Court reached a decision regarding the future of Tellico Dam, the fate of the snail darters, and the scope of Section 7. In a 6 to 3 opinion, the Court affirmed the decision of the Sixth Circuit, holding that Section 7 constituted an absolute bar against any actions authorized, funded, or carried out by federal agencies that would jeopardize the continued existence of a listed species.[97] In this way, the Supreme Court transformed Section 7 from what many had thought of as a purely procedural requirement to a substantive command, making it one of the most powerful provisions of the act and in all of environmental law. The holding left no room for economic or social considerations, and the Court upheld the injunction against the completion of Tellico Dam.[98]

Chief Justice Warren Burger, writing for the majority, offered several reasons for the decision. First, he believed that "one would be hard-pressed to find a statutory provision whose terms were any plainer than those in § 7 of the Endangered Species Act."[99] According to Burger, the act's "very words affirmatively command all federal agencies 'to *insure* that actions *authorized, funded*, or *carried out* by them do not *jeopardize* the continued existence' of an endangered species or '*result* in the destruction or modification of habitat of such species.'"[100] He believed that this language "admits of no exception."[101] To allow the dam to be completed, Burger wrote, would be to ignore the ordinary meaning of plain language.

The Court also turned to the legislative history to support the holding. Burger concluded that the "plain intent of Congress in enacting this statute was to halt and reverse the trend toward species extinction, whatever the cost."[102] In reaching this conclusion, he pointed to several statements by members of Congress in 1973 describing the loss of a single species as "incalculable."[103] Burger also pointed to the language of the consultation requirements found in predecessor acts to the ESA. The Endangered Species Conservation Act of 1966, for example, had required federal agencies to protect species only "insofar as is practicable and consistent with their primary purposes."[104] Similar qualifications were found in the House version of the 1973 bill, but the Conference Committee adopted the stronger language of the Senate version.[105] To the majority, this evidence seemed conclusive that Congress intended Section 7 as a substantive bar rather than simply a procedural requirement.

The Court also rejected TVA's other arguments. First, it held that the dam was not exempt from the requirements of the ESA just because construction on the dam began before the passage of the act. Second, the Court dismissed TVA's arguments that continuing appropriations for the dam created an implied exception to Section 7. In this, it relied on what it characterized as clear precedent rejecting implied amendments to existing statutes.[106] According to the Court, only those exceptions explicitly provided for in the act itself could be considered legitimate.

The three dissenters disagreed with the majority's reasoning and conclusions. Justice Lewis Powell, joined by Justice Harry Blackmun, warned that the Court's decision "casts a long shadow over the operation of even the most important projects serving vital needs of society and national defense."[107] According to Powell, Section 7 could not reasonably be interpreted to halt projects substantially completed. He objected to the majority's position that Congress could have intended such an "absurd result."[108] Powell dismissed the majority's reasoning by calling it an "extreme" example of literalist construction not required by the language of the act and contrary to congressional intent.[109] Instead, he believed the act should be interpreted in a way that accorded with common sense and the public weal.[110] Powell concluded by warning that he had little doubt Congress would amend the ESA in response to the Court's decision.[111]

Writing his own dissent, Justice William Rehnquist also disagreed with the majority's conclusion that once there is a finding of jeopardy, federal agencies have no recourse but to halt or modify their projects to avoid jeopardy. According to him, federal district courts like the one in this case should be allowed to exercise their traditional equitable powers to enjoin or not to enjoin such projects depending on the facts of each case.[112] For Rehnquist, as for Powell, Section 7 analysis required a balancing of factors by the district court, weighing, in this case, the value of preserving the snail darter and its habitat against the economic value of Tellico Dam. In his opinion, the district court had not abused its discretion when it sided with the dam.[113]

Despite the reasoning of the dissenters, the majority opinion became the law of the land. The holding meant foremost that if the services determined that a proposed agency action would jeopardize a listed species following a Section 7 consultation, then the agency could not continue its action without modification sufficient to protect that species. The holding promised to have a profound impact on any federal development project or any local government or private project requiring federal funds or federal authorization. Again, the Court reasoned that the plain meaning of the statute as well as congressional intent derived from the legislative history supported this holding. The dissent, the administration, and many in Congress disagreed with this interpretation.

Most in Congress in 1973 never even contemplated such an interpretation of Section 7. How then can the evidence that the majority opinion relied upon be explained? As for the plain language reasoning, one could argue that the language was not all that plain—even the Carter administration interpreted Section 7 consultation as a discretionary, procedural requirement prior to the Sixth Circuit's decision. Moreover, Congress could have made its language much clearer if it had intended the holding that the Court ultimately reached. Rather than labeling Section 7 "Interagency Cooperation" and instructing federal action agencies to "consult" with the Department of the Interior, Congress could have placed Section 7 under "Prohibited Acts," alongside Section 9. Section 7 could have read: "Federal agencies shall not take actions, nor shall they authorize or fund actions, that jeopardize endangered species; the Department of the Interior will determine whether jeopardy exists." This instruction would have been much clearer. The so-called plain language of Section 7 was not particularly plain at all.

The majority's reliance on legislative history is only slightly more persuasive. The evolution of the consultation requirement language seems, at first glance, to be particularly convincing. Nevertheless, to observe that Congress abandoned the explicitly discretionary language found in predecessor acts and in the House version of the bill is not to say that the language actually adopted withdrew all action agency discretion or transformed the consultation provision from a procedural requirement to a substantive one. Even if a few in Congress intended such a change in meaning, they did not share this intention with the rest of the members; almost no debate occurred over Section 7. Indeed, in the one instance during deliberations over the ESA in which Congress discussed Section 7, the Senate manager of the bill (the version eventually adopted by Congress) explained that after consultation, the federal action agency had the ultimate say on whether a project should continue or not, even if completing the project meant jeopardizing a species.[114] The majority ignored this crucial bit of legislative history—the only piece of evidence directly relevant to the issue before the Court in *TVA v. Hill.*

The Court also relied on legislative history to show that Congress intended to prevent species extinction no matter the cost. This evidence, however, does not necessarily support the conclusion that Congress intended Section 7 to be a powerful prohibition on federal agency action. Again, few in Congress contemplated how the ESA might significantly impact development or economic growth in the country. Most in Congress thought the act did little more than prohibit the direct killing of endangered species and halt the trade in the products of such species. Moreover, whenever Congress in 1973 mentioned the incalculable loss of species, it always referred to species of charismatic megafauna, not to species like the snail darter. On this point, the Court held Congress accountable for its rhetoric.

This discussion leads to a final point. By the time the Supreme Court considered *TVA v. Hill* in 1978, scientific understanding about the scope and cause of the extinction crisis had grown substantially, largely due to the passage of the ESA itself. By the end of the 1970s, scientists, the general public, and presumably even the members of the Supreme Court appreciated the necessity of preserving habitat to an extent not shared by Congress in 1973. Although the 93d Congress certainly recognized the need to protect habitat, it spoke even more about the need to stop the hunting of endangered species and the national and international trade in such species. It was possible, therefore, that when it discussed congressional intent regarding Section 7 and the ESA generally, the Court ascribed to the 93d Congress an appreciation of habitat conservation that it did not have. For the Court in 1978, if Congress had really wanted to save endangered species, then this meant saving habitat, which included limiting the development of private and public property—a conclusion not seriously considered by Congress in 1973. Again, this is not to say that in 1973, Congress and the courts had no understanding of the need to protect habitat in order to save species. Rather, by the late 1970s such an understanding was more widespread, even universally accepted.

This appreciation for habitat conservation stemmed in large part from scientific inquiry into the plight of endangered and threatened species of plants. Prior to 1973, scientists knew little about this subject, so little that with the ESA Congress specifically directed the Smithsonian Institution to prepare a report on endangered and threatened plants and the methods of adequately conserving them.[115] The Smithsonian completed this report early in 1975.[116] Soon after, FWS began taking steps to list and protect plant species, even though the ESA provided less protection for plants than for fish and wildlife.[117] A flurry of nongovernment-sponsored scientific studies on endangered plants soon followed the release of the Smithsonian report and the beginning of regulatory actions.[118] As a result of these plant studies, many scientists began to stress the need for "ecosystem conservation," which meant a shift in focus from protecting individual species to preserving whole habitats.[119]

Scientists soon began to apply the notion of ecosystem conservation with equal emphasis to species of fish and wildlife. Zoologist Clayton White, for example, concluded in one study that "the only clear way to preserve animals is, of course, to preserve or maintain habitat in large enough blocks of land to maintain the species diversity."[120] Norman Myers, in his popular and influential book *The Sinking Ark*, wrote that there is "no doubt" that habitat disruption poses the greatest threat to wildlife species. According to Myers, this had not been the case prior to the passage of the ESA: "Until a few decades back, the principal threats were of a more direct and deliberate kind, notably over-hunting."[121] By 1978, scientists understood that protecting endangered and threatened species meant foremost protecting habitat. The Supreme Court in *TVA v. Hill* interpreted the ESA to better reflect this new understanding.

CHAPTER FOUR

Dammed Fish

On June 16, 1978, the day after the U.S. Supreme Court's decision in *Tennessee Valley Authority v. Hill*, the *New York Times* ran a front-page story about the case. The paper reported that the Court had faced a "David and Goliath" choice and had ultimately decided that the strong language of the ESA required halting the completion of the $120 million Tellico Dam to save the last survivors of an "obscure kind of tiny fish."[1] The *Times* warned that the Court's interpretation of the act could be used to halt other major government projects, including the construction of the new space shuttle, which might jeopardize the habitat of the brown pelican and peregrine falcon. The newspaper also reported that both the majority and minority opinions of the justices acknowledged that Congress might exempt the dam from the ESA and thus allow the destruction of the total population of ten to fifteen thousand snail darters. Indeed, the article described efforts already under way on Capitol Hill to achieve this end by weakening Section 7.

These efforts included a bill introduced in the Senate on April 12, 1978 by Senator John Culver (R-IA), Senator Howard Baker (R-TN), and others.[2] The bill would have created a seven-member Endangered Species Interagency Board composed of the secretaries of the interior, agriculture, army, and transportation, the administrator of the Environmental Protection Agency, the chair of the Council on Environmental Quality, and the secretary of the Smithsonian Institution. The board would have been empowered to exempt a project from the requirements of Section 7 with a 5 to 2 vote. As expected, during hearings on the bill held in April, a number of environmental organizations testified against the amendment, while several commercial interests argued in favor of this and other proposals to weaken the ESA. The director of the U.S. Fish and Wildlife Service opposed the amendment, but development agencies within the federal government offered more ambivalent testimony.[3] In addition, several senators who were not members of the Committee on Environment and Public Works testified passionately in support of weakening the ESA in this way.

In May and June 1978, the House of Representatives conducted its own oversight hearings on the ESA, which also focused on ways to deal with the crisis created by the judicial interpretations of Section 7 in the ongoing snail darter litigation. The hearings, begun on May 24, extended until June 28 and thus overlapped with the Supreme Court's final decision in *TVA v. Hill.* Indeed, on June 20, the House Subcommittee on Fisheries and Wildlife Conservation and the Environment had the entire Court opinion read into the record of the oversight hearings.[4] That same day, the attorney for the plaintiffs in *TVA v. Hill,* Zygmunt Plater, testified before Congress that he and other environmentalists were disturbed to discover that they had to justify the Supreme Court's decision further to avoid debilitating amendments to the ESA.[5] Indeed, as a result of the Court's decision, criticism against the inflexibility of the ESA intensified manifold.

In particular, many in Congress seemed outraged by the presumption of the Court's decision, which claimed to interpret what Congress itself had intended when it passed the act into law just a few years earlier. Representative John Duncan (R-TN) exclaimed that contrary to the Court's decision, Congress never "intended for this act to afford any single-purposed interest a potential veto over virtually any federally funded or authorized project, at virtually any state of construction."[6] Congressman Jamie Whitten (D-MS) said, a bit more bluntly, "Congress never intended that this act be used to stop the development of our country."[7] Senator Malcolm Wallop (R-WY), an original cosponsor of the ESA, worried that the decision would lead to a wave of lawsuits designed "to stop Federal projects as a primary goal and in a way never intended by Congress."[8] Congressman Trent Lott (R-MS) declared that hardly any member of Congress had escaped the effects of the ESA and that all members had a vested interest in having the implementation and interpretation of the act conform with congressional intent.[9] Most congressmen believed that the Supreme Court had misinterpreted Section 7.

Others in Congress were less concerned with whether the Supreme Court had misinterpreted congressional intent and more worried about the immediate practical implications of the Court's decision. Representative Wesley Watkins (D-OK) fretted, "There is a serious possibility that a mutation or long-distant cousin of the snail darter or something in my district will prevent any type of economic growth for our people."[10] Senator Jennings Randolph (D-WV), chair of the Senate Committee on Environment and Public Works, warned that following the Court's decision, "some environmentalists, armed with section 7, will be able to literally shut down Federal construction programs by finding a remote species of mussel, snail, or fish at any project site."[11] He concluded that the recent Supreme Court decision demonstrated that the law was no longer flexible enough.

Some members of Congress offered arguments from the biblical to the environmental to support weakening the ESA. Senator William Scott (R-VA) complained that the act failed to give sufficient emphasis to human welfare, "to the fact that mankind is superior to animals and plant life, that both are under the dominion of man."[12] He backed up this claim with a quotation from the book of Genesis, which he read into the congressional record:

> And God said, let us make man in our image, after our likeness: And let them have dominion over the fish of the sea, and over the fowl of the air, and over the cattle, and over all the earth, and over every creeping thing that creepeth upon the earth . . . and God said unto them, be fruitful and multiply, and replenish the earth, and subdue it: And have dominion over the fish of the sea, and over the fowl of the air, and over every living thing that moveth upon the earth.[13]

For Senator Scott, completing Tellico Dam at the expense of the snail darter was humanity's God-given prerogative.

Senator Jake Garn (R-UT), on the other hand, used an environmental argument in support of amending the ESA and allowing the completion of Tellico Dam. According to him, man was, after all, part of nature: "There is no justification for calling his actions unnatural, whether those actions involve building a dam or a birdhouse. Beavers build dams, too. I do not know what is any more natural about a beaver building a dam than a man building a dam." Garn claimed, based on personal observation, that many beaver dams he had seen were "rather destructive," altogether "not very environmentally sound."[14]

Of course, not all in Congress wanted to weaken the ESA. Senator Gaylord Nelson (D-WI) believed that the Court had correctly interpreted the intent of Congress, and he blamed the press for exaggerating the Tellico Dam crisis and oversimplifying the conflict. He urged his colleagues to reauthorize the ESA without amendment, pleading that they did not have the wisdom to decide what species should live and what species should die.[15] Senator Patrick Leahy (D-VT) also praised the ESA, describing it as "the hub from which all our environmental protection and ecological awareness incentives radiate." According to Leahy, "No matter how I look at this issue, a dam is transitory, but extinction of a species is eternal. . . . we must draw the line somewhere."[16] Others in Congress echoed the sentiments of Senators Nelson and Leahy.

Nevertheless, support for amending the ESA was overwhelming. The Supreme Court's ruling provoked congressional outrage and contributed to a popular perception of the act as inflexible and antidevelopmental. To many in Congress and to average citizens across the country, the fact that an almost unknown, unimportant fish could stop a $120 million dam in the midst of an energy crisis and rampant inflation seemed ridiculous. The controversy, moreover, galvanized the industrial lobby, which by the late 1970s began to prove a formidable counterweight to the environmental lobby that had so successfully shepherded sweeping environmental laws through Congress earlier in the decade. Even most liberals in Congress sided with the dam, remaining faithful to the New Deal promise that the Tennessee Valley Authority stood for a new kind of democracy and lasting economic prosperity. In the ongoing fight between the fish and the dam, it seemed that the dam would surely win.

On July 19, 1978, the Senate voted 94 to 3 to amend the ESA.[17] Three months later, the House of Representatives voted 384 to 12 in support of its own version of ESA amendments but soon thereafter agreed to adopt the Senate version of the bill.[18] On November 10, 1978, President Jimmy Carter signed the amendments into law. He did so reluctantly and apologetically. During the signing ceremony, Carter noted that "while I believe that this new exemption process is not necessary, I hope that as the Committee carries out its responsibilities it will make the utmost efforts to protect the existence of the species inhabiting this planet." He further warned that "destruction of the life of an endangered or threatened species should never be undertaken lightly, no matter how insignificant the species may appear today."[19] He also attempted to assuage the environmental community by pointing out that some provisions of the 1978 amendments actually benefited endangered species. Environmentalists responded dubiously, although subsequent history revealed that Carter's claim had some merit.

The Carter administration had been exceedingly ambivalent about the proposed amendments to the ESA in 1978. On the one hand, FWS and to a lesser extent the Department of the Interior opposed amendments creating any exemptions from the requirements of Section 7. Federal development agencies, including most notably TVA, however, supported these amendments. Carter himself did little to resolve this conflict within his administration. According to historian Samuel Hays, he was more sincerely sympathetic to the environmental movement than any president from Nixon to Reagan. Nevertheless, Hays believes that advisers stressing economic development eventually created a rift between Carter and the environmental movement,[20] and his signing of the 1978 amendments to the ESA contributed to that rift.

Congress designed the 1978 amendments specifically to counteract what many believed to be the Court's expansive interpretation of Section 7 in *TVA v. Hill*. To this end, the amendments created the Endangered Species Committee (ESC) and gave it the power to allow a development project to be completed even if doing so would jeopardize the continued existence of a listed species. The committee consisted of the secretaries of the interior, agriculture, and army, the chairman of the Council of Economic Advisers, the administrator of the Environmental Protection

Agency, the administrator of the National Oceanic and Atmospheric Administration, and an individual nominated by the governor of the state in which a project was affected by the ESA. In granting an exemption, the ESC must conclude that there were no "reasonable or prudent alternatives" to the proposed action, the benefits of the agency action "clearly" outweighed the benefits of conserving the species or its habitat, and the agency action was of regional or national significance. An exemption could be granted on the approval of five out of the seven members.[21]

Congress anticipated that the ESC would promptly exempt Tellico Dam. Indeed, the 1978 amendments contained a provision requiring the committee to reach a decision regarding Tellico Dam within ninety days of the amendments' passage into law. In addition, some speculated that the new exemption process would also be applied to the Grayrocks Dam in Wyoming because of its potential impact on whooping crane habitat along the Platte River. According to one article by the *New York Times*, more than $400 million had already been invested in the Grayrocks project, and halting construction would cost two thousand jobs. Although most of the attention focused on the fate of Tellico Dam, a team of FWS biologists worked to determine whether Grayrocks Dam might jeopardize the whooping crane in violation of Section 7.[22]

The 1978 amendments contained significant provisions aside from the Section 7 exemption process. First, the amendments reauthorized appropriations for the act, which had expired on September 30, 1978. They also created new funds to purchase endangered plant habitat, and the provision for enforcement against commercial violators of the act was improved.[23] In addition, the 1978 amendments contained provisions not recognized as particularly important at the time. In particular, they required the secretary of the interior to designate critical habitat at the time that a species was listed.[24] Moreover, the amendments required the secretary to develop and implement recovery plans for listed species.[25] These last two provisions especially reflected an evolving scientific understanding of the extinction crisis and supplemented the ESA's prohibitive protections with affirmative actions to save endangered species.

At the time, however, all those involved with endangered species policy believed that the primary if not sole function of the 1978 amendments was to create an exemption process to the Section 7 requirements. Environmentalists and most ESA supporters believed this would significantly weaken the act, and viewed the passage of the amendments as a substantial defeat. Proponents of the amendments, on the other hand, expected that they would make the act more flexible and accommodating to social and economic concerns. In particular, Congress and others saw the creation of the ESC as a way to allow the completion of Tellico Dam under the guise of a legitimate process, so as to avoid the responsibility of simply granting outright a legislative exemption for the dam. Perhaps Congress in 1978 hesitated to be the direct instrument of a species' destruction.

The exemption process failed to function as Congress had anticipated. The ESC met in January 1979, and its seven members included the governor of Tennessee. Despite congressional expectations, the committee voted unanimously not to exempt Tellico Dam. In a letter to Congress, the chair of the ESC, Secretary of the Interior Cecil Andrus, explained that Tellico Dam could not be justified on economic grounds alone. Although the ESC found that there were no reasonable or prudent alternatives to finishing the dam and that its completion was of regional significance, the committee concluded that the economic and social benefits of the dam would not "clearly outweigh" the benefits of conserving the snail darter and its habitat. Interestingly, the committee ignored biological considerations, like the impact of the dam on the snail darter and the success of transplant efforts, and examined only economic factors. According to the ESC, Tellico Dam made no economic sense, and the costs of completing and maintaining the dam would exceed its benefits.[26]

Not only did the ESC foil specific congressional expectations in 1979, but throughout the 1980s and 1990s, it failed to operate as Congress had envisioned. Since its creation in 1978, the ESC, eventually dubbed the "God Squad," has seldom convened and in only one instance has it granted an exemption from the Section 7 requirements.[27] That exemption involved timber sales on federal lands affecting the habitat of the northern spotted owl in the early 1990s. In 1993, however, a federal court overturned the committee's decision in that case.[28] The ESC, therefore, never became the bogeyman environmentalists had feared, and it never became an effective means to make the ESA more considerate of social and economic concerns, as Congress had hoped it would in 1978.

During its deliberations over the snail darter early in 1979, the ESC also considered the case of the whooping crane and Grayrocks Dam in southeastern Wyoming. Eventually, the committee voted unanimously to exempt the Grayrocks project, but only if the Rural Electrification Administration abided by a federal court agreement that it reached in December 1978 with the State of Nebraska and several environmental protection groups. In effect, the ESC agreed to the completion of Grayrocks Dam if its builders guaranteed that enough water would be released from the dam to maintain adequate stream levels on the Platte River where it passed the Nebraska feeding grounds of the seventy-five endangered whooping cranes.[29] The ESC's "exemption" of Grayrocks Dam, therefore, was not really an exemption at all, but an administrative approval of a court order. If the project as stipulated by the court order required stream flows adequate to support the whooping cranes, then the agency action (completing the dam) would not "jeopardize" the continued existence of the crane. Therefore, Section 7 would not require halting completion of the dam, and the ESC would not need to exempt it.

Congress was unconcerned and uninterested in the committee's decision regarding Grayrocks Dam, perhaps because that decision had no practical effect. Many in Congress, however, were incensed at the ESC's refusal to exempt Tellico Dam. Senator John Johnston (R-LA) exclaimed that the "government of the United States has done some 'dam-fool' things" and, referring to the committee's decision, declared that "this has to be the most 'dam-fool' thing they have ever done."[30] Exasperated after having been thwarted by both the Supreme Court and the ESC, Senator John Chafee (R-RI) proclaimed, "We who voted for the ESA with the honest intention of protecting such glories of nature as the wolf, the eagle, and other natural treasures have found that others with wholly different motives are using this noble act in conjunction with science's present inability to place a relative value on any particular species for merely obstructive ends."[31] It was Senator Baker from Tennessee, however, who led the assault to save Tellico Dam, once and for all, from the ESA.

Early in April 1979, the Senate Subcommittee on Resource Protection conducted hearings on the reauthorization of the ESA. Those hearings centered on the ESC's decision and on proposals to circumvent it. In his opening statement, Senator Baker called the committee's decision "faulty" and out of line with congressional intent. He said that if allowed to stand, the ESC would set a "bad precedent."[32] Senator Baker concluded by informing the subcommittee that he had introduced legislation to specifically exempt Tellico Dam and authorize its completion.

An editorial in the *New York Times* lambasted Baker's plan to legislatively exempt Tellico Dam. The editorial supported the ESC's decision, agreeing with Interior Secretary Andrus that the dam was "ill-conceived and uneconomic in the first place."[33] The *Times* described Baker simply as a "sore loser,"[34] pointing out that he had been one of the chief architects and supporters for the 1978 amendment creating the ESC, and that for him to now attack the committee for failing to perform as he expected was unconscionable. The editorial concluded by stating that Baker's proposal might make good politics in Tennessee, but that it was a poor way to administer the ESA.

To his credit, Baker took the criticism with good humor. He informed the press that the snail darter had long been the "bane" of his existence and the "nemesis" of what he had fondly hoped would be his golden years. He described having been "locked in mortal combat with the lowly snail darter for what now seems an eternity" and admitted that in his fight with the darter he had "taken a sound thrashing."[35] But he assured the press that the fight was not yet over.

Senator Baker's efforts received significant support in Congress.

Baker commanded much power as a Senate Republican leader and as a presidential prospect for the Republican Party. Initially, he had reacted to the ESC's decision by drafting a bill to abolish the committee, but then decided he would be satisfied by merely circumventing their decision. Despite Baker's influence in Congress, however, he again met defeat, at least in the short term. The Senate Environment and Public Works Committee voted 8 to 3 to defeat his motion to introduce the amendment granting Tellico Dam an outright exemption.[36]

Baker did not give up, and his proposal eventually met with success in the House of Representatives. In June 1979, his Republican colleague from Tennessee, Congressman Duncan, submitted a nongermane rider to the Energy and Water Development Appropriations Act of 1980, granting Tellico Dam a legislative exemption from the ESA and from any other legal impediment.[37] The move was "sly," as the *New York Times* later called it in another editorial. The amendment was unpublished at the time, and only a handful of members of the House Subcommittee on Energy and Water Development voted on the bill as part of routine consent in many such appropriation of funds cases. The *Times* believed that when the full House later passed the entire bill, few understood the Tellico provision. For this deception, the *Times* castigated the dam sponsors for "reaching low indeed" and warned that such "legislative sleight-of-hand" endangered more than fish.[38]

The *Times* was probably correct in its opinion of the situation. The amendment allowing the completion of Tellico Dam was just a few lines long and was buried in a lengthy, uncontroversial appropriations bill for energy and water development projects nationwide. The language of the amendment did not mention the ESA or the snail darter at all but merely stated that TVA was authorized to complete Tellico Dam. Representative Duncan's rider was accepted in committee without dissent, and the House did not debate the rider prior to voting on June 18, 1979; 359 members of the House supported the bill, while 29 voted against it.[39]

By the time the bill reached the Senate in July 1979, that house of Congress had learned the import of the rider and debated it fiercely. Senator Culver, another original sponsor of the 1978 amendment creating the ESC, opposed granting Tellico Dam a direct legislative exemption. He argued that to do so would subvert the administrative exemption process, undermine the ESA, and inappropriately give precedent for congressional resolution of every future conflict between the ESA and a development project.[40] Culver introduced an amendment to withdraw the Duncan rider from the energy and water development appropriations bill, which the Senate supported with a vote of 53 to 45.[41]

The competing House and Senate versions of the bill then proceeded to the Conference Committee. The House rejected the Senate amendment on a vote of 258 to 156, and the Conference Committee returned the bill to the Senate having reinstated the legislative exemption for Tellico Dam. Senator James Sasser, a Democrat from Tennessee, and his colleague across the aisle, Senator Baker, led the fight in support of the exemption, while many others spoke in opposition. Ultimately, the Senate realized that an energy and water development appropriations bill would not be passed in the House without the Tellico exemption. On September 10, the Senate finally agreed to the rider with a vote of 48 to 44.[42]

The *New York Times* and other national newspapers closely followed this most recent episode in the snail darter controversy.[43] In an editorial the Sunday following the Senate vote, the *Times* called Tellico Dam an "ill-conceived pork-barrel project" and wrote that environmentalists could learn from the tricks and disingenuousness of those in Congress opposed to a strong ESA.[44] The editorial described the most recent vote as a victory for the Tennessee delegation, but warned that "if the Tennesseeans prevail, they will have created a precedent for further efforts to exempt pork-barrel projects from all laws and rational review."[45] The editorial urged President Carter to veto the bill.

Carter claimed that despite having fought against Tellico Dam for two and a half years, the Energy and Water Development Act of 1980 posed a difficult decision for him.[46] However reluctant, he signed the bill into law on September 25, 1979. He claimed that he did so in part because he feared that Congress would not let go of this issue and either override his veto or attempt other ways to exempt Tellico Dam. In particular, Carter hoped that by allowing the Tellico Dam exemption, he might prevent a more substantive and comprehensive weakening of the ESA.[47] Environmentalists, however, interpreted his decision to sign the bill into law as yet another sellout by the administration.

Zygmunt Plater, the attorney for the plaintiffs in *TVA v. Hill*, represented the reaction of many environmentalists. Plater had remained closely involved in the snail darter controversy even after the Supreme Court's decision. He had testified in Congress against the 1978 amendments creating the ESC and had personally lobbied President Carter to veto the energy and appropriation bill exempting Tellico Dam. Before the signing ceremony, Plater received a phone call from Carter informing him that he would not veto the bill. According to Plater, "Carter was like Pontius Pilate wanting me to wash his hands of blood."[48] Carter's decision left many environmentalists feeling abandoned and angry.

On November 30, 1979, the Tennessee Valley Authority completed construction of Tellico Dam, and the Little Tennessee River Valley was inundated with water. The *New York Times* printed a brief history of the project, reporting that TVA first proposed building the dam in 1965 at an estimated cost of $10 million. Fourteen years, $116 million, and eleven lawsuits later, TVA had finally finished its dam. According to the *Times*, TVA and the Tennessee congressional delegation had finally won, while environmentalists, scientists, farmers formerly living in the now inundated valley, the Cherokee nation, the ESA, and the snail darter had lost.[49]

Newspaper editors nationwide were not pleased. In one editorial, entitled "The Ultimate Corruption," the *New York Times* claimed that the actions of Senator Baker and others to complete Tellico Dam had done permanent damage "to the country, to faith in the system . . . Foiled by the new rules he had helped to draft, Senator Baker simply eliminated the rules." For the *Times*, Baker's behavior in the Tellico Dam affair helped explain why millions of Americans had come to despair of politics. But Baker was not the only target of attack. The newspaper also singled out President Carter for not having "the courage to do what he knew was right."[50] While not as harsh, other national newspapers echoed these sentiments.[51]

As for the ultimate fate of the snail darters, scientists and environmentalists had long predicted that the inundation of the Little Tennessee River Valley would mean certain doom for the species. New facts, however, soon muddied these predictions. To begin with, as early as 1978, FWS had attempted to transplant snail darters from the Little Tennessee River to locations on the Elk, Holston, and Hiwassee Rivers. Although transplanted populations in the Elk and Holston Rivers failed, those in the Hiwassee River seemed to thrive. More tellingly, in 1980 David Etnier, the ichthyologist who had first identified the darter in 1973, discovered healthy populations of darters outside of the Little Tennessee River Valley. The fish were found about eighty miles east from Tellico Dam in a creek called the South Chickamauga.[52] Etnier believed that the Chickamauga site represented natural but heretofore unknown habitat for the snail darter, concluding that the fish had not migrated there from any of the transplanted locations.[53]

FWS and TVA biologists, of course, tracked the discovery closely. TVA biologist Charles Saylor estimated that at least two hundred snail darters inhabited South Chickamauga Creek.[54] As a result of this discovery, FWS began looking for snail darters elsewhere and by early 1983 began to consider reclassifying the species.[55] By the summer of 1983, FWS had discovered healthy snail darter populations in four other locations in Tennessee, Georgia, and Alabama.[56] A year later, in an ironic epilogue to the snail darter controversy, FWS downlisted the species from endangered to threatened.[57] As the *Washington Post* put it, despite Tellico Dam, the tiny snail darter had swum off the endangered list.[58]

The news, of course, was good for the darter, good for the goal of biological diversity, and good for scientists like David Etnier. Environmental activists, however, received the revelation with mixed emotions. While they certainly did not want to see a species go extinct, the discov-

ery of additional habitat and the eventual downlisting of the darter un-
dermined their credibility. After all the fighting and fuss, it seemed that
the snail darter would survive despite the dam. The press, of course,
picked up on the irony. The *Los Angeles Times* ran an editorial entitled,
"Those Ungrateful Little—!" and hoped that environmentalists might
find "worthier, more grateful, symbols" for future efforts to protect vanishing species from oblivion.[59]

The snail darter controversy had many significant consequences for
endangered species policy specifically and for the environmental movement generally. Most important, the controversy fundamentally altered
congressional and public perception of the ESA. No longer did the American people or their politicians view the act as a costless tool used exclusively to preserve charismatic species representative of the national
heritage. The controversy also created an abiding opposition to the ESA
within Congress and helped produce a permanent and coordinated lobby
against it. Moreover, the perception of the controversy probably contributed to a more general backlash against the environmental movement
during the early 1980s. On the other hand, while the judicial decisions
that provoked the controversy made the ESA a target, they also transformed the law into a powerful tool for species preservation.

Congressional debates over the reauthorization of the ESA late in
1979 exposed this new generalized opposition to the act. Despite the recent resolution of the snail darter controversy, some in Congress attempted to use the reauthorization consideration to fundamentally
weaken the ESA. Representative Donald Young (R-AK), for example, offered an amendment to redefine "fish and wildlife" so as to exclude all
invertebrate species from ESA protection and thus "conform the act with
the original intent of Congress."[60] Others joined Young in attacking some
of the core protections offered by the law. These attacks, however, failed
for the time being, and Congress extended funds for the ESA through
1982 without debilitating amendments.[61] On December 28, 1979, claiming
that reauthorization of the act had been one of his highest legislative priorities, President Carter enthusiastically signed the bill into law.[62]

The snail darter controversy also had a profound impact on the way
the Fish and Wildlife Service and the National Marine Fisheries Service
implemented the ESA. Most significant, the services became much more
cautious about listing species, using their administrative discretion to
avoid the strict language of Section 4 requiring that species be listed based
solely on the best scientific knowledge available. The first evidence of the
abuse of agency discretion in listing arose even before the resolution of the
snail darter crisis. A 1979 report to Congress by the General Accounting
Office concluded that FWS had on several occasions delayed or refrained
from listing species or designating critical habitat to avoid controversy.[63]

In one instance, the GAO report claimed that FWS had deliberately delayed listing two species of cave harvestman (spiderlike invertebrates also known as daddy longlegs), which, based upon the best scientific knowledge available at the time, were known to be endangered. FWS feared that listing the insects would have posed a serious threat to the New Melones Dam in California. Interestingly enough, the service claimed that its reluctance stemmed not from support for the dam, but from the possibility that yet another controversy might push Congress to eviscerate the Endangered Species Act.[64] Again in 1980, in an oversight report on the administration of the ESA, the House Subcommittee on Fisheries and Wildlife Conservation and the Environment criticized the services for "inconsistently" applying the policies and procedures of the act in the listing of species.[65] This abuse of agency discretion, if not the agency's sympathetic stance toward the ESA, foreshadowed practices common under the Reagan and Bush administrations.

Although sometimes critical of the extent to which the administration used its discretion, Congress was partly responsible for increasing administrative power over implementing the ESA. The 1978 amendments creating the ESC essentially gave the administration exclusive power over the Section 7 exemption process, but they also increased administrative power in other ways. Most significant, Congress instructed the administration to designate critical habitat only to the "maximum extent prudent" and allowed the services to consider economic factors in the designation of such habitat.[66] This amendment in particular helped change the listing process from a purely biological inquiry to a subjective one balancing biology, economics, and other social considerations.

Aside from these more direct consequences for the administration, the snail darter controversy may also have contributed to the antiregulatory sentiment that helped elect Ronald Reagan to the presidency in 1980. Reagan rode into the White House as part of the sagebrush rebellion, an antienvironmental movement originating in the West. Reagan called himself a "Sagebrush Rebel" and pledged "'to work toward a Sagebrush solution'" for the nation's environmental problems.[67] Part of this solution meant appointing James Watt, a known antienvironmentalist, as the secretary of the interior. Watt led, in the words of historian Sam Hays, "a massive assault on environmental policies,"[68] and his appointment had a profound affect on the implementation of the ESA.

In December 1981, environmentalists voiced a host of complaints against the new administration to the congressional ESA oversight committee. To begin with, they protested that the services had not listed one new species since Reagan came into office. They also complained that the administration was focusing unduly on protecting "higher life forms" while ignoring so-called lesser species. Environmentalists opposed Reagan's executive order requiring the White House Office of Budget Management to conduct cost-benefit analyses for all federal programs, including each new ESA listing. They believed that compelling such economic analysis contravened Section 4's requirement that species be listed based solely on the best scientific knowledge available.[69]

Soon after these hearings, the national press began to publicize the changes Watt brought to the Department of the Interior. According to one insider, Watt had made administrative changes and encouraged new interpretations of environmental laws so as to shift the department's emphasis from resource conservation to resource development.[70] With regard specifically to endangered species, the *Washington Post* reported that not only had the Department of the Interior refused to list new species in recent years, but it also had been "shedding" species from the endangered and threatened lists. In particular, the *Post* noted that the Interior Department had recently downlisted the alligator and African leopard from endangered to threatened and that it now proposed removing the Minnesota timber wolf from the list entirely.[71] Watt responded that the lack of listings, the downlistings, and the delistings could all be explained by the "tremendous success" of the endangered species program.[72]

Not all of those within the Department of the Interior agreed with Watt's statement or with his new policies. One department lawyer, who asked not to be identified by the press, reported that according to Watt there were two categories of persons within the department, "liberals and Americans."[73] This lawyer had been told not to bother considering any management option out of line with the administration's prodevelopment policies. Moreover, early in 1982, John Spinks, the head of Interior's Office of Endangered Species, wrote a "blistering memo" that ripped into his superiors for what he called "nit-picking delays" in listing endangered species. According to the *Washington Post*, Spinks's co-workers were astounded that a career official would send such a memo. "They could ship him to Guam tomorrow for writing that stuff," said one policy analyst.[74]

The conservative attack on the ESA and other environmental laws, however, had consequences unforeseen by Reagan, Watt, and their fellow sagebrush rebels. The extreme actions of the Reagan administration aroused nationwide concern over the fate of the environment. As a result, membership in environmental organizations grew 200 to 300 percent in the early 1980s. In addition, the administration's unabashed antienvironmentalism transformed some relatively conservative environmental groups, like the National Wildlife Federation, into activist organizations. In general, the administration's stance helped unite and galvanize environmentalists and the major environmental organizations.[75]

Environmentalists also adopted new strategies of activism to counteract the administration's environmental hostility—turning, in particular, to the courts to implement the ESA. In 1980, the National Wildlife Federation brought suit against the secretary of the interior, claiming that oil and gas leases on Alaska's North Slope violated Section 7 because of their adverse impact on the endangered bowhead whale.[76] A year later, Defenders of Wildlife used the ESA to challenge the administration's approval of bobcat exports.[77] In 1982, a coalition of environmentalists attacked the U.S. Forest Service's approval of a mineral exploration project in a Montana wilderness area, alleging that the project would jeopardize the grizzly bear.[78] Although these cases met with varying degrees of success, they demonstrate the growing trend of environmentalists during the 1980s to bring suits against the administration to implement and enforce the ESA and other environmental laws.

Eventually, this litigious strategy led to further controversy. This time the conflict centered not on the scope of Section 7 but on the meaning of Section 9. Section 9 prohibited the "take" of any species listed as endangered.[79] Congress defined the term "take" to mean "to harass, harm, pursue, hunt, shoot, wound, kill, trap, capture, or collect, or to attempt to engage in any such conduct."[80] The ESA did not define these terms further. To better explain at least one of these words, in 1975 the Department of the Interior had issued regulations defining "harm" to include "significant environmental modification or degradation" of an endangered species' habitat.[81] The administration, however, declined to use this broad definition in the actual enforcement and implementation of the act throughout the 1970s and 1980s.

Once again, using the citizen suit provision of the ESA, environmentalists stepped in where the administration remained reluctant. In the summer of 1979, the Sierra Club, the National Audubon Society, and other environmental organizations sued the Hawaii Department of Land and Natural Resources to enjoin it from maintaining populations of feral goats and sheep on certain state lands. The department supported the animals as a subsidy to big game hunters, but the environmentalists claimed that the goats and sheep destroyed the mamane-naio forests on the slopes of Mauna Kea, the only known habitat of the endangered Palila bird, a finch-billed member of the Hawaiian honeycreeper family.[82] In 1981, the Ninth Circuit Court of Appeals affirmed the district court's holding that the State of Hawaii had indeed violated Section 9 of the ESA by indirectly allowing the degradation of the Palila's critical habitat.[83]

Many were alarmed by the implications of the Ninth Circuit's decision. According to the court's interpretation of the administration's definition of harm, theoretically at least the ESA could be used to regulate activities on private or state lands as seemingly innocuous as maintaining cattle, plowing a field, or clearing a stand of trees. The *Washington*

Post reported that the Ninth Circuit's decision had generated much concern among private landowners. In response to the decision, FWS proposed to redefine "harm" to mean only an act that directly injured or killed wildlife. The *Post* reported the administration's plans and even provided readers with the FWS address to which they could send comments on the proposed redefinition of harm.[84]

Environmentalists, led by the Environmental Defense Fund, fought to block the proposed regulation. Surprisingly, they succeeded. After months of rulemaking, FWS ended up just about where it started. According to the slightly new definition, significant modification or degradation of a species' habitat constituted harm if it killed or injured fish or wildlife by upsetting breeding, feeding, or sheltering patterns.[85] The definition, therefore, remained a prohibition on land use activities that might indirectly kill or injure wildlife. Like the snail darter controversy, these environmental victories proved pyrrhic.

Prompted in part by these developments, late in 1981 Congress again considered amending the ESA. The administration pushed Congress for the most comprehensive changes. Robert Jantzen, the director of FWS, testified that Congress should revise the act to allow the services to place a priority on the management of higher life forms, to rescind the requirement for designating critical habitat, to apply economic analysis to the listing of species, and to make the exemption process more efficient.[86] All told, Secretary Watt and his staff recommended significant changes to twenty-seven sections of the act. Environmentalists, of course, were alarmed at the administration's sweeping proposals. Even Congress seemed unprepared to make such wholesale revisions.

Sensing congressional reluctance for comprehensive amendments in 1982, Watt decided to seek a one-year extension of the act with only minor changes. The *Washington Post* theorized that he did this to avoid a potentially divisive political issue in an election year and to await a more conservative Congress.[87] Environmentalists, however, continued to worry that the administration was eviscerating the act even without the help of debilitating amendments. They again complained that all sixty of the proposals for new listings under the ESA were bottled up in the solicitor general's office awaiting clearance under the Reagan administration's rules for cost-benefit analysis. Moreover, they noted that the budget for Interior's Office of Endangered Species had been slashed by more than 50 percent, from $4.1 million to $1.9 million. Sixteen major environmental organizations, therefore, united behind proposed amendments designed primarily to counter what they perceived as the administration's abuses in implementing the act.[88]

The national press also defended against what the *Washington Post* called the "sharpest attack" against the ESA since Congress enacted it in

1973.[89] The *Los Angeles Times* wrote that controversy over the act had been exaggerated, citing, for example, that of the 9,686 cases requiring Section 7 consultation over the last three years, only five projects could not be modified to avoid destroying a species. According to the *Los Angeles Times*, what was not exaggerated was the rapidly rising rate of global extinctions, now reaching perhaps one a day. The paper concluded that Congress should reauthorize the ESA for three more years without amendments that would weaken or destroy it.[90] Others, too, believed that in the face of inexorable human population growth and receding habitat, the ESA as then written represented an appropriate line in the sand.[91] Calling the act one of the "truly enlightened" laws, the *Washington Post* urged Congress to oppose the "quiet coalition" of mining interests, the wood products industry, furriers, and land developers bent on gutting the ESA of its key provisions.[92]

Scientists as well joined environmentalists and the press in trying to protect the ESA. Increasingly, they criticized the administration for "vertebrate chauvinism," arguing that the real reservoir of "genetic diversity" lay in the lower animals and plants and warning that this genetic diversity would supply the chemical potions that would be "the future's wonder drugs or untapped food supply."[93] Moreover, these scientists argued that biological diversity provided a fount of untapped knowledge, and that allowing species extinction was tantamount to "book burning."[94] Calling the rate of extinctions unprecedented in the history of life, scientists in 1982 warned that "by the year 2000," as many as 20 percent of species on the planet will have disappeared.[95] Against these dire predictions, the interests of "commercialists" were purely "shortsighted."[96]

Scientists spoke not only through the press but also testified directly before Congress. For example, Peter Raven, the director of the Missouri Botanical Garden, spoke to the House Subcommittee on Fisheries and Wildlife Conservation and the Environment on behalf of the forty scientific societies and eighty thousand members of the American Institute of Biological Sciences. He called the prevailing extinction crisis the most significant occurrence in the world at the time and urged Congress to support a strong ESA.[97] Thomas Eisner, a professor of biology at Cornell, attempted to explain to Congress the consequences of the loss of biological diversity resulting from the extinction crisis. He called proposals to remove protections for invertebrates and plants a misunderstanding of the reasons for preserving biological diversity so fundamental as to warrant the label "biological illiteracy."[98]

By spring 1982, debate over reauthorization and amendments to the ESA came to a head. On the one side, the administration and organized industrial interests like the American Mining Congress, the National Forest Products Association, and the American Fur Resources Institute argued for comprehensive amendments to make the act more "flexible," in other words, to substantially weaken it. Environmentalists and scientists united to defend the ESA and supported amendments that would decrease the administration's discretion in implementing it. Congress took a compromise position, drafting bills that reauthorized the ESA for three years without amendments to either seriously weaken it or to undermine administrative discretion. The compromise satisfied neither side.

Despite expectations that there would be a bitter fight over the ESA, Congress reauthorized and amended the act in June without significant dissension. Indeed, there was almost no opposition at all. The press reported the 1982 amendments as a modest success for environmentalists, primarily because they repudiated Secretary Watt's request for a one-year extension and for significant changes to weaken the act.[99] In one respect, the amendments actually strengthened the ESA by requiring the administration to take no more than twelve months to act on a petition to list a species, thus limiting the extent to which the administration could delay the listing process. Despite significant differences with Watt's recommendation, the Reagan administration supported the bill. According to the *Los Angeles Times,* this was evidence that the administration had "finally got the message" that there was strong public support for environmental protection.[100]

A closer look at the 1982 amendments, however, reveals that at least in one important respect, they made the ESA substantially more amenable to economic considerations. Specifically, the 1982 amendments created a permit process to allow the "incidental" take of listed species, so long as the applicant prepared a habitat conservation plan to minimize and mitigate the effects of such taking. In this way, for example, a timber company could obtain a permit to log its lands even if doing so destroyed critical habitat of an endangered species, thus "incidentally" or indirectly taking such species in what would otherwise be a violation of Section 9. This amendment seemed to be a direct response to the Ninth Circuit's holding in *Palila v. Hawaii Department of Land and Natural Resources* that Section 9 could be applied to prevent public or private land use activities that might indirectly kill or injure a species through habitat degradation. Like the 1978 amendment that had created an exemption from the Section 7 consultation requirement, the 1982 amendment created an exemption from the Section 9 prohibition against harming an endangered species.[101] Oddly, few in- or outside of Congress at the time noted the significance of this particular amendment.

The Department of the Interior, however, did not wait long to propose rules to implement the new permit process. As the *Washington Post* reported, the new rules would "allow developers to kill endangered species accidentally."[102] Despite some language to the contrary, the 1982 amendments failed to limit administrative discretion significantly in implementing the act. The services continued to list new species slowly and selectively, while early in 1983 they delisted fourteen species because they had gone extinct.[103] On the eve of the act's ten-year anniversary, FWS reported that there was now "less confrontation and more accommodation" in the implementation of the ESA.[104] Environmentalists agreed—the administration was confronting industry less and accommodating them more.

By the end of 1983, however, environmentalists could claim at least one substantial victory—Secretary Watt fell victim to his own big mouth. That fall, he had referred to the membership of his coal advisory board as "a black, a woman, two Jews, and a cripple."[105] With so many enemies among environmentalists and liberals, Watt could ill afford such gaffes. Under intense pressure, he was forced to resign. In an address to the nation, Reagan reported that Watt had always thought the enemies he would make as secretary of the interior would eventually push him out of office. Reagan, however, declined to mention any specifics about why Watt had chosen to resign.[106] In his three years as secretary of the interior, he had allowed the listing of an average of only seven species a year, significantly fewer than the annual average of twenty-seven species named under the Carter administration or the forty-seven species listed each year under Watt's successor, William Clark.[107]

Regardless of Watt's exodus, environmentalists continued to encounter administrative reluctance in enforcing and implementing the ESA throughout the 1980s. In June 1984, for example, administrative foot-dragging, coupled with sheer bureaucratic bungling, helped push the Palos Verdes blue butterfly closer to extinction. Because of lack of communication and coordination between FWS and the city of Rancho Palos Verdes in southern California, the city had built a baseball diamond on a stretch of the butterfly's only remaining habitat.[108] That same year, Defenders of Wildlife released a report claiming that despite the 1982 amendments, 3,827 species remained backlogged for consideration as either threatened or endangered.[109] Among these was the northern spotted owl.

PART III: THE SPOTTED OWL

CHAPTER FIVE

Spotty Wisdom

By the ten-year anniversary of its passage, the Endangered Species Act once again enjoyed widespread, if somewhat subdued, support. For many, the ESA seemed a success. Scientists like Thomas Lovejoy called the law terribly important in slowing the tide of extinctions. In particular, scientists credited it with saving the bald eagle, the rare primrose, and the green parrot.[1] For commercial interests, it was equally important that despite an average of two thousand Section 7 consultations each year, there had been no more standoffs like Tellico Dam. Ron Lambertson, the head of the Fish and Wildlife Service's endangered species program, claimed this was because government agencies and developers had finally embraced the goal of species preservation. Environmentalists, however, continued to believe that industry and agency satisfaction with the ESA stemmed primarily from the lack of aggressive implementation and enforcement.

Moreover, while supporters of the ESA lauded its successes, they worried that the act failed to do enough to halt the flood of global extinctions. Scientists in the mid-1980s estimated that ten million species inhabited the planet. They warned that two million of these might disappear by the year 2000, primarily due to loss of habitat. According to Edward O. Wilson, the loss of species and genetic diversity going on in the 1980s alone would take millions of years to correct, yet scientists feared that the ESA, at least as administered, seemed to do little to protect habitat. Alarm over the scope of the extinction crisis increased as scientists during the mid-1980s learned more about what the loss of biodiversity might mean for humans.[2]

Amid these general apprehensions, a group of ornithologists met in June 1984 to discuss the fate of one particular subspecies. They convened for the Fifty-fourth Annual Meeting of the Cooper Ornithological Society in Arcata, California, and formed a symposium to report on the northern spotted owl, *Strix occidentalis caurina*. Biologists had already identified it as one of three subspecies of spotted owl distributed in old-growth forests from British Columbia south into Mexico. The northern spotted owl lived in the old-growth, primarily Douglas-fir forests of southwestern British Columbia, western Washington and Oregon, and northwestern California. Scientists described it as a medium-size owl with dark eyes and dark to chestnut brown coloring, with whitish spots on the head and neck and white mottling on the abdomen and breast. The owl, scientists believed, was monogamous, long-lived, highly territorial, and site tenacious. It depended exclusively on old-growth forest habitat for survival.[3]

Because the Forest Service managed most of the owl's remaining old-growth habitat, that agency's biologists played a prominent role among members of the symposium. Although FWS had not yet listed the owl as either threatened or endangered under the ESA, the Forest Service had designated the species as "sensitive" and thus afforded the owl special management consideration. The Forest Service had also determined the owl to be a "management indicator species,"[4] which meant that it represented other species dependent on the old-growth forests and that the Forest Service would have to implement additional protections for the owl in accordance with the National Forest Management of 1976. As an indicator species, the health of the spotted owl reflected the health of the entire forest ecosystem.

Unfortunately for the owl, the logging industry also claimed dependence on old-growth forests. Timber harvesting increased dramatically during the 1980s, and as private and state lands became exhausted, the logging industry looked to the old-growth, previously unlogged lands owned by the federal government. To compound the problem, not only had scientists concluded that the owl could only survive in old growth, but they also discovered that one breeding pair used an average of over two thousand acres of habitat. They recommended that at a minimum the Forest Service protect one thousand acres from logging for a breeding pair to survive.[5] Although not yet able to estimate the remaining number of northern spotted owls in the Pacific Northwest, scientists at the Cooper Ornithological Society found that at least a thousand breeding pairs would need to be saved to prevent eventual extinction.[6] This meant that protecting the spotted owl would mean preventing timber companies from logging at least one million acres, and probably more.

This potential conflict, however, remained distant and unforeseen by most in Congress and the Reagan administration during the mid-1980s. In 1985, Congress again considered extending appropriation authorization for the ESA, and it did so in the absence of any significant debate about the owl. In February of that year, Representative John Breaux (D-LA) sponsored a bill to reauthorize the law through 1988. He admitted that the ESA had achieved both successes and failures and that Section 7, especially, kept the act controversial. Nevertheless, paraphrasing naturalist Aldo Leopold, he urged ESA reauthorization because "the first rule of intelligent tinkering is to save all the pieces."[7]

In a show of bipartisan support for reauthorization, Senator John Chafee (R-RI) cosponsored Breaux's appropriation bill, introducing it in the Senate. At the time, Chafee chaired the Senate Subcommittee on Environmental Pollution. He told his fellow senators that reauthorizing the

ESA would be one of his top legislative priorities. Once a proponent of weakening the act, Chafee now praised the ESA, calling it "one of the world's strongest and most important environmental laws."[8] He agreed with Representative Breaux that the law did not need to be amended. It was working well enough as written.

According to Breaux and Chafee, the 1982 amendments had corrected the primary failings of the ESA. Specifically, those amendments had required FWS and the National Marine Fisheries Service to respond to citizen petitions to list a species within one year. Breaux and Chafee believed that this requirement would correct the most egregious problem with the implementation of the ESA—the deliberate delay or refusal by the services to list species that needed protection. In what Breaux described as a "dramatic" increase in the number of listings since 1982, he noted that in the past year alone the services had listed forty-six species.[9] Significantly, Breaux, Chafee, and others in Congress in 1985 ignored the 1982 amendment provisions allowing for incidental take permits through habitat conservation plans. Later, these provisions and their implication—that the ESA could apply to private, seemingly innocuous land use activities—would stir controversy of their own.

In March 1985, the House held hearings on Breaux's bill to reauthorize the ESA. During these hearings, the directors of FWS and NMFS supported the bill, agreeing that the act needed reauthorization without additional amendments because earlier amendments had given it sufficient flexibility.[10] Although environmentalists supported reauthorization, they did not agree that the ESA was working well. Specifically, they continued to criticize the services for failing to list species quickly enough. They also attacked recovery plans as mere "pieces of paper" identifying actions necessary to recover listed species rather than accomplishing that recovery.[11] Environmentalists called for amendments to address these and other concerns.

Commercial interests testified against the ESA generally and in particular against environmental attempts to strengthen it. These interests included the American Farm Bureau, the American Petroleum Institute, and certain organizations representing water development projects in the West. The American Farm Bureau argued that the ESA be amended to compensate farmers and ranchers who suffered property depredations from protected species. The other organizations had more general complaints about the act.[12] What was particularly interesting about their testimony was that even in the absence of specific controversy, the ESA had permanent enemies providing an effective counterweight to the environmental lobby. Indeed, Congress failed to reauthorize the act in 1985, and for the next few years it survived on annual appropriations.

In the meantime, controversy began to brew over the spotted owl. As required by the National Forest Management Act, in the summer of 1986 the Forest Service announced its plan to protect the owl, estimating at the time that about two thousand pairs of owls inhabited the old-growth forests of Washington and Oregon. To protect and manage for these owls, the Forest Service identified 550 spotted owl habitats averaging 2,200 acres, or 1.2 million acres of old-growth in thirteen national forests throughout the Northwest. At the core of the Forest Service's proposal was a prohibition on logging in about 690,000 acres of old-growth forest within these habitat areas.[13]

The timber industry despised the plan, calling it "embarrassing" and "excessive."[14] In particular, they attacked the science upon which the Forest Service had based its conclusions, arguing that the northern spotted owl had been inadequately researched. Moreover, they claimed the plan would cost forty-eight hundred jobs. Responding to these criticisms, Forest Service Chief Forester Dale Robertson decreased the number of acres for each owl pair below twenty-two hundred acres, thus allowing more logging in old-growth forests. Robertson called the revised plan more flexible.[15]

Environmentalists, however, called the plan a recipe for the extinction of the northern spotted owl. According to their own scientific studies, the owl needed at least forty-five hundred acres of protected habitat per breeding pair.[16] Responding to the Forest Service's capitulation to logging interests, a small Massachusetts environmental organization called Greenworld filed a petition with FWS in January 1987 to list the northern spotted owl as a threatened or endangered species under the ESA. They expected that such a listing would force the Forest Service to protect the owl fully. The nation's major environmental organizations, however, hesitated in joining the petition, perhaps afraid to provoke Congress into weakening or repealing the act.

During the spring of 1987, Congress again considered bills to reauthorize the ESA. Fortunately for supporters of the act, the owl had not yet created enough controversy to intrude on these deliberations. Neither the House nor the Senate versions of the bill contained significant amendments to weaken the ESA; they merely authorized appropriations through 1992. During hearings on reauthorization, no representative of the timber industry came forward to testify against the bills, nor did the Forest Service mention the northern spotted owl in its own statements to Congress.[17] Perhaps just as important, environmentalists did not mention the owl. They asked only for minor amendments to strengthen the act and toned down their criticism of its implementation.[18] In this way, they hoped to get the ESA reauthorized without debate.

Frank Dunkle, director of FWS, also emphasized the lack of controversy over the ESA. He testified that since 1973, the service had conducted thirty-five thousand Section 7 consultations but had hindered less than 1 percent of all the projects reviewed. Dinkle also testified that FWS had accelerated its listing process, naming more than 150 species in 1985 as either threatened or endangered. Moreover, the service had developed over 211 recovery plans. According to Dinkle, the primary problem with the implementation of the ESA was lack of sufficient funding.[19]

Instead of demanding substantial amendments to strengthen the ESA or castigating the administration before Congress, environmental organizations decided to pursue their goals through nonlegislative means. In late May 1987, the Environmental Defense Fund announced it would sue the Department of the Interior for failing to make timely decisions in listing endangered species. Adopting a tone notably different from his testimony at the congressional hearings just a few months earlier, Michael Bean criticized FWS for consistently delaying the listing process. He explained that the delays resulted from pressure from developers whose projects might be affected and not because of lack of funding or scientific uncertainty.[20] In a letter to Secretary of the Interior Donald Hodel, Bean accused FWS of violating the 1982 amendments to the ESA by failing to act within one year on seventeen different petitions to list species.

A few months later, several dozen major environmental organizations joined Greenworld in petitioning FWS to list the northern spotted owl as threatened or endangered. A Sierra Club study cited in the petition estimated that only four to six thousand northern spotted owls remained alive in the Pacific Northwest. The study also concluded that the owl's population was declining at a rate of 8 percent annually due to the cutting of old-growth forests. The *Seattle Times* reported that if listed under the ESA, the Forest Service would have little discretion in managing for the owl. Such a listing would inevitably result in sharp decreases in logging throughout the Pacific Northwest.[21]

Because of these and other events, the spotted owl began to attract the attention of the national press. In September 1987, the *Washington Post* reported that over the last two decades, three hundred kinds of plants and animals had vanished waiting to be listed under the ESA, and nearly a thousand more, including the northern spotted owl, were still waiting. Conservationists, reported the *Post*, accused the government of engaging in a policy of "biological brinksmanship."[22] The newspaper noted that each species listed cost about $62,000 for field studies and paperwork, and that given current funding levels it would take FWS seventy-six years to review the thirty-eight hundred species currently on its candidate list. The *Post* warned, however, that the owl was unique—that it might eventually cost $6 billion to protect. In such a case, public and industry opposition might forever block listing.[23]

Despite these developments concerning the spotted owl, reauthorization of the ESA remained uncontroversial when the House of Representatives considered the issue in December 1987.[24] The House debated very little over the provisions of the bill and voted, 399 to 16, to reauthorize it. The House bill would have increased appropriations generously, from $39 million in 1987 to $57 million in 1988, $59 million in 1989, $61 million in 1990, $64 million in 1991, and $66 million in 1992.[25] The Senate, however, had yet to approve the bill, and growing controversy over the spotted owl threatened to jeopardize reauthorization.

Meanwhile, the Reagan administration attempted to defuse the situation. On December 23, 1987, FWS announced that it would not list the northern spotted owl as threatened or endangered, concluding that the listing was not warranted.[26] In addition, a few months later, President Reagan issued an executive order directing federal agencies to minimize interference with private property rights in the implementation of their regulations, an order intended in part to limit the application of the ESA to land use activities that might harm protected species.[27] Although environmentalists could do nothing immediately about the executive order, they did respond to the administration's refusal to list the owl. In May 1988, twenty-three environmental groups filed a lawsuit against FWS, alleging it had declined to list the owl due to political and economic considerations. Specifically, they accused FWS of violating Section 4 of the ESA by ignoring scientific evidence of the owl's condition.[28]

At the same time, however, environmentalists refused to advocate amending the ESA to deal with these and other perceived problems. Senator Simpson complained that environmentalists were putting "intense pressure" on members of the Environment and Public Works Committee not to introduce or to vote for any significant amendments to the act.[29] According to Simpson, these "extreme" environmental groups viewed the ESA as being "some form of holy document."[30] By opposing any significant amendments to either strengthen or weaken the law, environmentalists hoped to avoid controversy that might derail reauthorization. They continued to believe that they could achieve their goals with less risk through litigation.

In the short term, the strategy appeared to work. In July 1988, the Senate voted overwhelmingly, 92 to 2, to reauthorize the ESA. The final bill, however, approved appropriations far less generous than those first endorsed by the House—authorizing $35 million for 1988, $36.5 million for 1989, $38 million for 1990, $39.5 million for 1991, and $41.5 million for 1991.[31] The 1988 act ultimately did contain some amendments to the ESA, imposing specific requirements for the development and implementation of recovery plans and requiring the secretary of the interior to report to Congress every two years on the status of recovery efforts. These amendments, though, were relatively minor.

Environmentalists also began to win a number of important legal victories over the spotted owl and related issues. By the summer of 1988, environmentalists had coerced representatives of the timber industry, FWS, the Forest Service, and the Bureau of Land Management (BLM) into meeting to discuss short-term solutions to the spotted owl problem. The *Seattle Times* reported that this was not the first time that the threat of litigation had forced parties in dispute over Pacific Northwest timber practices to the bargaining table.[32] On other fronts, the Ninth Circuit held that Montana rancher Richard Christy did not have a constitutional right to shoot a grizzly bear, a species listed as threatened, which was eating his sheep.[33] Representative Ron Marlenee (R-MT) complained that the decision made private property rights a "sacrificial lamb" to the ESA.[34] The case represented yet another triumph for environmentalists.

The environmentalists' greatest victory, however, came in November 1988. In the case of *Northern Spotted Owl v. Hodel*, U.S. District Court Judge Thomas Zilly held that FWS's decision not to list the owl was "arbitrary and capricious and contrary to law."[35] Reviewing the record on a motion for summary judgment, Judge Zilly found that FWS had ignored its own scientific experts. In particular, the court wrote that FWS's decision not to list the owl contradicted the conclusions of its own staff biologist, Mark Shaffer. Shaffer's report on the owl had concluded that continued old-growth harvesting would likely lead to the extinction of the subspecies in the foreseeable future, "which argues strongly for listing the subspecies as threatened or endangered."[36] Aside from ignoring contrary evidence, the court found that FWS had cited no scientific evidence supporting its decision that listing was not warranted. The court, therefore, ordered FWS to reconsider its decision within ninety days and to provide scientific evidence if it again concluded that the owl should not be listed.

The timber industry called the decision "devastating."[37] The *Seattle Times* reported that because the owl required one thousand to forty-five hundred acres per pair for hunting, the decision could force a halt to logging in huge tracts of old growth on federal forestlands. FWS, however, decided not to appeal the district court's holding, instead stating that it would abide by the decision by redoing a 1987 study of the owl with new data that scientists had produced in 1988. Retreating from its earlier decision, FWS explained that its scientists had learned "quite a few things" about the owl in recent months that might no longer support its decision not to list the owl under the ESA.[38] FWS announced that its new finding would be available by May 1, 1989.

Bolstering the district court's findings in *Northern Spotted Owl v. Hodel*, a report by the General Accounting Office in February 1989 also concluded that FWS had intentionally ignored scientific evidence when it decided not to list the owl in December 1987. Specifically, the GAO found that FWS had actually ordered a spotted owl study rewritten to keep the bird from being named a threatened or endangered species.[39] Lawmakers responded quickly to the GAO report. Representative Peter DeFaxio (D-OR) said the GAO report revealed FWS's decision as a "simple case of political expediency winning out over sound scientific evaluation and good policy."[40] Representative Gerry Studds (D-MA) said that FWS had based its decision on the politics of a conservative administration, not on science or law.

In the meantime, perhaps in an attempt to convince FWS that the spotted owl did not need the protection of the ESA, the Forest Service announced a new management plan for the owl. According to this proposal, the Forest Service would reserve 1.6 million acres of old-growth forest for the owl, with habitat areas ranging from one to two thousand acres per breeding pair. Environmentalists called the Forest Service plan a farce. According to them, it would only protect about 9 percent of northern spotted owl habitat from logging. Forest Chief Robertson responded that while the plan had been an extremely difficult decision, it struck the right balance between science and economics.[41]

Regardless of the Forest Service's new plan, the court's holding practically forced it to reverse its earlier decision. In late April 1989, FWS announced that the owl would be proposed for listing as threatened. According to the requirements of the ESA, FWS could not simply list the owl at that time but had to allow for public review and comment before taking final action. The ESA, however, also required that a final decision be reached within one year, unless substantial disagreement existed among specialists, in which case a six-month extension could be granted.[42] James Geisinger, president of the Northwest Forestry Association, said that if the owl was eventually listed, as it appeared it would be, the impact on timber supply would be "potentially catastrophic."[43]

In an editorial following FWS's reversal, the *Seattle Times* called that agency's handling of the spotted owl "highly disturbing." The editorial also criticized the hyperbole of the timber industry, arguing that unrestricted cutting of old growth would not keep timber-dependent communities healthy in the long term. Instead, the editorial blamed the timber woes on exports, automation, and changing market trends. "Scapegoating the spotted owl doesn't address the powerful market forces that pose the biggest threat to the mill town and its way of life," wrote the *Times*.[44] The newspaper concluded by calling for a workable compromise that would protect the owl while minimizing impacts on the timber industry.

An earlier article by the *Seattle Times* posed an interesting contrast to this editorial and to the case of the spotted owl generally. In that article, the *Times* had featured the bald eagle's recovery as an example of the success of the ESA. The article did not specifically contrast the eagle's recovery with the owl's plight, but it did point out that FWS seemed to focus listing and recovery efforts on species with high public appeal.[45] What it did not mention was that, contrary to Section 4 of the ESA, FWS avoided listing and protecting species that lacked appeal or species whose protection would come at significant economic cost. If the recovery of the eagle represented the success of the ESA, the handling of the owl represented the act's failure.

In response to the proposed listing, federal land management agencies met to coordinate owl management pending a final decision. Forest Service Chief Dale Robertson, Robert Buford, director of the BLM, and James Ridenour, director of the National Park Service, attempted to coordinate their efforts. These agency heads, however, declined to take immediate action themselves. Instead, they drafted a joint letter to Susan Lamson, acting director of FWS, expressing the need for a decision on the harvest of the old-growth forests. Although not required by law, the proposed listing of the owl seemed to have shifted the locus of responsibility for managing old-growth forests in the Pacific Northwest from the Forest Service, BLM, and Park Service to FWS. In this way, these traditional land management agencies hoped to avoid responsibility for making the hard, controversial management decisions necessary to protect the owl.[46]

Environmentalists did not wait patiently while these federal agencies scrambled to respond to the proposed listing. Instead, they went to court, this time to halt directly the logging of old-growth forests pending a decision on the owl. In Seattle, nine environmental groups sued the Forest Service to enjoin proposed timber sales. They could not yet claim Section 7 or Section 9 violations under the ESA because the owl had not yet been officially listed. Instead, they relied on the National Forest Management Act, the National Environmental Policy Act, and the Migratory Bird Treaty Act to protect the owl. Environmentalists also brought similar claims against proposed timber sales by the BLM in Oregon.[47] The lawsuits succeeded in both cases.

In his opinion, District Court Judge William Dwyer in Seattle was unsympathetic toward the timber industry and the federal land management agencies that catered to it. According to Dwyer, the Forest Service had known of the owl's danger for a long time and should have taken action much earlier to protect the subspecies. As for the timber industry, he blamed the timber crisis on overcutting and on the enormous export of unprocessed logs to Asia. In total, Dwyer's injunctions blocked more than 140 timber sales, or nearly one billion board feet of old growth, which represented about a fifth of the Forest Service's planned sales program for fiscal year 1989.[48] The Forest Service indicated it would appeal the injunctions.[49]

In the meantime, industry groups throughout the Northwest warned of dire economic consequences if these injunctions stood and if the owl eventually was listed. First, the timber industry claimed that the injunctions were already boosting western lumber prices, thus raising the cost of new homes.[50] Moreover, the Northwest Forest Research Council claimed that a decision to list the owl could eventually result in the loss of 290,000 jobs.[51] The mining industry also felt the burden of owl conservation. In one case, it claimed that a pair of nesting owls threatened mining claims valued at up to $400 million.[52] Industry hoped that these economic arguments would win support in Congress for relief from the strict requirements of the ESA.

In an attempt to gain this support, the timber industry even hired a public relations firm. That firm created a simple message: jobs lost to the spotted owl were destroying families and small communities throughout the Pacific Northwest. In defense of their new tactic, timber industry representatives declared that they were now in a public relations war with environmentalists. According to the timber industry, this was a war that environmentalists had been waging without resistance for over a decade.[53]

The timber industry's strategy worked, at least on the congressional delegation from the Pacific Northwest. Representative Sid Morrison (R-OR), for example, joked, "In our area we need injunctive relief. That is relief from injunctions."[54] Representative Robert Smith (R-OR) proposed a law to defer protection of the spotted owl under the ESA for five years. Senator Mark Hatfield also criticized what he called the "litigate-legislate" cycle of the owl controversy and urged a timber summit to work out a compromise.[55] Although Smith's effort to defer owl listing for five years failed, Hatfield's timber summit met and negotiated a compromise in the summer of 1989.

At the heart of that compromise was a 4.2-billion-board-feet cap on the annual harvest of timber from federal forests in the Pacific Northwest. The timber industry, represented by the National Forest Products Association, reluctantly agreed to this plan. Environmentalists, however, rejected it, claiming that an annual harvest of 4.2 billion board feet exceeded sustainable levels. In an attempt to ameliorate the Northwest's congressional delegation, environmentalists said they were not opposed to the concept of a compromise plan, just to the specifics in this case. Senator Hatfield replied that while the summit delegation was willing to accept some of the environmentalists' arguments, it would not accept the "tidal wave of job loss" that they seemed to require.[56] His timber summit had failed after all.

In response, Congress considered several proposals to limit the economic impact of owl conservation. Senator Hatfield, joined by Senator Brock Adams (D-WA), proposed a bill lifting all injunctions on federal timber sales in Washington and Oregon for one full year.[57] Although Congress did not approve this bill as written, it did overwhelmingly approve a similar measure to temporarily limit the jurisdiction of federal courts over suits brought on behalf of the spotted owl. Perhaps wary of further amendments that might weaken the ESA itself, environmentalists reluctantly supported the one-year compromise.[58] Congress mostly intended the law to counteract recent court decisions by maintaining the status quo until FWS reached a final decision on the spotted owl.

Meanwhile, in April 1990, just a couple of months before FWS was due to announce its listing decision, the Forest Service's Interagency Spotted Owl Committee completed its report. That report was supposed to be a purely scientific inquiry into the status of the owl along with management recommendations that would identify the minimum protections necessary to prevent the owl from extinction. Jack Ward Thomas, Forest Service chief research wildlife biologist, chaired the committee, which consisted of sixteen scientists from various land management agencies, including most of the nation's foremost experts on the northern spotted owl. According to the so-called Thomas Report, only about seventeen hundred breeding pairs of northern spotted owls survived, an estimated 60 to 80 percent reduction since 1800. The report identified forty-three habitat areas in Washington, forty-eight in Oregon, and ninety-nine in California, with California having smaller areas because of lusher foliage. Most significant, the Thomas Report recommended a ban on logging in 30 to 40 percent of publicly owned land in the Pacific Northwest, or about eight million acres.[59]

Testifying before a Senate subcommittee, the heads of the affected land management agencies warned of the economic consequences if the plan were adopted. According to one executive summary, timber harvesting would decline by 2.4 billion board feet by 1995.[60] Forest Service Chief Dale Robertson claimed that by 1995 the Thomas Plan would cost more than twenty-five thousand jobs and $148 million in revenue from canceled timber sales on both Forest Service and BLM lands.[61] An independent study by Oregon State University found that if implemented, the Thomas Plan would cost twelve to fifty thousand jobs.[62] To many in Congress, such a price was unacceptable.

Representatives and senators, particularly those members of the Northwest congressional delegation, voiced concern and outrage over the Thomas Report. Although Senator Hatfield accepted the scientific conclusions of the Interagency Committee, he said that it was ultimately up to Congress to create sound policy that recognized social and economic needs. Specifically, Hatfield believed that any forest management plan for the owl must include greater protection for the livelihood of Northwest loggers.[63] Senator James McClure (R-ID) attacked the science of the report itself, calling it unclear and unsupported.[64] Senator Malcolm Wallop (R-WY) agreed, saying the Thomas Report was one of the "most outrageous" examples of the abuse of science and public policy that he had ever seen.[65]

Attacks on the science of the Thomas Report, however, proved to be without merit. To ensure objectivity and accuracy, the Interagency Committee had its final report reviewed by other scientists selected by the National Academy of Scientists, the Society of American Foresters, the American Ecological Society, the National Wildlife Federation, the Society for Conservation Biology, and the American Ornithology Union. These experts agreed with the scientific findings of the report. Still dissatisfied, however, the Bush administration appointed another panel of independent scientists to review it. They also confirmed the findings and recommendations of the report, calling them prudent, fair, and accurate. Congress and the Bush administration, declared one news editorial, could no longer ignore the science.[66]

Yet, they continued to do just that. In one interview, Representative Denny Smith (R-OR) rejected the conclusion that logging was the primary cause of the spotted owl's demise. Instead, he blamed predation by the great horned owl: "There are millions of owls in this world. This little puppy just happens to be kind of a passive kind of owl that's being run over by the great horned owl."[67] Senator Wallop also took his outrage over the Thomas Report to the public, saying to one newspaper that the report's recommendations were "utterly unacceptable to the American people, except for the hot-tub crew with their special agenda."[68] Regardless of the reaction by these and others in Congress, the report seemed unassailable from a scientific standpoint and therefore represented a serious blow to the forest industry.

Faced with the Thomas Report recommendations and the imminent listing of the owl and battered by litigation, the administration itself finally spoke out in opposition to the ESA. In a newspaper interview in May 1990, Secretary of the Interior Manuel Lujan questioned the need to save every subspecies and argued that the ESA should be weakened. "It's just too tough an act," said Lujan. "We've got to change it."[69] As a basis for this position, he cited the Forest Service report estimating that twenty-five thousand loggers would lose their jobs if prohibited from cutting old-growth forests on federal lands in the Pacific Northwest. For these reasons, Lujan announced that the administration would support legislation in Congress to weaken the ESA and end the spotted owl controversy.[70]

Much as the Thomas Report had provoked opponents to the act, Lujan's comments drew sharp responses from ESA supporters in Congress. Representative Bruce Vento (D-MN) accused Lujan of misunderstanding the law, arguing that the ESA was not about protecting a single species like the spotted owl but about maintaining biological diversity in ecological communities. As an indicator species, Vento warned, the owl represented the health of entire old-growth forests.[71] Representative Meldon Levine (D-CA) responded to Lujan's question about the need to save every subspecies with an emphatic yes, "of course we need to save every subspecies."[72] In support for his position, Levine read into the congressional record an article by biologist Donella Meadow on the importance of preserving all species, subspecies, and distinct population segments.[73]

Others in Congress criticized Lujan's remark that the ESA was "frequently" used to block development or threaten jobs. According to Representative George Mitchell (D-ME), for example, less than 1 percent of the 48,538 biological opinions issued from 1979 to 1986 resulted in jeopardy decisions requiring modification or cancellation of a proposed agency action. In total, during that time period only three projects in ten thousand were withdrawn or canceled following Section 7 consultation. Representative Mitchell also cited a GAO report concluding that in over three thousand consultations on water projects in the West, only about 2 percent actually had any effect on the project, and no project was actually terminated by the ESA. The ESA, he concluded, was far from being too tough— instead it was balanced, flexible, and should not be changed.[74]

Despite Mitchell's testimony, by 1990 the ESA had begun to threaten development projects throughout the West. In Colorado, the protected squawfish was interfering with the Animas–La Plata irrigation project on the Colorado River. In Arizona, the Mount Graham red squirrel had halted construction of a seven-telescope observatory. In Utah, the mottled-bellied spotted frog blocked the completion of the Central Utah Irrigation Project. The spotted owl, however, differed from these species in that its protection threatened not a single project in one state but an entire industry in several states.[75]

Increasing controversy over the ESA and election-year politics eventually forced President George Bush to address the spotted owl controversy himself. Predictably, while campaigning for fellow Republicans in Oregon during the spring of 1990, Bush attempted to please both sides, saying he was looking for a middle ground in the owl debate.[76] "I am interested in the owl, but I'm also interested in the American family. . . . I want to be known as the environmental president. I also want to be concerned about a person's ability to hold a job and have a job."[77] To achieve this end, Bush called for a balance between economic and biological concerns in the spotted owl controversy, saying in particular that his administration should not totally ignore the economic consequences of listing.[78] Although this response may have sounded reasonable to President Bush, to many environmentalists it seemed like an attack on one of the key provisions of the ESA.

Finally, on June 22, 1990, FWS announced that the northern spotted owl would be listed as threatened under the ESA effective July 23. In its decision to list, the service recognized the controversy surrounding the decision, reporting that during the public review period it had received over twenty-three thousand comments on the listing proposal.[79] At the same time, the service admitted that scientific evidence indeed warranted the listing, noting that it had identified only about two thousand breeding pairs of owls, even though it believed the total population to be between three and five thousand pairs.[80] Although FWS said it would take some time to design a recovery plan for the owl, it described the Thomas Report as the "most scientifically credible plan" yet advanced for protecting the owl and promised to consider it closely before developing a plan. In the meantime, because of the high degree of public uncertainty over the effects of the listing, FWS agreed to publish a procedural manual describing the steps that federal, nonfederal, and private entities would have to take to comply with the ESA. Interestingly, nowhere in the listing announcement did the service mention the role of the courts in compelling the decision.

Both the local and national press carried the story on the front page. In what it called a "landmark decision," the *Seattle Times* reported that the listing would surely lead to battles in Congress over the act's application.[81] The *Washington Post* warned of the potentially dire consequences associated with the listing, noting too that FWS might take up to two more years before it completed a recovery plan for the owl. Although FWS would place a high priority on developing that recovery plan, wrote the *Post*, the process would be complicated by the fact that the owl required an unprecedented amount of habitat for survival. The press also warned that litigation and congressional attempts to rewrite the ESA might further delay the designation of critical habitat and the completion of a recovery plan.[82]

FWS's listing decision also provoked quick responses from higher-ups in the administration. Just four days after the announcement, Secretary of Agriculture Clayton Yeutter and Secretary of the Interior Manuel Lujan put forth an alternative proposal to the Thomas Report. Their recovery plan had less to do with protecting the owl than with protecting the interests of the timber industry in the Pacific Northwest. Their proposal essentially instructed BLM and the Forest Service to continue logging at historic levels while taking artificial measures to support the owl, like supplemental feeding and setting out nesting boxes. If contravened by court decisions, their plan called for convening the God Squad to grant exemptions from Section 7 of the Act.[83] The White House also announced its opposition to the Thomas Report, claiming that it was discouraged by the "rigidity" of the ESA and that it preferred a plan that would preserve more jobs.[84]

Environmentalists and the timber industry also responded quickly to the listing decision. Although environmentalists welcomed the long-awaited listing, they warned that they would not be satisfied with an owl recovery plan less extensive than the management plan proposed by the Thomas Report. They strongly opposed the proposal put forward by the secretaries of the interior and agriculture and threatened to continue their strategy of litigation if necessary to protect the owl. They also promised to fight any attempts in Congress to weaken the ESA. Moreover, environmentalists criticized what they called exaggerated estimates of job losses associated with the owl listing. According to their own calculations, the listing and the protection of the owl under the Thomas Plan would only result in the loss of four thousand jobs.[85]

The timber industry, on the other hand, vehemently opposed the listing. In sharp contrast to projections by environmentalists, the industry now claimed that the listing decision would cost fifty thousand jobs. Gary Jones, president of Summit Timber, said somberly that the owl listing heralded "a dark day in the history of the Northwest."[86] Not long after the decision, the timber industry sponsored rallies in the Pacific Northwest against it. At one such rally, a journalist observed T-shirts and bumper stickers emblazoned with slogans like "Save a Logger—Eat an Owl," "I Love Spotted Owls—Fried," and "Save the Trees—Wipe Your Ass with a Spotted Owl."[87] Rather than resolve the controversy over the northern spotted owl, the listing decision seemed to provoke more conflict.

CHAPTER SIX

Giving a Hoot

The listing of the northern spotted owl as threatened under the Endangered Species Act provoked Congress into action. In July 1990, Congress held hearings on the administration's plan to reject the Thomas Report recommendations in favor of a scheme that allowed for more harvesting of old-growth forests. The chairman of the House Subcommittee on Fisheries and Wildlife Conservation and the Environment, Representative Gerry Studds (D-MA), called the administration's proposal "partly incomprehensible, partly indefensible, and partly impossible."[1] Other members of the subcommittee, however, disagreed with the chairman. For example, Representative Don Young (R-AK) supported the administration's efforts to protect "the working man" and called environmentalists "sanctimonious elite."[2] As the spotted owl controversy deepened, Congress grew increasingly divided over not only the fate of the owl but also the future of the ESA.

At first, Congress only considered bills directed at resolving the spotted owl controversy and did not contemplate modifying the ESA itself. In the summer of 1990 alone, the House of Representatives considered four bills addressing the spotted owl crisis. First, Representative Robert Smith (R-OR) and Representative Young introduced a bill to permit timber sales in federal forests at historic levels during a five-year study period on the status of the spotted owl. In a similar, if less drastic, attempt to limit the economic impacts of the listing, Representative Peter DeFazio (D-OR) and others introduced a bill to counteract the Forest Service's decision to implement the Thomas Report while awaiting the Fish and Wildlife Service's recovery plan. The DeFazio bill would have required the Forest Service to once again consider conservation options other than the Thomas Report before taking action.[3] Both of these bills, if passed, would have delayed owl conservation efforts and allowed the timber industry to continue logging the old-growth forests of the Pacific Northwest.

Supporters of spotted owl conservation introduced bills of their own. Representative James Jontz (D-IN), joined by 107 cosponsors, introduced the Ancient Forest Protection Act of 1990, designed to set aside the remaining old-growth forests in the Pacific Northwest for the preservation of the owl and for other conservation purposes. Representative Bruce Vento (D-MN) and others introduced a similar bill to allow the secretary of the interior and the secretary of agriculture to create an ancient forest reserve system and to provide rural logging communities with economic assistance.[4] Environmentalists testified in favor of both bills, although they indicated their preference for the more expansive Jontz bill.[5] Meanwhile, the administration declined to take any position on these bills and, retreating from its earlier proposal, announced that it would form yet another task force to examine the spotted owl issue.[6]

None of these House bills earned enough support to become law, nor did a Senate bill introduced by Bob Packwood (R-OR) in the fall of 1990 fare any better. Packwood's proposal would have allowed federal land management agencies like the Forest Service to appeal to the Endangered Species Committee, the so-called God Squad, to obtain Section 7 exemptions from timber sales within ninety days rather than the full year allowed under the ESA. With such a bill, Packwood hoped to make the committee a more efficient and effective means of bypassing the ESA's requirements regarding the spotted owl. Majority Leader George Mitchell (D-ME) warned that the Packwood amendment would "hamstring" the ESA by allowing land management agencies to obtain easy exemptions from the act's safeguards.[7] Senator Al Gore (D-TN) also opposed the bill, arguing that the God Squad would be composed of Bush administration officials opposed to the preservation of the owl. Ultimately, the Senate rejected the bill by a vote of 62 to 34.[8]

During this time, Congress also held hearings on proposals to extend unemployment benefits and to provide job retraining for victims of spotted owl conservation. These hearings were confounded by the continuing discrepancies in job-loss estimates. Environmentalists claimed that protecting the owl would cost ten thousand jobs, the federal government believed twenty thousand jobs would be lost, while the state of Oregon predicted fifty thousand lost jobs. Above all, the timber industry claimed that saving the owl would cost one hundred thousand jobs.[9] Such widely varying estimates tended to further polarize Congress between liberals who accepted the lower numbers and conservatives who adopted the higher numbers.

Although Congress failed to resolve the owl controversy with legislation in 1990, the administration continued to procrastinate its own solution. To begin with, the White House task force did not produce conservation recommendations by its self-imposed deadline of September 1990. President Bush, therefore, called for yet another study, this time broadening its scope to include a review of the federal government's overall public land policy. To complete this study, Bush convened a multiagency planning team consisting of representatives from the Department of the Interior, FWS, Bureau of Land Management, White House Council of Economic Advisers, and White House Council on Environmental Quality. Their report was due by December 1991.[10] In such a manner, the administration put off making hard choices.

Many factors contributed to administrative delay and indecision in the early 1990s. To begin with, for economic and political reasons the administration was simply reluctant to implement a scientifically valid plan for preserving the spotted owl. The administration, however, was also confused and hampered by an array of federal laws guiding different federal agencies responsible for managing federal lands in the Pacific Northwest. With the listing, the ESA became superimposed over these laws, forcing strict safeguards to protect the owl. Yet, land management agencies like the Forest Service and the BLM still had to comply with their own organic acts and the administrative procedures associated with those acts. ESA compliance was further complicated because FWS had not yet produced a recovery plan to protect the owl. Meanwhile, court-ordered injunctions affecting millions of acres throughout the Pacific Northwest also hindered the development of a coherent, comprehensive interim management plan. As a result of all these factors, the administration chose to delay.[11]

Faced with congressional and administrative inaction and inspired by their opponents' tactics, the timber industry sued. In one of their first cases, *Gifford Pinchot Alliance v. Butruille*, the timber industry tried to compel the Forest Service to offer 7.7 billion board feet of timber for harvest from national forests in Washington and Oregon. The industry argued that irrespective of the ESA, a relevant appropriations act passed in 1990 for the Department of Agriculture required the Forest Service to offer up such timber. The U.S. District Court, however, disagreed, holding that the Forest Service was required only to make every reasonable effort both to offer timber for sale and to comply with the ESA.[12] In a related suit, a group of logging companies petitioned FWS to list Olympic Peninsula loggers as a threatened species under the ESA and warned that it would sue the agency if its petition were denied.[13] This symbolic effort, of course, also failed in the courts, though it generated good publicity for the plight of the logger.

Environmentalists met with more success as they continued to appeal to the courts to force the administration to implement the ESA. Not long after FWS listed the owl as a threatened species, the Sierra Club Legal Defense Fund, the Audubon Society, and other environmentalists again sued FWS. This time they complained that the agency had violated the act because it had failed to designate critical habitat at the same time it had listed the owl. Although the 1982 amendment to the ESA did not require that critical habitat designation coincide with a listing decision in all cases, it did direct the secretary of the interior, "to the maximum extent prudent and determinable," to designate critical habitat concurrently with a listing decision.[14] FWS responded that the owl's critical habitat was not yet determinable. On February 26, 1991, U.S. District Court Judge

Thomas Zilly, sitting in Seattle, disagreed, citing the Thomas Report as evidence that the owl's critical habitat could be determined. He held that FWS had again abused its discretion and ordered the service to designate critical habitat for the northern spotted owl.[15]

Compelled by the court order, on May 6, 1991, FWS published its proposed rule to list critical habitat for the spotted owl. Based largely on the findings of the Thomas Report, FWS identified 11.6 million acres of old-growth forest for this purpose. Although the ESA required this initial designation to be based solely on scientific evidence, it also allowed the amount of critical habitat to be reduced if economic and social factors outweighed its importance to the species' survival. The designation of critical habitat itself did not prohibit particular activities, but the disruption of such habitat did make it more likely that FWS (or the courts reacting to an ESA citizen suit) would find a Section 7 or Section 9 violation.[16] In this way, the designation of critical habitat provided environmentalists and their lawyers with further ammunition with which to attack suspect forest management practices.

After several months of public comment to determine the economic and social impacts of the critical habitat designation, FWS revised its proposal. Most significant, it decreased the acreage to be protected from 11.6 million to 8.2 million acres, removing 3 million acres of private land and 400,000 acres of federal land from critical habitat designation. FWS estimated that protecting the owl's habitat would cost thirty-three thousand timber-related jobs by 1995.[17] The timber industry, loggers, and local politicians criticized the revised proposal, complaining that it did not go far enough in decreasing the number of acres to be designated. Washington State Representative Bob Basich (D-Aberdeen) told a federal panel, "We don't like somebody from the East Coast who doesn't know a board foot from a Bigfoot telling us what the hell to do."[18] Environmentalists also criticized the revision, claiming that it did not provide for enough critical habitat to protect the owl.

Meanwhile, environmentalists pursued litigation on other fronts. In the spring of 1991, the Seattle Audubon Society and others sued the Forest Service, claiming that by allowing timber sales of northern spotted owl habitat the service had violated provisions of the National Forest Management Act (NFMA). The environmentalists sought a permanent injunction on the sale of such timber until the Forest Service developed and implemented a management plan for the owl as required by NFMA. In an opinion highly critical of the administration, U.S. District Court Judge William Dwyer determined that "the problem here has not been any shortcoming in the laws, but simply a refusal of administrative agencies to comply with them."[19] For this and other reasons, Judge Dwyer ordered an injunction compelling the Forest Service to produce a management plan for the owl by March 5, 1992, and preventing the service from selling additional logging rights in spotted owl habitat until that time. In December 1991, the Ninth Circuit Court of Appeals upheld Judge Dwyer's injunction.[20]

In another case, the Lane County Audubon Society and others sued the BLM seeking injunctions on planned timber sales. In September 1990, the BLM had adopted management guidelines for the conservation of the northern spotted owl, called the Jamison Strategy, which allowed the sale of 750 million board feet of timber during 1991 and 1992. Environmentalists complained that the BLM had violated Section 7 of the ESA because it had failed to consult FWS regarding the impact of the Jamison Strategy on the spotted owl. U.S. District Court Judge Robert Jones agreed, finding that the strategy was an "action" within the meaning of the statute and that the BLM had therefore violated Section 7. On September 11, 1991, Judge Jones enjoined the BLM from implementing the Jamison Strategy, including the proposed timber sales, until it had completed a Section 7 consultation with FWS.[21] The BLM appealed, but in the spring of 1992, the Ninth Circuit upheld the district court's findings and its injunction.[22]

The timber industry and individual loggers responded to this onslaught of environmental litigation in a variety of ways. First, the industry launched a media campaign to obtain broader, national support from the American people. This campaign focused not only on the plight of loggers and their communities but also on how conserving the owl would affect all Americans. In one article, the timber industry warned that recent court decisions would not only result in lost timber-related jobs, but they also would significantly increase the costs of wholesale timber, thus affecting the price of many products, especially new homes, purchased by Americans nationwide.[23] While the timber industry did not, of course, orchestrate all such news articles, it began to mimic its environmental opponents by manipulating the media to win public support.

The timber industry and individual loggers also pursued litigation of their own, in some cases taking more direct action. For example, logging communities in Sweet Home and Mill City, Oregon, backed by the timber industry, filed their own citizen suit under the ESA. In it, they claimed that FWS had overstepped its legal mandate in issuing regulations regarding the owl, and that the plain language and legislative history of the act did not support the service's broad definition of "harm."[24] Moreover, in a few isolated incidents, activists deliberately killed spotted owls and displayed their remains. Organized timber interests sought to distance themselves from such illegal actions and, in at least one case, offered a $7,500 reward for information leading to the arrest of a perpetrator.[25]

The successes of environmentalists in court also pushed the administration into action. The most drastic reaction came after the BLM, forced by court order, consulted with FWS on the timber sales provided for in the Jamison Strategy. Following the consultation, FWS determined that of the 175 timber sales approved by the BLM, 52 would jeopardize the owl and must therefore be permanently halted. The director of the BLM appealed to Secretary of the Interior Lujan, asking him to convene the Endangered Species Committee, or God Squad, to exempt the timber sales from Section 7.[26] Reflecting administrative frustration far greater than warranted by a few blocked BLM timber sales, Secretary Lujan agreed to convene the ESC. Interested parties around the country warned that the God Squad's ultimate decision would have a far greater effect on the continuing spotted owl dispute.[27]

In the short term, just the mere decision to convene the God Squad aroused enthusiastic support from some, outraged opposition from others, and general interest from Americans nationwide. Senator Packwood applauded the decision, saying that the God Squad, unlike the ESA, would take into account human needs and concerns. Representative Les AuCoin (D-OR) retorted that a "frantic yank on the emergency rip cord of the Endangered Species Act" should not be a substitute for a sound, long-range forest policy.[28] The decision to convene the committee also piqued the interest of those so far uninvolved with the spotted owl controversy. Wrote one *Washington Post* journalist, "When Washington decides to play God, it appoints—what else?—a committee."[29] The notion that a group of high-level bureaucrats could meet and decide the fate of a species intrigued many across the country.

The decision to convene the ESC, however, upset and even horrified environmentalists. The Sierra Club Legal Defense Fund warned that granting an exemption might push the owl over the brink of extinction. Greenpeace called the administration's decision to convene the committee an act of "all-out war by the government to cut down this country's landmark Endangered Species Act."[30] The National Audubon Society agreed, calling the decision "a purely political move" designed to help Senator Packwood's campaign to gut the ESA by demonstrating the inflexibility of the act.[31] Environmentalists worried that convening the God Squad would have dire consequences for both the owl and the ESA.

While the administration deliberated over habitat designation and considered convening the ESC, Congress consulted leading scientists for alternatives to managing the owl and old-growth forests. In May 1991, the House of Representatives had asked four leading forestry and wildlife scientists to advise them on how best to protect the owl and its habitats. This so-called "Gang of Four" included Jerry Franklin, chief plant ecologist with the Forest Service and a professor of ecosystem management at the University of Washington, John Gordon, the dean of the School of Forestry and Environmental Studies at Yale, Jack Ward Thomas, chief research biologist at the Forest Service's Forestry and Range Science Lab, and K. Norman Johnson, an associate professor of forest management at Oregon State University. To accomplish their task, the panel met for two weeks in Portland, Oregon, to consult with each other and with over one hundred other scientists. They worked alone and did not hear from special interest groups or agency line officers.[32]

The Gang of Four presented their findings to Congress in October 1991. Their report outlined fourteen alternatives to managing old-growth forests in the Pacific Northwest, ranging from protections for 2.3 to 5.7 million acres of federal land. One of the alternatives was based entirely on the Thomas Report. Private lands were not included in the study. Although the panel presented a broad range of ecosystem-based alternatives to forest management, it admitted that no alternative could provide both abundant timber harvest and a high degree of protection for old-growth forests. The report also estimated job losses from four to sixteen thousand and criticized current forest plans for failing to adequately protect owl habitat and for overestimating the remaining amount of harvestable timber in the Northwest.[33] Some in Congress hoped that this report would form the foundation for a legislative effort to resolve the owl crisis.

Meanwhile, ESA supporters in the House of Representatives again attempted to reauthorize the act without debilitating amendments. In late fall of 1991, Representative Studds introduced legislation to reauthorize the ESA through 1996. He opposed the convening of the God Squad and any amendments that might weaken the act. Arguing in support of his bill, he quoted from naturalist Charles Beebe: "When the last of a species breathes no more, another heaven and another Earth must pass before such a one can be again."[34] According to Studds, the ESA as written recognized that humans do not have the luxury of waiting for another heaven and another earth to pass.

Others in Congress, however, continued their opposition to the ESA. Inspired by claims from some scientists and from the timber industry, many began to question FWS management practices and the scientific legitimacy of the law itself.[35] Representative Steven Symms (R-ID), for example, read into the record three articles highly critical of FWS and the science of the ESA. In the first article, author Robert Gordon challenged the scientific assumption made by the act that protecting subspecies and distinct populations was necessary to prevent extinction. The second article, also by Gordon, called FWS's recovery record abysmal and criticized the service for doing little more than listing species while accumulating power through land acquisitions and budget increases.[36] In the third article, Warren Brooks accused FWS of using the ESA merely to expand its budget, turf, and power.[37]

In response to such concerns, in November 1991, a coalition of ESA supporters and opponents asked the National Research Council to evaluate the legitimacy of the science of the act. This powerful bipartisan coalition included Senator Mark Hatfield (R-OR), Representative Studds, Speaker of the House Thomas Foley (D-WA), and others. Specifically, they asked the National Research Council to review and evaluate the way that the act defined and protected species. They also asked the council to review the role of habitat conservation in species protection, the recovery planning process, and the way the ESA and FWS dealt with potential conservation conflicts among species. In addition, the coalition wanted the council to evaluate how the act defined risk and describe how FWS implemented policy according to the definition. For example, what were the threshold requirements sufficient to justify the listing of a species as threatened or endangered, and what were the bases for findings of jeopardy, adverse modification, reasonable and prudent alternatives, and take? Finally, the coalition asked the council to examine issues related to timing in the designation and management of species.[38]

Meanwhile, on December 16, 1991, the administration's latest task force, the Spotted Owl Recovery Team, delivered its report and recommendations. During the previous three years, various government agencies and independent scientific organizations had produced overlapping reports on the status of the owl with recommendations on how to protect it from extinction. The administration heads, including cabinet-level secretaries and the president himself, had consistently rejected these reports because of the economic consequences of their implementation. This report, however, promised to be different because Secretary Lujan, supported by the president, had handpicked the Spotted Owl Recovery Team. Their report and recommendations, however, disappointed the administration.[39]

The Spotted Owl Recovery Team refused to ignore scientific evidence about the plight of the northern spotted owl and the conservation measures necessary to protect it. As a result, the team's report closely resembled the earlier Thomas Report, concluding that to protect the owl, timber harvest levels would have to drop as much as 45 percent from 1980 levels, resulting in about thirty-one thousand lost jobs over the next few years. Still, the administration refused to accept the "indisputable science" of spotted owl conservation.[40] Instead, Secretary Lujan unabashedly announced that he would convene yet another task force to examine the issue.[41]

Predictably, the administration's stubbornness provoked much criticism. In one editorial, the *Seattle Times* castigated the administration for its lack of guidance, declaring that Lujan's stalling on an owl plan was not helping area loggers: "How many more studies do we need to tell us the same thing?"[42] The paper went on to accuse Lujan of denying scientific reality for thinking that yet another study would produce a different result. Lujan responded by claiming that the new task force would not duplicate previous studies or current efforts by FWS to develop a recovery plan. According to him, the new team's recommendations would not necessarily have to comply with the ESA or other environmental laws. When questioned, Lujan admitted that any such recommendations would require congressional approval before implementation.[43] The administration, therefore, implied that the ESA would have to be weakened before it could get its forest plan approved.

In the spring of 1992, Congress held hearings on the administration's response to the spotted owl crisis. During these hearings, the Democratic leaders attacked the administration for not only failing to resolve the crisis but also for contributing to it. Representative Vento, Chair of the Subcommittee on National Parks and Public Lands, blamed the crisis on what he called a "leadership vacuum."[44] He also accused the Bush administration of repeatedly violating the nation's environmental laws in dealing with the old-growth issue. "How do we know?" Vento asked rhetorically. "Because the Bush administration has lost every lawsuit brought before the courts concerning the old-growth forests."[45] Finally, he and others attacked the administration for consistently ignoring the scientific recommendations of its own agencies and independent scientific task forces. According to Vento and others, if the administration had provided the necessary leadership four years earlier, if it had followed the nation's environmental laws, and if it had listened to its own scientists, there would not be a crisis.[46]

Not all in Congress agreed with these criticisms of the administration. Senator Slade Gorton (R-WA) admitted that if the administration had applied the ESA the way environmentalists wanted, there would be no spotted owl crisis—but there would be widespread unemployment and depression throughout the Pacific Northwest and beyond.[47] Moreover, he praised the administration for considering the social and economic consequences of owl protection, even if he conceded that the administration had so far failed to adopt a coherent plan. Eventually, Gorton warned, Congress would be faced with a choice between allowing the implementation of a recovery plan that would jeopardize the economy of the Northwest or passing into law a proposal by the secretary of the interior that would save jobs and still provide some protections for the owl. He urged his colleagues to accept the second alternative, even if it meant creating a legislative exception from the requirements of the ESA and other environmental laws.[48]

Also in the spring of 1992, the Senate considered the larger issue of ESA reauthorization, continuing the effort spearheaded by Representative

Studds in the House of Representatives a few months earlier. Senator Max Baucus (D-MT), chair of the Subcommittee on Environmental Protection, opened one reauthorization hearing by calling the ESA "fundamentally sound" but "far from perfect."[49] Although opposing drastic revisions, he said that the ESA should be changed to better recognize economic and social concerns. Baucus, however, stated that such considerations could not come at the expense of species preservation. Unfortunately, he did not offer any suggestions as to how this might be done.

Other senators voiced more specific concerns and opinions. Senator Mitchell, for example, urged reauthorization of the ESA without amendment and criticized the administration for failing to give its unqualified support for reauthorization.[50] In contrast, Senator Alan Simpson (R-WY) said that environmentalists had hijacked the ESA, using it to halt economic development across the country. According to Simpson, the law needed to be rewritten to correct such abuses.[51] Representative Rodney Chandler (R-WA) agreed, calling the ESA inflexible and a "tool for radicals."[52] Senator Packwood also believed the act had gone too far, declaring that it now threatened to "shut down" entire communities.[53]

Although the hearing in April 1992 focused on ESA reauthorization, the Senate dedicated a separate hearing specifically to the spotted owl in May 1992. Senator Baucus again chaired this committee, but this time his opening statement was more focused and forceful. According to him, the economic and social crisis in the Pacific Northwest could be blamed not so much on the owl as on larger trends in the national economy that had begun in the early 1980s. Unfortunately, said Baucus, the Reagan and Bush administrations had resisted necessary changes, and now the Pacific Northwest faced a more painful but inevitable transition. He declared that the current task before Congress was to lead the Northwest through this crisis with the least amount of human suffering and environmental degradation.[54] While continuing to be short on details, Senator Baucus nevertheless provided vision and leadership notably lacking in the administration. Others, of course, strongly disagreed with his interpretation, and by the spring of 1992, it seemed that the spotted owl crisis had irreconcilably divided Congress over the fate of the ESA.

The media, naturally, tracked these and other developments. In April, the *Seattle Times* printed Vento's statement blaming the Reagan and Bush administrations for the current owl crisis and also reported FWS Director John Turner's defense of the ESA against accusations of inflexibility.[55] On the subject of predicted job losses, the press also repeated the findings of two recent reports. In one, the American Forestry Association concluded that the owl was wrongly being blamed for job losses and pointed instead to long-term declines and changes in the timber industry predicted twenty years ago. In the other study, Thomas Power, chairman of the University of Montana's economics department, said that protecting the old-growth forests would not have an adverse effect because a recreation-based economy would essentially replace a timber-based one.[56]

The media also closely followed the proceedings of the God Squad as it deliberated over granting exemptions to forty-four BLM timber sales from the requirements of Section 7. In January 1992, an administrative law judge oversaw a hearing to collect evidence from the interested parties about the proposed exemptions. Those involved included not only the BLM and FWS but also the Northwest Forest Resource Council, the Portland Audubon Society, the Association of Oregon and California Counties, the Oregon Lands Coalition, and others. A month later, the ESC held a public hearing in Portland, where it heard oral comments from nearly a hundred citizens and collected eighteen hundred letters and petitions. Finally, in April 1992, the secretary of the interior submitted his recommendation to the ESC on the proposed exemptions.[57]

The God Squad reached its decision soon after receiving the Interior Department's report. As required by law, the committee consisted of the secretary of the interior, the secretary of agriculture, the secretary of the army, the chair of the Council of Economic Advisers, the administrator of the Environmental Protection Agency (EPA), the administrator of the National Oceanic and Atmospheric Administration, and one member appointed by the president from each state affected by the decision. In this case, President Bush had appointed Oregon citizen Tom Walsh. Before reaching its final decision, the committee made several determinations required by the ESA. First, it found that no reasonable or prudent alternative existed for thirteen of the timber sales. Second, it decided that in at least thirteen cases the benefits of the timber sales clearly outweighed the benefits of owl preservation, and that those sales were in the public interest. Finally, the ESC determined that the timber sales were of regional significance. Based on these determinations, the God Squad voted 5 to 2 to exempt thirteen of the proposed forty-four timber sales from the requirements of Section 7. EPA Administrator William Reilly and Oregon citizen Tom Walsh were the only two members of the committee to vote against the exemptions.[58]

Interior Secretary Lujan announced the decision along with a belated administrative plan for resolving the larger conflict. Basically, this plan proposed to preserve 2.8 million acres of old-growth forest sufficient to protect thirteen hundred pairs of owls, the administration claimed. It also entailed capturing owls in certain areas and relocating them to existing parks and preserves. According to Lujan, "Owls die every day, just like people," but the administration's proposal would give the owl more than a 50 percent chance of surviving for the next one hundred years.[59] Lujan conceded that this plan would fall below what was currently required by the ESA and that it would be up to Congress to enact the plan by amending the law itself or by passing special legislation superceding it in the case of the spotted owl. In the meantime, he promised to expand the Section 7 exemption process to other timber sales if necessary.

At the same time that Lujan announced the decision of the ESC and unveiled the administration's forest plan, FWS published its draft recovery plan for the spotted owl. In it, the service proposed to preserve 5.5 million acres of habitat, protecting about twenty-three hundred breeding pairs of owls. This amount was 2.7 million acres less than what FWS had designated as critical habitat for the owl and what the Thomas Report had identified as the minimum necessary for the owl to survive. The service expected that if implemented, the draft recovery plan would reduce total board feet production to about 2.3 billion, less than half the average levels of the 1980s. Secretary Lujan claimed that such a reduction would result in the unacceptable loss of thirty thousand jobs in the Pacific Northwest. This curious administrative conflict between Secretary Lujan's plan and FWS's recovery plan can be explained. Lujan's proposal, the administration's preferred plan, required congressional authorization because it would otherwise violate the ESA, while FWS's plan, at least according to the agency itself, would comply with the act. These three developments—the decision by the God Squad, the administration's extralegal proposal, and even FWS's draft recovery plan—left environmentalists stunned and outraged.[60]

The *Seattle Times* also criticized the ESC's decision and the administration's plan for the owl, if not FWS's draft recovery plan. According to one editorial, the God Squad had betrayed the long-term public interest "for fleeting political benefit."[61] Lujan's "cavalier" comments about how owls die every day, wrote the editor, showed he did not comprehend the nature of the problem. Specifically, the paper criticized Lujan for failing to understand that the owl was an indicator species and that its demise might mean the breakdown of the entire old-growth forest ecosystem. The newspaper stressed that the owl required preservation for the sake of the entire ecosystem, despite the economic costs.

In June 1991, a report by the General Accounting Office also criticized the administration's implementation of the ESA. According to that report, agency officials purposefully gave critical habitat designation a low priority, lamely explaining that designating critical habitat provided little additional benefit for a species. Moreover, in reviewing all Section 7 consultations between 1987 and 1991, the GAO determined that in over 90 percent of the cases, FWS had allowed the agency action to proceed without any modification to the plan. The findings also confirmed the inefficiency of the listing process, noting that it would take FWS until the year 2006 to consider for listing the six hundred species currently identified as candidates, to say nothing of the potential three thousand species that might need protection in the near future.[62] Another GAO report a year later examined more closely how pressure from higher-ups in the Bush administration contributed to delays in the listing of species by FWS.[63] These reports helped confirm to environmentalists that short of a change in administration or a strengthening of the ESA through amendments, they would have to continue their strategy of litigation to force what they considered a correct implementation of the act.

A speech in the summer of 1992 by Agriculture Secretary Edward Madigan, another member of the God Squad, provided more evidence of the administration's growing hostility toward the owl and the ESA. Speaking before an American Farm Bureau gathering, Madigan said that the federal government could do nothing to prevent the eventual extinction of the northern spotted owl because it interbred with the barred owl: "We can protect every tree in the United States and it isn't going to stop [the spotted owl] from disappearing."[64] In anticipation of upcoming elections, he also joked that the Republican platform would include an agriculture plank calling for "more money, higher income, more markets. String all the environmentalists up."[65] Statements like these helped convince environmentalists that, aside from litigation, they might benefit from getting involved in the upcoming presidential election.

As the elections approached, President Bush described the ESA as a "broken" law that must be "fixed."[66] He vowed not to sign an extension of the act unless it was amended to require greater economic sensitivity. Bush also advocated a specific proposal for the northern spotted owl, a species he once described as "that little furry, feathery guy."[67] He urged Congress to pass into law his administration's plan reducing the number of acres to be set aside for owl habitat from 5.4 million to 2.8 million. He did this even though his own administration had acknowledged that the change would "highly likely" result in the extinction or near extinction of the owl after a century had passed. To cheering timber workers in Colville, Washington, Bush said, "It is time to make people more important than owls."[68] The *Washington Post* noted that the owl crisis seemed to have forced Bush to retreat from his claim four years earlier that he would be the "environmental president."[69]

Indeed, Bush seemed to voluntarily abdicate the title, directly contrasting himself with Bill Clinton and his running mate, Al Gore. In one speech, Bush read a passage from Gore's environmental book, *Earth in the Balance*, where Gore argued that the spotted owl should be protected because the timber jobs would be lost anyway. Bush adamantly disagreed, then challenged Clinton to say whether or not he agreed with his running mate. Others, too, used the spotted owl to contrast the presidential candidates. Congressman Walter Herger (R-CA), for example, said Gore "seems to put people last" and went on to accuse Clinton of waffling over the spotted owl.[70] In contrast, Herger praised President Bush for being the only candidate who believed people were more important than owls.[71]

Responding to such criticisms, Clinton promised that if elected he would break the logjam over the owl. He said that within ninety days of his administration, he would convene a summit to resolve the crisis. Promising to preside over the summit himself, Clinton assured quick and decisive action. He also rejected what he called the owls versus jobs choice as a false dichotomy, pledging to find a compromise solution that would protect both owls and jobs. Although Clinton's promises sounded good to some, to environmentalists long involved in the owl controversy, the summit seemed little more than additional administrative delay in the face of conclusive scientific evidence. Meanwhile, funding for the ESA expired in September 1992, and Congress chose to extend the act by just one year so as to avoid debate on reauthorization or amendment until after the election.[72]

The Bush administration ended in January 1993 with no federal plan in place for managing the northern spotted owl. Secretary Lujan announced that he would leave office without approving FWS's draft recovery plan for the owl, passing that controversial decision on to the Clinton administration.[73] Both environmentalists and the timber industry lauded the decision, because both hoped that the Clinton administration would adopt a recovery plan more amenable to their interests. The Bush administration's legislative plan to protect only 2.8 million acres also died when America elected Clinton to the presidency. Pending the implementation of a recovery plan or amendment to the ESA, most federal forests in the Pacific Northwest remained under court orders banning logging.

Environmentalists had not retreated from litigation during the presidential elections. Indeed, just days after the God Squad reached its decision to exempt thirteen timber sales from the ESA, the Portland Audubon Society and others sued the administration. In its suit, the Audubon Society accused the cabinet-level members of the ESC of improperly communicating with President Bush and with members of his staff. In doing so, the environmental plaintiffs argued that the ESC had violated the Administrative Procedure Act's prohibition against ex parte communications. The Ninth Circuit Court of Appeals agreed and effectively overturned the God Squad's decision to exempt the thirteen timber sales from the ESA.[74] Once again, environmentalists had triumphed in court, foiling administrative attempts to weaken the act.

As a result of yet another lawsuit, in March 1993 a scientific analysis team led by Jack Ward Thomas submitted a viability and management report for the owl and other species dependent on old-growth forests.[75] The chief of the Forest Service had formed the team, but only after being compelled to do so by U.S. District Court Judge William Dwyer. In a legal decision related to the owl, Dwyer had expressed problems and concerns with the science behind the Forest Service's "Final Environmental Impact Statement on the Management for the Northern Spotted Owl," completed in 1992. The team and its report, therefore, resulted not from administrative initiative but from environmentalists who yet again had gone to court and convinced a federal judge to compel a federal agency to conduct more scientific investigation so as to be able to develop a better management plan for the owl and other species. Both directly and indirectly, environmentalists used the courts to shape endangered species policy.

The team's report had an important impact on the owl controversy and on the implementation of endangered species policy. Most important, the report contributed significantly to the development of the Northwest Plan and to the emergence of ecosystem management within the national forests. It did so in part by focusing not only on the spotted owl, but also on the 482 plant and animal species it determined to be associated with old-growth forests. The scientific analysis team claimed that any successful management plan for the owl must provide protection for a panoply of species and all their assorted habitats. In this way, environmentalists used the courts to shape policy and relied on the ESA to convince the court of their position. The court compelled the Forest Service to assemble scientists to study the owl issue, and they told the Forest Service that the agency must begin managing for ecosystems, not just for individuals and certainly not just for the timber companies.

In the midst of this sea change in land use management, on April 2, 1993, President Clinton convened his promised timber summit in Portland, Oregon. Aside from the president himself, Vice President Al Gore and a half-dozen cabinet members attended, including most importantly the secretaries of the Interior and Agriculture. For eight hours, the administration heard testimony from scientists, environmentalists, timber industry representatives, local citizens, and others. Although Clinton said he felt sympathy for the jobless and their distressed families, he also said he could not "repeal the laws of change."[76] Following the conference, Clinton directed his cabinet to develop a forest plan within sixty days "to end the warfare between timber and environmental interests."[77] The president said that he preferred an administrative solution to the current crisis over a legislative one.

The same day as the summit, the *Washington Post* reported that the spotted owl was not the cause of the Northwest timber and job crisis. Instead, the *Post* blamed other factors, including timber exports, increased mechanization, overcutting for short-term profits, and a shift in industry investment from the Northwest to the Southeast and overseas. According to the newspaper, between 1979 and 1988 the timber industry in Washington and Oregon had eliminated more than twenty-five thousand jobs, which occurred well before court injunctions halted logging in remaining old-growth forests.[78] Such reports helped shape the contours of the recovery plan.

To develop a comprehensive management plan for the owl, the Clinton administration formed an interagency team of scientists, managers, and technicians that was called the Forest Ecosystem Management Assessment Team (FEMAT). The president instructed FEMAT to develop a series of options for the management of federal lands within the owl's habitat range. To assist them, the new secretaries of the interior and agriculture asked an independent team of scientists to produce a summary of all the existing demographic studies on the northern spotted owl.[79] Along with President Clinton's pledge to complete a plan within sixty days, a court order required the administration to produce a plan by July 16, 1993.

Two weeks before this deadline, FEMAT presented its ten management options to the president and his cabinet. Option 1 provided the greatest protection for the owl, reserving 11.4 million acres of habitat and limiting the harvest of timber on federal lands in the Northwest to about 100 million board feet annually. Option 7, the least restrictive option, would still have reserved 5.4 million acres and limited timber sales to 1.8 billion board feet. The president and his administration, however, endorsed Option 9, which would reserve about 10 million acres of old-growth habitat for the owl and would limit logging to about 1 billion board feet per year.[80] Option 9, the administration promised, would provide enough habitat to protect thirty-five hundred breeding pairs of owls.

In late July 1993, the Forest Service and the BLM, in cooperation with FWS and other agencies, issued a draft environmental impact statement on Option 9 soliciting public comment.[81] Predictably, the timber industry and area loggers were not pleased with the plan—they expressed outrage, frustration, and a sense of betrayal over the decision.[82] In the first of a series of public hearings, the timber industry attacked the Clinton plan as excessive and warned of the dire economic consequences should it be adopted. Outside of this hearing, loggers protested the plan, including Clinton's promise to provide funds and resources for the retraining of loggers. "Retrain Clinton," read one sign.[83]

Environmentalists also attacked the plan. Despite the fact that Option 9 appeared to protect 10 million acres of owl habitat—far more than the 5.5 million acres proposed by FWS under Bush or the 2.8 million acres proposed by former Secretary Lujan—many environmentalists found this choice unappealing. To begin with, environmentalists correctly worried that the administration would use its discretion in implementing the plan to dilute its recommendations. They also accused Option 9 of doing little to protect the owl on private and state lands. Indeed, in reducing the protective circles around nesting trees on private and state lands from five hundred to seventy acres, environmentalists charged the administration with effectively destroying 116 owl sites.[84] Jay Hair, president of the National Wildlife Federation, said of the environmentalists' relationship with the Clinton administration, "What started out as a love affair now quite frankly feels more like date rape."[85]

For several years, environmentalists had used the courts to effectively sidestep the administration and to halt virtually all logging of old-growth forests in the Pacific Northwest. Although environmentalists had long criticized the Bush administration for failing to develop an owl plan, they had also grown used to tight restrictions on logging imposed by court-ordered injunctions. With the adoption of Clinton's new forest management plan, these injunctions would finally be lifted. Environmentalists knew, although did not admit, that no administrative plan could protect the owls as effectively as injunctions halting all logging. Moreover, any administrative plan would shift power and discretion in implementation from the environmental lawyers and the courts back to the federal land management agencies.

Despite criticisms from the timber industry and environmentalists, in April 1994 the administration formally adopted Option 9, then called the Pacific Northwest Forest Management Plan. Clinton himself announced that the plan marked the beginning of a new era for the Pacific Northwest and for forestry management across the nation because it incorporated ecosystem management principles. He said that the plan fulfilled the commitment he had made over a year ago and would move the management of federal forests "out of the courts and into the hands of professional resource managers."[86] The administration believed, or at least hoped, that it had finally resolved the crisis the spotted owl had created for federal land management in the Northwest and for the ESA itself.

Environmentalists and timber industry representatives had other ideas. Ironically, shortly after the adoption of the Pacific Northwest Forest Management Plan, the two competing interest groups joined forces to challenge the plan in court, claiming that it failed to meet the requirements of several environmental laws. Judge Dwyer disagreed and granted the administration's motion for summary judgment. According to the court, the administration had acted within the lawful scope of their discretion in adopting the plan. "The question," wrote Judge Dwyer, "is not whether the court would write the same plan, but whether the agencies have acted within the bounds of the law."[87] Answering yes to that question, Judge Dwyer observed that for the first time in several years, old-growth forests in the Pacific Northwest would be managed by the responsible federal agencies rather than by court injunctions. Although environmentalists and the timber industry appealed, the Ninth Circuit Court of Appeals upheld Judge Dwyer's decision.[88]

As the administration developed its Pacific Northwest Forest Management Plan, Congress held a series of hearings on the reauthorization of the ESA. In the first of these, the chair of the Subcommittee on Environment and Natural Resources, Representative Studds, promised that consideration of ESA reauthorization would prove to be "one of the most riveting environmental debates" ever held in Congress.[89] In the first hearing, Studds hoped to educate his subcommittee on the act itself by hearing the testimony of administrative experts. In subsequent field hearings held in Texas, the subcommittee heard not only from national interest groups but also from a broad range of local business interests. From these hearings, it became clear that controversy over the ESA was no longer limited to the Pacific Northwest.[90] In the fall of 1993, Representative Studds held yet another hearing to address in particular the degree to which the law now seemed to intrude on private property rights.[91] In part because of the urging of the timber industry to wait until Clinton had developed his forest plan, Congress refused to reauthorize the ESA during 1993.[92]

By 1994, however, the spotted owl crisis had helped convince many Democrats, including Senator Baucus, now chair of the Senate Committee on Environment and Public Works, that the ESA needed to be changed.[93] Baucus and other moderates proposed relatively modest changes to the law, while the more conservative members of Congress called for sweeping revisions that they believed necessary to protect the economy and private property rights. Secretary of the Interior Bruce Babbitt defended the act, saying that despite claims by some in Congress and by private property rights groups, there had not been one case filed alleging an unconstitutional take of private property because of the ESA. Calling it "the most innovative, wide-reaching, and successful environmental law which has been enacted in the last quarter century," Babbitt opposed efforts to gut the act.[94] The division within Congress resulted in a stalemate, and yet another year passed without a reauthorization for the ESA.

In the fall of 1994, the nation elected a conservative majority to the 104th Congress that was openly hostile to the ESA. According to Senator Packwood, for decades the "liberals in Congress" had distorted the original intent of the law to further their "extreme agendas," but "in November, the voters cried foul and asked Republicans to restore rationality to our environmental laws."[95] Led by Speaker of the House Newt Gingrich, these Republicans pledged to rewrite the ESA.[96] Indeed, just months into their first session the House passed a bill allowing private landowners to be compensated for any losses in property value due to the ESA or other environmental laws.[97] Although that measure failed to become law, Congress did impose a temporary moratorium on the listing of species under the ESA by withdrawing funds from listing activities.[98] Congress later extended the moratorium through September 1996.[99]

In 1995 alone, Congress held over twenty-five hearings on the ESA. In the first of these, the Senate Subcommittee on Drinking Water, Fisheries, and Wildlife, now under the leadership of Dirk Kempthorne (R-ID), examined recent, "unfortunate" court holdings that forest plans required consultation under Section 7 of the ESA.[100] A series of hearings throughout the spring and summer examined local impacts of the law in Washington, northern California, Oregon, Idaho, and Wyoming.[101] Congress also formed a Special Task Force on the ESA composed of members of the House Committee on Resources to oversee three hearings on the impact of the act on the nation.[102] These hearings revealed a Congress and a nation bitterly divided over the ESA in part as a result of judicial interpretations of it.

Embittered by their experience with the spotted owl, members of the Pacific Northwest congressional delegation led efforts to revise the ESA. Senator Packwood, like many in Congress, believed that the law had "gone awry" and was "wreaking havoc on our communities and economies, particularly in the Pacific Northwest, but increasingly nationwide." If the ESA had been law one hundred years ago, he said, "we would not have developed the West."[103] To fix perceived problems with the act, Senator Packwood and his colleague Slade Gorton (R-WA) introduced a bill to weaken it. If passed, the bill would have allowed economic and social considerations in listing decisions and in recovery planning, limited the definition of "take" to just those acts that directly killed or injured a species, compensated landowners for property depreciation due to species protection, and created incentives for private species conservation efforts.[104] Enough members of Congress, however, opposed these and similar amendments to prevent Republicans from permanently weakening the ESA in 1995.

The administration also fought against attempts to undermine the act.[105] During a town hall meeting in Billings, Montana, a local resident asked President Clinton if he would veto any Republican attempt to revise the ESA. The president responded that it depended on the language of the bill, but that he opposed attempts to gut the act. Although admitting that the ESA might need some revising, he stressed its successes and his administration's commitment to strong species protection.[106] Indeed, when the bill to impose a moratorium on the listing of species finally reached the president's desk in December 1995, he called the moratorium "misguided" and vetoed it.[107] Congress, however, overrode his veto.

Meanwhile, as the Republican Congress struggled to rewrite the ESA, the timber industry continued to pursue litigation it had begun a few years earlier. In 1992, a coalition of logging communities backed by the timber industry had unsuccessfully sued the secretary of the interior, claiming that the ESA did not support FWS's broad interpretation of "harm."[108] The timber interests appealed, and in 1994 the D.C. Circuit of the U.S. Court of Appeals reversed the district court's holding. According to the appellate court, in the definition of "take," the word "harm" should be read as applying only to "the perpetrator's direct application of force" against the species taken.[109] In other words, Section 9 could not be applied to limit activities that might indirectly take listed species. Secretary Babbitt appealed the decision to the U.S. Supreme Court. The nation's highest court accepted the administration's petition for certiorari not only because of the potential implications for the ESA but also because the D.C. Circuit's holding contradicted an earlier decision by the Ninth Circuit, thus creating a confusing split among the courts.[110]

In the late winter and early spring of 1995, the Supreme Court considered the parties' briefs. The administration argued that the D.C. Circuit's decision should be overturned because the Interior Department's interpretation of "harm" was based on a reasonable construction of the ESA.[111] The timber industry responded that the language, structure, and history of the ESA did not support the administration's expansive interpretation of the word. Among other arguments, the timber industry noted that "harm" should not prohibit activities that indirectly killed or injured listed species, because all of the other words included in the definition of "take" applied only to direct, purposeful actions.[112] The administration disagreed, arguing that the other verbs defining "take"—to harass, pursue, hunt, shoot, wound, kill, trap, capture, or collect—could also be interpreted to prohibit indirect activities.[113] A significant share of the ESA's scope and power hinged on the Court's definition of one word.

In April 1995, the Supreme Court heard oral arguments in the case of *Babbitt v. Sweet Home Chapter of Communities for a Greater Oregon*. During these arguments, the Court initially appeared to favor the timber industry, as conservative Justice Antonio Scalia pummeled the deputy solicitor general, Edwin Kneedler, with question after question challenging the administration's interpretation of the word "harm."[114] Compared to the interrogation of Kneedler, John Macleod's arguments on behalf of the timber industry went smoothly. From the oral arguments alone, it appeared that the Court favored the timber industry's position. The *Washington Post* reported on its front page the day after oral arguments that the case could decide the future of the act.[115]

Despite appearances during oral arguments, on April 17, 1995, in a 7 to 3 decision, the Supreme Court reversed the holding of the court of appeals. According to the majority opinion written by Justice John Stevens, the secretary of the interior's expansive definition of "harm" was a reasonable and permissible interpretation of the ESA.[116] The Court based its decision on an ordinary understanding of the word itself, the broad purpose of the law to protect species, and the fact that in 1982 Congress had amended the ESA to allow for incidental take permits—thereby indicating that indirect actions could result in an illegal take. In her concurring opinion, Justice Sandra Day O'Conner agreed with the majority's holding, but only with the understanding that ordinary principles of proximate causation and foreseeability limited the administration's regulation.[117] Justice Scalia, Chief Justice William Rehnquist, and Justice Clarence Thomas dissented from the decision.

The *Washington Post* called the *Sweet Home* decision "one of the most important environmental cases in a generation." Environmentalists and property rights advocates had anxiously awaited the decision not only because of its potential effect on the implementation of the act but also because of how the decision might influence congressional deliberations over ESA reauthorization and amendment. Although pleased that the high court and "good science" supported a strong interpretation of the ESA, the Sierra Club, for example, worried that the decision would further provoke conservatives in Congress to simply bypass the Court's decision by legislative amendment.[118] The decision convinced property rights advocates that they would find no support with the courts and that they would therefore have to redouble their efforts for a legislative solution.

Indeed, demands for major revisions of the ESA increased significantly as a result of the Court's decision. Eventually, Don Young (R-AK) and Richard Pombo (R-CA) introduced a bill designed explicitly to reverse *Sweet Home*. Their bill not only redefined "take" but also required cost-benefit analysis in the listing process and provided compensation for private landowners whose property values would diminish because of regulatory actions taken under the ESA and other environmental laws.[119] Secretary Babbitt quipped of the Young-Pombo bill, "If Noah had to follow all the rules in this bill, he wouldn't have needed an ark. He could have fit all the animals he was allowed to save in a canoe."[120] President Clinton also spoke out in opposition to the bill, saying that it weakened or abandoned the most important provisions of the ESA. Despite this opposition, however, the Young-Pombo bill passed through the Resources Committee in the fall of 1995 and seemed likely to clear the entire House of Representatives.[121]

Supporters of the ESA in Congress, however, soon received help from an unlikely source—evangelical Christians. In the winter of 1996, the Evangelical Environmental Network (EEN), representing over a thousand churches nationwide, launched a campaign to keep Republicans in Congress from weakening the law. With TV, radio, and print ads appearing in eighteen states, the group stressed the connection between biblical teachings and endangered species. In particular, the EEN relied on the Genesis story of Noah, calling his ark and God's covenant following the flood "the first endangered species act proclaimed in written history."[122]

The group equated the Republican assault on the ESA to a "modern-day sinking of Noah's Ark."[123] The evangelists hoped their campaign would mobilize thirty to fifty million Christians in support of the act.

National and local newspapers covered the story, inadvertently assisting the EEN. In one article on the evangelists' efforts, the *Los Angeles Times* quoted Ron Sider, a professor of theology at Eastern Baptist Theological Seminary: "The Earth is the Lord's and human beings are called to be stewards of God's gorgeous garden."[124] The *Portland Oregonian* also followed the story, quoting from an opportunistic secretary of the interior who stressed the story of Noah, "in which endangered animals are put into a protective ark as part of the covenant between God and 'all living things on Earth,' not just man."[125] The *Washington Post* even reprinted the EEN's "Evangelical Declaration on the Care of Creation," which quoted from the Bible to argue that humans had an obligation to preserve and protect all species.[126] Other papers around the country helped spread the message.

As part of their campaign, the EEN attempted to counter contradictory interpretations of the Bible. In particular, these Christians emphasized stewardship for God's creatures over other passages in the Bible granting humans "dominion" and "rule."[127] They also fought the specter of former Secretary of the Interior James Watt. In 1981, Watt had said, "I do not know how many future generations we can count on before the Lord returns—my responsibility is to follow the scriptures, which call upon us to occupy this land until Jesus returns."[128] Many at the time interpreted his statement as a biblical justification for his antienvironmentalism: "We don't need to worry about saving the forests or the animals, because the world will end soon anyway." The founder of the EEN, Calvin DeWitt, said that at the time he was "surprised and dismayed" by Watt's remarks. "Only the Creator has the right to destroy His creation," said DeWitt.[129]

Evangelists, however, were not the only Christians to oppose Republican attempts to undermine the ESA. While the EEN targeted evangelical and fundamentalist churches, an organization called the Ministry of God's Creation sent literature to other mainstream Protestant churches, like the United Church of Christ. The group designed the literature, entitled "A Call to Defend God's Creation," to be an insert for weekly bulletins that quoted from the Bible and from theologians to support its message of stewardship. "The Endangered Species Act," read the insert, "has been an important way that we as a nation exercise our God-given responsibility to serve as guardians and protectors of God's creation."[130] It also included an "action alert" warning that Congress was set to dismantle the ESA: "An analysis of the bills before Congress reveals that the primary motive behind these bills is not to protect God's creation." The action alert supplied concerned Christians with addresses and phone numbers and urged them to write or call their representatives and senators to "support our biblical covenant to be 'stewards, protectors, and defenders of all Creation'" by protecting the ESA.[131]

Meanwhile, Democrats also went on the offensive, appealing to the American public for help in defending the ESA. At a news conference on the Republican environmental record, Minority Leader Richard Gephardt (D-MO) noted that Speaker Gingrich liked to visit zoos but warned that he better "hurry up, because if Republicans had their way a lot of those animals would be extinct before much longer."[132] At another news conference on the Contract with America, Representative George Miller (D-CA) called the environmental record of the 104th Congress an "outright shame and scandal." "We need the ESA," Miller said, "and we'll fight to keep it."[133] The administration joined in this offensive, saying that of all the nation's environmental laws, Republicans most wanted to eliminate the ESA. In speech after speech, publication after publication, Secretary Babbitt used the Christian message to defend the act, accusing Republicans of violating God's "Commandment to protect creation in all its diversity."[134]

Republicans in Congress got the message, at least temporarily. House Speaker Newt Gingrich agreed to meet privately with representatives from the Evangelical Environmental Network. Soon after, he indicated that the Republican Party had begun to rethink its position on the ESA and other environmental issues.[135] In an address on the "Republican Environmental Agenda" in April 1996, Gingrich called for a "new environmentalism" that was more creative, decentralized, less bureaucratic, incentive-based, and less litigious. At the same time, with regard to the ESA specifically, Gingrich said, "We have nonetheless a firm standard; that our goal is, in fact, to ensure the maximum bio-diversity." "Frankly," he continued, "every species we lose is a level of knowledge about life which is irreplaceable." The Speaker then pledged that he was "deeply committed to maximizing the bio-diversity" of the planet.[136]

These efforts by church groups, of course, failed to convert most conservatives in Congress into champions of a strong ESA. They did, however, help to derail Republican-led attempts to revise the act in 1996. Aggressive Democratic opposition in Congress, firm administrative support for the ESA, and concerted effort by environmentalists also roused national sympathy for the act. Although the public may have elected a conservative Congress in 1994, it did not abide the wholesale dismantling of the ESA or other environmental laws. Nevertheless, while opponents of the ESA failed to weaken it, proponents were yet again unable to secure a reauthorization of appropriations. In the wake of the spotted owl, Congress deadlocked over the future of the ESA.

Conclusion

In the nineteenth century, scientists began to warn Americans that certain species faced extinction because of human activity. These warnings became increasingly dire by the late twentieth century. Sometimes it was the scientists themselves, like William Hornaday and Rachel Carson, who directly inspired political responses to this crisis. More frequently, the disciples of science, conservationists and environmentalists, worked to convince Congress to create federal endangered species law. These laws reflected not any one scientific truth, however, but an evolving scientific understanding about the nature of the modern extinction crisis. Changes in scientific perception influenced the way the administration implemented endangered species law and the way the judiciary interpreted it.

In 1973, federal endangered species law culminated in the ESA. Since then the act has changed dramatically, but not so much because of legislative amendment. Various administration have used, and sometimes abused, their discretion in implementing the law. In exercising their discretion, these administrations have determined which species get protected and how they get protected. Environmentalists have monitored administrative action through the ESA's citizen suit provision. Frequently, they have sued to force the administration to implement the act in certain ways and to expand its scope. The judiciary often accommodated the environmentalists in these lawsuits. Deeper changes in science, culture, and politics have profoundly affected this interplay among Congress, the administration, and the courts over the fate of endangered species.

Litigation, in particular, has played an important but overlooked role in the history of the ESA and other environmental laws. Even though the judiciary was never the mere puppet of environmentalism, most of the important ESA court decisions favored environmentalists, in part because of administrative abuses in implementing the act, especially during the Reagan and Bush administrations. Administrative foot-dragging aside, judges interpreted the act's provisions beyond what Congress intended or anticipated when it passed the ESA in 1973, although this did not occur because the judiciary actively and intentionally ignored the language of the law or the intent of Congress.

Rather, judges interpreted the text of the ESA broadly because they overlooked changes in scientific understanding that gave new meaning to words written in 1973. When the law was drafted and adopted, concepts like biodiversity and ecosystem integrity were relatively unknown. Today, most schoolchildren are familiar with these words—certainly federal judges have some idea of their meaning. Basically, what they mean for observers today is that the ESA can do little to stop extinction if interpreted solely to protect certain isolated species from hunters and furriers. Instead, the act must protect interrelated species and, most important, the habitats upon which they depend. In 1973, many in Congress and elsewhere knew that habitat was important for species preservation but felt it would be enough to create a few wildlife refuges and to prevent people from killing listed species directly. Most folks in 1973 lacked the later–twentieth century appreciation for the importance of habitat in species preservation.

What did this mean for judicial interpretation over the course of the act's history? In 1973, a judge familiar with basic biological and ecological concepts of the day would likely interpret the "take" prohibition of Section 9 to mean little more than that a person could not just go out to hunt, kill, or otherwise directly destroy a listed species. By the late 1970s, however, the American public began to absorb new scientific evidence that habitat degradation was the overwhelming cause of species extirpation. Judges writing opinions during the 1980s and 1990s who accepted science as a constant were more likely to infer that because Congress in 1973 wanted to save species from extinction, it must have intended the take prohibition to prevent private actions that might indirectly harm a species by modifying that species' habitat. Changes in the way that scientists understood why species were becoming extinct resulted in changes in the way that judges interpreted important provisions of the ESA, like the Section 7 consultation requirement and the Section 9 prohibition against take.

Evolution in scientific understanding affected not only judicial interpretation of the ESA but also legislation and legal interpretation throughout the history of federal endangered species law. In the nineteenth century, Darwinian science seemed to excuse human society from responsibility for species extinction. Such was the incidental cost of progress. State and local governments, of course, passed fish and game laws so as not to deplete limited resources, but they did this primarily for economic and recreational reasons. Not until the end of the century and the near elimination of the bison did Americans grow to care about the loss of a species for aesthetic or cultural reasons. While still anthropocentric, such reasoning marked a change in the way Americans viewed the extinction crisis. By the end of the nineteenth century, the nation had the luxury of at least contemplating the preservation of a species merely because of what that species represented—our American heritage.

As the new science of ecology emerged in the early twentieth century, Americans learned of the growing scope of the extinction crisis and what it might mean to humanity. The national government responded to this concern by usurping power from the states to regulate endangered fish and wildlife. Progressive conservationists sincerely believed that only federal protection could save species like migratory birds, which did not respect state boundaries. The national government pushed its way into traditional state domain not just by making new laws but also by convincing the courts to accept broad interpretations of the Constitution's commerce clause and treatymaking powers. In this way, the law gradually reflected the new scientific consensus that species preservation required national effort, which contributed, incidentally, to the growth of the federal government during the twentieth century.

Throughout the first half of the twentieth century, national laws to protect wildlife focused only on particular groups of species or certain individual species. Federal protection for migratory birds made obvious sense. Much like it had attempted to do during the nineteenth century with the bison, the national government provided legislative protection for the bald eagle because of its symbolic worth. The role of the federal government during the first sixty years of the twentieth century, however, remained limited. The birth of the environmental movement during the 1960s changed this situation.

The environmental movement gave unprecedented political power to scientists, ecologists foremost among them. By the 1960s, these scientists began to warn of the plight of not just a few individual species, but of an extinction crisis unprecedented in the history of life on this planet. Inspired by the oracles of science, environmentalists clamored for broad legislative protection for these endangered species, much like they pushed for legislation to protect the nation's air, water, and other natural resources. Protection for species, however, remained uniquely biocentric because its connection to human health and happiness was tenuous compared to efforts to protect air, water, timber, and other resources. Scientific and aesthetic reasons aside, many Americans began to want to protect species based on philosophical, moral, and even religious grounds. Scientists and environmentalists eventually convinced Congress and the Nixon administration that comprehensive species protection legislation would abate this crisis at seemingly little cost.

Nearly thirty years after its passage, many wonder if the Endangered Species Act has succeeded. The answer depends again on science. What history has taught, however, is that science offers different truths at different times for different peoples. Science, especially the science of life, is not exact. Sometimes it is little more than a cultural projection, a social construction. It is difficult, therefore, to assess the act's success. Nevertheless, it is worth an effort.

At the end of the twentieth century, most scientists agree more or less with the following account of the history of the current extinction crisis. Since life began on this planet about 4 billion years ago, the number of species has grown steadily, perhaps reaching as many as 100 million.[1] Our species, *Homo sapiens*, emerged only about 100,000 years ago, at the time of the greatest biodiversity in the history of life.[2] Since then, however, the number of species on this planet has plummeted, especially over the last few centuries, chiefly as a result of human activity.[3] We destroy species three ways: by overhunting or harvesting; by introducing nonnative species to new areas, including the spread of disease; and, most important, by destroying habitat. Because of human activity, biodiversity today has fallen to its lowest level in 65 million years, about the time that the dinosaurs died out.[4]

As the fate of the dinosaurs attests, however, extinctions occurred long before humans existed. Specifically, scientists have identified five periods of mass extinctions within the last 500 million years. The most well known of these include the Permian-Triassic extinctions 245 million years ago, the Cretaceous-Tertiary extinctions 65 million years ago, and the Pleistocene-Holocene extinctions only 11,000 years ago. Approximately 65 percent of terrestrial species perished during the Permian-Triassic, while 90 percent of terrestrial and marine reptiles, including the dinosaurs, disappeared during the Cretaceous-Tertiary.[5] During the Pleistocene-Holocene, climate change and prehistoric human overhunting killed off many large mammal species, like the giant sloth, the mastodon, and the sabertooth tiger.[6] A period of massive species extinction, therefore, is nothing new.

Nevertheless, scientists at the end of the twentieth century believe that the modern extinction crisis differs in important ways from earlier events. First, modern extinctions occur at an unprecedented rate, prompting many scientists to conclude that the present situation has reached "crisis" proportions.[7] Second, with the possible exception of the Pleistocene-Holocene extinctions, major physical events like climate change precipitated earlier periods of mass extinction, while the activities of one species alone have caused the current crisis. And third, modern extinctions threaten all groups of organisms, not just particular groups like dinosaurs or large mammals.[8] Although extinction may be the natural end of evolution, humans have altered and accelerated the process.

The precise rate of modern extinctions, however, is difficult to estimate. At the end of 2000, the U.S. Fish and Wildlife Service had listed 1,792 species worldwide as either endangered or threatened with extinction; 1,234 of these could be found in the United States. At the same time, 155 species were candidates for listing.[9] These numbers, however, only dimly reflect the number of species actually facing extinction. One late-twentieth-century estimate places the current global extinction rate somewhere between one hundred and one thousand times the prehuman level.[10]

The number of species listed under the ESA has also grown steadily. Prior to the passage of the act in 1973, 119 species were listed. The Nixon and Ford administrations listed an average of 14 species each year; the Carter administration, 27 species a year; the Reagan administration, 32 species annually (only 7 per year under the leadership of Secretary of the Interior Watt); the Bush administration, 57 species each year; and the Clinton administration, 69 species annually through 1999.[11]

Scientists and environmentalists at the turn of the millennium have given many reasons why we should care about the scope and rate of modern extinctions. To begin with, many of our modern drugs derive from plants and animals. For example, the rosy periwinkle, a tropical flower, supplies compounds necessary for a chemotherapy treatment that has increased dramatically the remission rates of certain cancers. Plants and animal products provide medical and pharmaceutical benefits to humans in countless other ways, even though scientists have studied only a small fraction of species for their potential uses. The overall economic value of plant- and animal-derived drugs and pharmaceuticals exceeds tens of billions of dollars annually.[12]

Biodiversity also preserves genetic diversity, essential for protecting and improving our food supply. Only about 130 plant species supply virtually all of the world's food crops and feed grains. Modern agriculture has achieved unprecedented productivity among these crops, in part because of the uniformity of crop strains, but this uniformity has left modern crops vulnerable to quickly evolving pests and blights. Genetic diversity supplied by the wild cousins of commercial crops help protect them, thus safeguarding our food supply. To cite just one example, scientists added disease-resistant genes from a seemingly useless strain of wild wheat grass from Turkey to commercial wheat in the United States for a savings of $50 million annually.[13]

Furthermore, biodiversity contributes to ecosystem stability, sustaining natural resources and energy flows upon which we all depend. For example, through the process of photosynthesis, plants supply oxygen to the air we breathe. Forests reduce evaporation, limit erosion, and protect our water supplies. Bugs and microorganisms feed on the wastes of animals, supplying nutrients to the soil from which we grow the food we eat. Species extinctions erode this ecological foundation. Some scientists even claim that if enough species die out, our planetary ecosystem may collapse to the point where it can no longer support human life.[14]

Biodiversity is also important for less ominous reasons. Many people simply enjoy plants and animals and feel that extinction causes irreparable loss. "I wish to know an entire heaven and an entire earth," wrote Henry David Thoreau.[15] Less poetically, over one hundred years later, Congress declared that species of fish, wildlife, and plants possess aesthetic, educational, historical, and recreational value.[16] Even for those who do not take direct pleasure from contact with endangered species, just knowing that wild things thrive in faraway places provides some sufficient reason for preservation.

Finally, many simply believe that species should be protected for their own sake, that life has inherent value. Hindus, for example, hold all life sacred, while Judeo-Christians believe that humans are to be stewards for the earth and the living things upon it. Al Gore, for example, interprets the Old Testament story of Noah's ark as a modern commandment: "Thou shalt preserve biodiversity."[17] For many environmentalists, the human-caused loss of a species is both incalculable and immoral.

Nevertheless, the need to protect biodiversity may seem less obvious than the need to protect other resources, like clean air and water, in part because scientists often cannot quantify the loss of any particular species. No one knows exactly the worth of the snail darter or the spotted owl, or what effect their disappearance may have on human welfare. When confronted with palpable costs—like lost jobs—the history of the ESA has taught that enthusiasm for species preservation often fades.

The Endangered Species Act is now nearly thirty years old and remains the "broadest and most powerful law" in the world for the protection of species.[18] Yet it is still unclear whether the law has been successful. A recent report by the National Research Council found that the ESA has prevented the extinction of some species and slowed the decline of others, but that by itself, it cannot prevent the loss of many species and their habitats. Nevertheless, despite some ambivalence, the report concluded that the act is based on sound scientific principles.

If success means that the ESA has halted the global flood of modern extinctions, however, then the act has failed. Of the 1,263 U.S. species listed since 1967, FWS has removed 6 species due to extinction, while another 8 still listed are probably extinct.[19] Yet, since the ESA's passage in 1973, an average of 85 species has been added to the list every year.[20] Moreover, scientists believe that 60 species of mammals have died out in the recent past, and that about 40 species of freshwater fishes in the United States have become extinct over the last one hundred years.[21] Given the scope of the modern crisis, the ESA may seem to have had a negligible impact on the rate of global extinctions.

Yet these numbers do not tell the whole story. Endangered and threatened species are better off with the ESA than without it. When originally listed, virtually all species were declining in numbers. After listing, however, many species have stabilized and improved. One statistical estimate concludes that for every year of listing, 3 out of 200 listed species formerly declining in number began to increase. To date, listing appears to have turned the fortunes of about half of the species protected by the act.[22] FWS has actually delisted 11 species because of recovery.[23] Slowly, the ESA seems to be making a contribution, if not a significant difference, in the rate of global extinctions.

If Congress primarily intended the ESA to save charismatic megafauna, then it has indeed succeeded. In May 1998, Secretary of the Interior Bruce Babbitt announced: "In the near future, many species will be flying, splashing and leaping off the list. They made it. They're graduating."[24] The 29 species to be upgraded from endangered to threatened, or removed from the list altogether, included the gray wolf, the Columbian white-tailed deer, and the bald eagle. The graduating class, however, included few species that could not fly, splash, or leap. The ESA may not have halted the flood of global extinctions, but it has helped save those species most representative of our national heritage and dearest to the American people. Despite the act's unanticipated consequences, perhaps it has achieved what Congress intended it to do after all.

Notes

INTRODUCTION

1. See the Endangered Species Act of 1973, 16 U.S.C. § 1531–1544 (1999).
2. Bruce Babbitt, "The Endangered Species Act and Takings: A Call for Innovation within the Terms of the Act," *Environmental Law* 24 (1964): 356.
3. *Tennessee Valley Authority v. Hill*, 437 U.S. 153, 180 (1978).
4. See Roderick Nash, *Rights of Nature: A History of Environmental Ethics* (Madison: Univ. of Wisconsin Press, 1989), 175.
5. Statement of Senator Bob Graham (D-FL), U.S. Congress, Senate, Committee on Environment and Public Works, *Endangered Species Act Amendments of 1993*, hearings, 103d Cong., 2d sess., 23 July 1994 (Washington, D.C.: GPO, 1994), 2.
6. See 16 U.S.C. § 1540(g).
7. See 16 U.S.C. § 1533(b)(1)(A).
8. See 16 U.S.C. § 1532(16).
9. See 16 U.S.C. § 1532(6), (20).
10. See 16 U.S.C. § 1532(8).
11. See 16 U.S.C. § 1536(a)(2).
12. See 16 U.S.C. § 1538(a). The Section 9 prohibition does not automatically apply to threatened species; rather threatened species are protected by regulations that the secretary deems "necessary and advisable" (16 U.S.C. § 1533[d]).
13. See 16 U.S.C. § 1532(19). This broad prohibition applies only to the taking of fish and wildlife. Weaker prohibitions apply to the taking of plants; see 16 U.S.C. § 1538(a)(2)(B).
14. See 40 *Federal Register* 44412, 44416 (1975), current version at 50 *Code of Federal Regulations*, sec. 17.3 (1975).
15. J. B. Ruhl, "Section 7(a)(1) of the 'New' Endangered Species Act: Rediscovering and Redefining the Untapped Power of Federal Agencies' Duty to Conserve Species," *Environmental Law* 25 (1995): 115.
16. See *Palila v. Hawaii Department of Land and Natural Resources*, 471 F.Supp. 985 (D. Haw. 1979), affirmed by 639 F.2d 495 (9th Cir. 1981); see also *Babbitt v. Sweet Home Chapter of Communities for a Greater Oregon*, 515 U.S. 687 (1995).
17. Heather Dewar, "Gingrich Is Going for the Green," *Wisconsin State Journal*, 25 Apr. 1996, 3A.
18. See John Cushman, "Linking Endangered Species Act to Spending," *New York Times*, 10 Oct. 1998, A1.
19. See *Tennessee Valley Authority v. Hill*, 437 U.S. 153, 173 (1978).

CHAPTER 1. BISON TO BALD EAGLES

1. Charles Darwin, *The Origin of Species* (1859; reprint, New York: Penguin Books, 1982).

2. See Peter Matthiessen, *Wildlife in America* (New York: Viking Press, 1959), 281.

3. *Martin v. Waddell,* 41 U.S. 367, 416 (1842).

4. *Martin v. Waddell,* 41 U.S. at 412.

5. See *Pollard v. Hagan,* 44 U.S. 212, 223 (1845); see also *Ward v. Race Horse,* 163 U.S. 504 (1896). In *Ward v. Race Horse,* the Court applied the equal footing doctrine, that all states shall be admitted with the same rights and powers held by the existing states, to the question of state authority over wildlife.

6. Constitution of the United States, art. 4, sec. 3, cl. 2.

7. See U.S. Congress, *Act of July 27, 1868,* ch. 273, 15 Stat. 240 (repealed 1944).

8. See U.S. Congress, *Act of February 9, 1871,* 16 Stat. 593 (repealed 1964).

9. See U.S. Congress, *Act of March 3, 1891,* ch. 561, sec. 24, 26 Stat. 1103 (repealed 1976).

10. "The Congress shall have power . . . To regulate Commerce with foreign Nations, and among the several States, and with the Indian Tribes" (Constitution of the United States, art. 1, sec. 8, cl. 3).

11. See *Gibbons v. Ogden,* 22 U.S. 1 (1824).

12. See *Smith v. Maryland,* 59 U.S. 71, 76 (1855).

13. See Lawrence Friedman, *A History of American Law,* 2d ed. (New York: Simon and Schuster, 1985), 261.

14. See *Gibbons v. Ogden,* 59 U.S. at 76.

15. See *Gibbons v. Ogden,* 59 U.S. at 75.

16. *McCready v. Virginia,* 94 U.S. 391, 395 (1876).

17. See James Trefethen, *An American Crusade for Wildlife* (Alexandria, Va.: Boone and Crockett Club, 1975), 16.

18. See Richard White, "Animals and Enterprise," in *The Oxford History of the American West,* ed. Clyde A. Milner et al. (New York: Oxford Univ. Press, 1994), 249.

19. "The Buffalo Meat Business," *New York Times,* 26 Mar. 1871, 6.

20. "The Buffalo Meat Business," 6.

21. "Extinction of the Buffalo," *New York Times,* 22 July 1872, 3.

22. "The Buffalo Meat Business," 6.

23. "Buffalo Slaughter," *New York Times,* 7 Feb. 1872, 2.

24. "Buffalo Slaughter," 2.

25. See *Congressional Record,* 43d Cong., 2d sess., 10 Mar. 1874, p. H2105.

26. *Congressional Record,* 43d Cong., 2d sess., 10 Mar. 1874, p. H2106.

27. See *Congressional Record,* 43d Cong., 2d sess., 10 Mar. 1874, p. H2108.

28. *Congressional Record,* 43d Cong., 2d sess., 10 Mar. 1874, p. H2107.

29. *Congressional Record,* 43d Cong., 2d sess., 10 Mar. 1874, p. H2107.

30. Columbus Delano, *Report of the Secretary of the Interior for 1872* (Washington, D.C.: GPO, 1873), 7.

31. *Congressional Record,* 44th Cong., 1st sess., 23 Feb. 1876, p. H1238.

32. *Congressional Record,* 44th Cong., 1st sess., 23 Feb. 1876, p. H1241.

33. *Congressional Record,* 44th Cong., 1st sess., 23 Feb. 1876, p. H1239.

34. See "The Buffalo Slowly Disappearing," *New York Times,* 10 Sept. 1883, 5.

35. "The End of the Buffalo," *New York Times,* 26 Dec. 1884, 3.

36. "Killing of the Buffalo," *New York Times,* 26 July 1896, 20.

37. See U.S. Congress, *Act of May 7, 1894,* 28 Stat. 73 (Washington, D.C.: GPO, 1895); see generally Alfred Runte, *National Parks: The American Experience,* 2d ed. (Lincoln: Univ. of Nebraska Press, 1987), which describes the importance of national parks for wildlife preservation.

38. "Bison Preserves," *New York Times*, 3 Nov. 1907, 8.

39. See U.S. Congress, *Act of May 23, 1908*, 35 Stat. 267 (Washington, D.C.: GPO, 1909).

40. See *Geer v. Connecticut*, 161 U.S. 519 (1896).

41. *Geer v. Connecticut*, 161 U.S. at 523.

42. *Geer v. Connecticut*, 161 U.S. at 529.

43. *Geer v. Connecticut*, 161 U.S. at 530.

44. See the statement of Representative Lacey, *Congressional Record*, 56th Cong., 1st sess., 1900, vol. 33, p. H4871.

45. See U.S. Congress, *Act of May 25, 1900* (Washington, D.C.: GPO, 1901), sec. 3.

46. See, for example, *Rupert v. United States*, 181 F. 87 (8th Cir. 1910).

47. See *People of the State of New York v. Henry Hesterberg*, 211 U.S. 31, 41 (1908). In that case, the Court held that "laws passed by the states in the exertion of their police power, not in conflict with laws of Congress upon the same subject, and indirectly or remotely affecting interstate commerce, are nevertheless valid laws."

48. See generally Samuel Hays, *Conservation and the Gospel of Efficiency: The Progressive Conservation Movement, 1890–1920* (Cambridge: Harvard Univ. Press, 1963).

49. See John F. Reiger, "Wildlife, Conservation, and the First Forest Reserve," in *The Origins of the National Forests*, ed. Harold K. Steen (Durham, N.C.: Forest History Society, 1992), 106; see generally John F. Reiger, "Wildlife, Conservation, and the First Forest Reserve," in *American Forests*, ed. Char Miller (Lawrence: Univ. Press of Kansas, 1997).

50. See Christopher McGrory Klyza, *Who Controls the Public Lands? Mining, Forestry, and Grazing Policies, 1870–1990* (Chapel Hill: Univ. of North Carolina Press, 1996).

51. See "White Heron Victim of Woman's Vanity," *New York Times*, 13 Aug. 1905, 4.

52. See "Prohibited Plumage Law," *New York Times*, 1 June 1906, 1.

53. See "To Save the Heath Hen," *New York Times*, 3 June 1907, 2.

54. See "States Favor Bird Laws," *New York Times*, 27 Mar. 1912, 7.

55. "Shall We Give Posterity a Gameless Country?" *New York Times*, 5 Feb. 1911, 5.

56. "Bird Law In Effect," *New York Times*, 8 Oct. 1913, 10.

57. See William S. Haskell, "Will Federal Courts Assure Birds Free Use of Air?" *New York Times*, 22 May 1913, 7.

58. See A.W. Schorger, *The Passenger Pigeon: Its Natural History and Extinction* (Norman: Univ. of Oklahoma Press, 1955), 199, 205, 214, 224–230.

59. See U.S. Department of State, "Convention for the Protection of Migratory Birds, United States–Great Britain (on Behalf of Canada)," 16 Aug. 1916, TIAS no. 628.

60. See U.S. Congress, *Migratory Bird Treaty Act of 1918*, 40 Stat. 755 (Washington, D.C.: GPO, 1918).

61. See U.S. Congress, *Migratory Bird Treaty Act of 1918*, sec. 2.

62. See Constitution of the United States, art. 2, sec. 2, cl. 2.

63. See Constitution of the United States, amend. 10.

64. See *Missouri v. Holland*, 252 U.S. 416, 434–435 (1920).

65. See U.S. Congress, *Migratory Bird Conservation Act of 1929*, 45 Stat. 1222 (Washington, D.C.: GPO, 1929).

66. See "Long Islanders Fight Club Hunters," *New York Times*, 20 Jan. 1920, 19.

67. See "Needless Hunting and Fishing Laws," editorial, *New York Times*, 22 Apr. 1926, 24.

68. See William Hornaday, "Hunters Menace All Birds," *New York Times*, 29 Mar. 1925, 11.

69. "More Ground for Ducks," *New York Times*, 4 Feb. 1925, 20.

70. See "Rise in Poaching Laid to Depression," *New York Times*, 8 Dec. 1931, 31.

71. "Hoover Asks Hunters to Keep Duck Season; Would Avoid 'Calamity of Extermination,'" *New York Times*, 27 Aug. 1931, 9.

72. "Hoover Backs Move to Preserve Game," *New York Times*, 2 Dec. 1930, 32.

73. See U.S. Congress, House, Special Committee on Conservation of Wildlife, *Conservation of Wildlife*, hearing, 73d Cong., 2d sess., 23 Mar. 1934 (Washington, D.C.: GPO, 1934), 7.

74. See Special Committee on Conservation of Wildlife, *Conservation of Wildlife*, 13.

75. See Special Committee on Conservation of Wildlife, *Conservation of Wildlife*, 13.

76. See Special Committee on Conservation of Wildlife, *Conservation of Wildlife*, 129.

77. See Special Committee on Conservation of Wildlife, *Conservation of Wildlife*, 13, 20.

78. See U.S. Congress, *Act of March 10, 1934*, 48 Stat. 401 (Washington, D.C.: GPO, 1935).

79. U.S. Congress, *Act of March 10, 1934*, secs. 2 and 3.

80. U.S. Congress, *Act of March 10, 1934*, secs. 1 and 3.

81. See "President Pledges New Wild Life Aid," *New York Times*, 2 Oct. 1936, 2.

82. See U.S. Congress, Senate, Special Committee on Conservation of Wildlife Resources, *Wildlife Restoration and Conservation: Proceedings of the North American Wildlife Conference*, report, 74th Cong., 2d sess., 3–7 Feb. 1936 (Washington, D.C.: GPO, 1936), 1.

83. See Special Committee on Conservation of Wildife Resources, *Wildlife Restoration and Conservation*, 639.

84. U.S. Congress, Senate, Special Committee on Conservation of Wildlife Resources, *Wildlife and the Land: A Story of Regeneration*, report on S. Res. 246, 71st Cong., 1st sess., January 1937 (Washington, D.C.: GPO, 1937), 81.

85. Special Committee on Conservation of Wildlife Resources, *Wildlife and Land*, 81.

86. U.S. Congress, House, Select Committee on the Conservation of Wildlife Resources, *Conservation of Wildlife: Hearings on House Resolution 11*, hearing, 75th Cong., 3d sess., 5 May 1938 (Washington, D.C.: GPO, 1938), 192.

87. Select Committee on Conservation of Wildlife Resources, *Conservation of Wildlife* (1938), 193.

88. See U.S. Congress, House, Select Committee on Conservation of Wildlife Resources, *Conservation of Wildlife: Hearings on House Resolution 65*, hearing, 76th Cong., 1st sess., 31 Mar. 1939 (Washington, D.C.: GPO, 1939), 28–29.

89. See Select Committee on Conservation of Wildlife Resources, *Conservation of Wildlife* (1939), 30.

90. See "Says Nation Seeks Game Fish Surplus," *New York Times*, 3 Dec. 1931, 31.

91. U.S. Congress, Senate, Special Committee on Conservation of Wild Life Resources, *Brown Bear of Alaska*, hearing, 72d Cong., 1st sess., 18 Jan. 1932 (Washington, D.C.: GPO, 1933), 24.

92. Special Committee on Conservation of Wildlife Resources, *Wildlife Restoration and Conservation*, 650.

93. See U.S. Congress, House, Committee on Agriculture, *American Eagle Protection*, hearing, 71st Cong., 2d sess., 31 Jan. 1930 (Washington, D.C.: GPO, 1930), 1.

94. Committee on Agriculture, *American Eagle Protection*, 2.

95. Committee on Agriculture, *American Eagle Protection*, 21, 26–27.

96. U.S. Congress, *Bald Eagle Protection Act*, 54 Stat. 278 (Washington, D.C.: GPO, 1940), sec. 1.

97. *Bald Eagle Protection Act*, sec. 1.

98. See Michael Bean and Melanie Rowland, *The Evolution of National Wildlife Law*, 3d ed. (Westport, Conn.: Praeger, 1997), 162.

99. U.S. Congress, House, Select Committee on Conservation of Wildlife Resources, *Conservation of Wildlife: Hearings on House Resolution 65*, hearing, 76th Cong., 3d sess., 19 Mar. 1940 (Washington, D.C.: GPO, 1940), 1.

100. Select Committee on Conservation of Wildlife Resources, *Conservation of Wildlife* (1940), 3.

101. U.S. Congress, House, Select Committee on Conservation of Wildlife Resources, *Conservation of Wildlife: Hearings on House Resolution 49*, hearing, 77th Cong., 1st sess., 25, 28 Nov., 9 Dec. 1941 (Washington, D.C.: GPO, 1942), 182.

102. See Glover M. Allen, *Extinct and Vanishing Mammals of the Western Hemisphere* (Cambridge, Mass.: American Committee for International Wildlife Protection, 1942), 2.

103. See Select Committee on Conservation of Wildlife Resources, *Conservation of Wildlife* (1942), 72.

104. See U.S. Congress, House, Select Committee on Conservation of Wildlife Resources, *Conservation of Wildlife*, hearing, 79th Cong., 2d sess., 1 Nov. 1945, 10–12 June 1946 (Washington, D.C.: GPO, 1946), 1.

105. See Select Committee on Conservation of Wildlife Resources, *Conservation of Wildlife* (1946), 1.

106. See U.S. Congress, House, Select Committee on Conservation of Wildlife Resources, *Conservation of Wildlife*, hearing, 79th Cong., 1st sess., 19–20 June 1945 (Washington, D.C.: GPO, 1945), 45.

107. See generally U.S. Congress, House, Committee on Merchant Marine and Fisheries, Subcommittee on Conservation of Wildlife Resources, *Promoting the Conservation of Wildlife*, 80th Cong., 1st sess., 2 July 1947 (Washington, D.C.: GPO, 1947).

108. U.S. Congress, House, Committee on Merchant Marine and Fisheries, Subcommittee on Fisheries and Wildlife Conservation, *Protection of the Bald Eagle*, hearing, 81st Cong., 2d sess., 9 Feb. 1950 (Washington, D.C.: GPO, 1950), 14.

109. See Subcommittee on Fisheries and Wildlife Conservation, *Protection of the Bald Eagle*, 13.

110. See Subcommittee on Fisheries and Wildlife Conservation, *Protection of the Bald Eagle*, 1.

111. See U.S. Congress, *Act of Oct. 24, 1962*, 76 Stat. 1246 (Washington, D.C.: GPO, 1962).

112. U.S. Congress, Senate, Committee on Commerce, Subcommittee on Senate Joint Resolution 105 and House Joint Resolution 489, *Protection for the Golden Eagle*, hearing, 87th Cong., 2d sess., 26 June 1962 (Washington, D.C.: GPO, 1962), 2.

113. Subcommittee on Senate Joint Resolution, *Protection for the Golden Eagle*, 12.

114. See generally Ellen Swallow, *Sanitation in Daily Life* (New York: J. Wiley and Sons, 1910).

115. See generally Frederic Clements, *Plant Succession* (Washington, D.C.: Carnegie Institute, 1916).

116. See Arthur Tansley, "The Use and Abuse of Vegetational Concepts and Terms," *Ecology* 16 (1935): 284, 306.

117. See Eugene P. Odum, "The Strategy of Ecosystem Development," *Science* 164 (1969): 262, 270. Since the 1960s, much to the chagrin of environmentalists, the field of ecology has changed dramatically, emphasizing chaos and randomness rather than equilibrium and harmony. See generally Daniel Botkin, *Discordant Harmonies: New Ecology for the Twenty-First Century* (New York: Oxford Univ. Press, 1990).

118. Aldo Leopold, *A Sand County Almanac*, commemorative ed. (New York: Oxford Univ. Press, 1989), 224–225.

119. See Leopold, *A Sand County Almanac*, 108–110.

120. "Scientists Aloof on U.S. Wolf Hunt," *New York Times*, 17 June 1953, 29.

121. Leopold, *A Sand County Almanac*, 130.

122. Leopold, *A Sand County Almanac*, 130.

123. Leopold, *A Sand County Almanac*, 130.

124. See "A New Wildlife Policy," editorial, *New York Times*, 7 July 1965, 36; see also "Cry Coyote," editorial, *New York Times*, 27 Feb. 1972, sec. 4, 12.

125. See Richard Nixon, *Public Papers of the Presidents of the United States, 1972* (Washington, D.C.: GPO, 1974), 183; see also Galdwin Hill, "A Polite Nudge on Environment," *New York Times*, 9 Feb. 1972, 21.

126. U.S. Congress, House, Committee on Merchant Marine and Fisheries, *Wildlife Refuge Disposal Policy*, hearing, 84th Cong., 2d sess., January 1956 (Washington, D.C.: GPO, 1956), 1.

127. See, for example, U.S. Congress, House, Committee on Merchant Marine and Fisheries, Subcommittee on Fisheries and Wildlife Conservation, *Miscellaneous Fish and Wildlife Legislation*, hearing, 87th Cong., 1st sess. 9, 10, 11 May; 28, 29 June; 19 July 1961 (Washington, D.C.: GPO, 1962).

CHAPTER 2. CONGRESS AND CHARISMATIC MEGAFAUNA

1. See Rachel Carson, *Silent Spring* (1962; reprint, New York: Fawcett Crest, 1966).

2. See Robert Gottlieb, *Forcing the Spring: The Transformation of the American Environmental Movement* (Washington, D.C.: Island Press, 1993), 81.

3. "New Fund Seeks to Save Near Extinct Species," *New York Times*, 8 Nov. 1961, 37.

4. See "New Fund Seeks to Save Near Extinct Species," 37.

5. See U.S. Congress, House, Committee on Merchant Marine and Fisheries, Subcommittee on Fisheries and Wildlife Conservation, *Miscellaneous Fish and Wildlife Legislation*, hearing, 87th Cong., 1st sess., 9, 10, 11 May; 28, 29 June; 19 July 1961 (Washington, D.C.: GPO, 1962), 7.

6. See William M. Blair, "U.S. Studying Way to Save Wildlife," *New York Times*, 7 July 1964, 16.

7. See U.S. Congress, *Wilderness Act of 1964*, 78 Stat. 890 (Washington, D.C.: GPO, 1964).

8. See U.S. Congress, House, Committee on Merchant Marine and Fisheries, Subcommittee on Fisheries and Wildlife Conservation, *Miscellaneous Fisheries and Wildlife Legislation*, hearing, 89th Cong., 1st sess., 27 May, 20 July 1965 (Washington, D.C.: GPO, 1965), 34.

9. See Subcommittee on Fisheries and Wildlife Conservation, *Miscellaneous Fisheries and Wildlife Legislation* (1965), 134–135.

10. U.S. Congress, Senate, Committee on Commerce, Subcommittee on Merchant Marine and Wildlife, *Conservation, Protection, and Propagation of Endangered Species of Fish and Wildlife*, 89th Cong., 1st sess., 12 Aug. 1965 (Washington, D.C.: GPO, 1966), 5.

11. See "Wildlife Species Face Extinction," *New York Times*, 9 Jan. 1966, 48.

12. "Man, the Endangered Species," editorial, *New York Times*, 26 Jan. 1966, 36.

13. "Man, the Endangered Species," 36.

14. See U.S. Congress, *Endangered Species Preservation Act of 1966*, 80 Stat. 926 (Washington, D.C.: GPO, 1967).

15. See *Endangered Species Preservation Act of 1966*, sec. 1(c).

16. *Endangered Species Preservation Act of 1966*, sec. 1(b).

17. *Endangered Species Preservation Act of 1966*, sec. 2(d).

18. *Endangered Species Preservation Act of 1966*, sec. 4.

19. *Endangered Species Preservation Act of 1966*, sec. 4(c).

20. U.S. Congress, Senate, Committee on Commerce, Subcommittee on Merchant Marine and Fisheries, *Endangered Species*, hearing, 90th Cong., 2d sess., 24 July 1968 (Washington, D.C.: GPO, 1968), 25.

21. See U.S. Congress, Senate, Committee on Merchant Marine and Fisheries, Subcommittee on Fisheries and Wildlife Conservation, *Fish and Wildlife Legislation*, hearing, 90th Cong., 1st sess., 4 Oct. 1967 (Washington, D.C.: GPO, 1967), 38.

22. See "78 Species Listed Near Extinction," *New York Times*, 12 Mar. 1967, 46.

23. Civilization's Prey, editorial, *New York Times*, 9 Sept. 1967, 30.

24. See "Traffic in Savagery," editorial, *New York Times*, 19 Sept. 1968, 46.

25. U.S. Congress, House, Committee on Merchant Marine and Fisheries, Subcommittee on Fisheries and Wildlife Conservation, *Endangered Species*, hearing, 91st Cong., 1st sess., 19, 20 Feb. 1969 (Washington, D.C.: GPO, 1969), 21.

26. See Tom Garrett, "Wildlife," in *Nixon and the Environment*, ed. James Rathlesberger (New York: Taurus Communications, 1972), 131.

27. See Garrett, "Wildlife," 133, 153; see also generally U.S. Congress, Senate, Committee on Commerce, Subcommittee on Energy, Natural Resources, and the Environment, *Endangered Species*, 91st Cong., 1st sess., 14, 15 May 1969 (Washington, D.C.: GPO, 1969).

28. See U.S. Congress, *Endangered Species Conservation Act of 1969*, 83 Stat. 275 (Washington, D.C.: GPO, 1969).

29. See *Endangered Species Conservation Act of 1969*, sec. 3(a), sec. 2.

30. See *Endangered Species Conservation Act of 1969*, sec. 2.

31. See *Endangered Species Conservation Act of 1969*, sec. 7(a).

32. See *Endangered Species Conservation Act of 1969*, sec. (2).

33. "Washington Records: The President," *New York Times*, 6 Dec.1969, 25.

34. See *A. E. Nettleton Co. v. Diamond*, 27 N.Y. 2d 182, 264 N.E. 2d 118, 315

N.Y.S. 2d 625 (1970); see also *Palladio, Inc. v. Diamond*, 321 F.Supp. 630 (S.D.N.Y. 1970), affirmed by 440 F.2d 1319 (2d Cir. 1971).

35. See James Fisher et al., *Wildlife in Danger* (New York: Viking Press, 1969), 7.

36. Fisher, *Wildlife in Danger*, 11, 13.

37. See Walter Sullivan, "Scientist Urges Rearing Lost Species' Relatives," *New York Times*, 17 Mar. 1970, 24.

38. Bayard Webster, "Plants Called Endangered, Along with Rare Animals," *New York Times*, 11 Nov. 1971, 49.

39. U.S. Congress, *Wild Free-Roaming Horses and Burros Act*, 85 Stat. 649 (Washington, D.C.: GPO, 1971).

40. *Kleppe v. New Mexico*, 426 U.S. 529, 541 (1976).

41. See Michael Bean and Melanie Rowland, *The Evolution of National Wildlife Law*, 3d ed. (London: Praeger, 1997), 110–111.

42. See U.S. Congress, *Marine Mammal Protection Act*, 86 Stat. 1027 (Washington, D.C.: GPO, 1973).

43. See, for example, *Fooke Co. v. Mandel*, 386 F.Supp. 1341 (D.Md. 1974).

44. See U.S. Congress, Senate, Committee on Commerce, Subcommittee on the Environment, *Endangered Species Conservation Act of 1972*, hearing, 92d Cong., 2d sess., 4, 10 Aug. 1972 (Washington, D.C.: GPO, 1972), 253.

45. Prince Bernhard, "Man and the Natural World," *New York Times*, 26 Mar. 1972, sec. 4, 13.

46. See William S. Boyd, "Federal Protection of Endangered Wildlife Species," *Stanford Law Review* 22 (1970): 1289.

47. Richard Nixon, *Public Papers of the Presidents of the United States, 1972* (Washington, D.C.: GPO, 1974), 183.

48. Nixon, *Public Papers, 1972*, 183.

49. See U.S. Congress, House, House Resolution 13081, 92d Cong. (Washington, D.C.: GPO, 1972).

50. See U.S. Congress, Senate, Senate Bill 3199, 92d Cong. (Washington, D.C.: GPO, 1972).

51. See U.S. Congress, House, House Resolution 37, 93d Cong. (Washington, D.C.: GPO, 1973); see also U.S. Congress, House, Committee on Environment and Public Works, *Legislative History of the Endangered Species Act of 1973*, report prepared by the Congressional Research Service (Washington, D.C.: GPO, 1982), 72.

52. See U.S. Congress, Senate Bill 1983, 93d Cong. (Washington, D.C.: GPO, 1973).

53. See Richard Nixon, *Public Papers of the Presidents of the United States, 1973* (Washington, D.C.: GPO, 1975), 94, 101, 285–286; see also U.S. Congress, House, House Resolution 4758, 93d Cong. (Washington, D.C.: GPO, 1973); U.S. Congress, Senate, Senate Bill 1592, 93d Cong. (Washington, D.C.: GPO, 1973).

54. See U.S. Congress, Senate, Committee on Interior and Insular Affairs, *Congress and the Nation's Environment: Environmental and Natural Resource Affairs of the 93d Congress*, Committee Print 1950 (Washington, D.C.: GPO, 1973), 561.

55. See Committee on Environment and Public Works, *Legislative History*, 385.

56. See the statement of Lawrence Jahn, vice president of the Wildlife Management Institute, printed in U.S. Congress, Senate, Committee on Commerce, Subcommittee on the Environment, *Endangered Species Act of 1973*, hearing, 93d Cong., 1st sess., 18, 21 June 1973 (Washington, D.C.: GPO, 1974), 108; see also George Wilson, "Hill Vote Set on Bill to Save Animals from Extinction," *Washington Post*, 16 Sept. 1973, A2.

57. See the statement of Representative Grover, reprinted in Committee on Environment and Public Works, *Legislative History*, 199.

58. See the statement of Representative Dingell, reprinted in Committee on Environment and Public Works, *Legislative History*, 194.

59. Statement of Senator Williams, reprinted in Committee on Environment and Public Works, *Legislative History*, 362.

60. See "Protecting Endangered Species," editorial, *Washington Post*, 26 June 1973, A22; see also Stephen Seater, Defenders of Wildlife, "Letter to the Editor: Protection of Wildlife," *Washington Post*, 4 July 1973, A27.

61. Statement of Senator Stevens, reprinted in Committee on Environment and Public Works, *Legislative History*, 361.

62. See Committee on Environment and Public Works, *Legislative History*, 409–410.

63. Statement of Representative Grover, reprinted in Committee on Environment and Public Works, *Legislative History*, 200.

64. Statement of Representative Dingell, reprinted in Committee on Environment and Public Works, *Legislative History*, 196.

65. See Committee on Environment and Public Works, *Legislative History*, 30, 167–168.

66. See U.S. Congress, House, Conference Report No. 93-740, 93d Cong. (Washington, D.C.: GPO, 1973).

67. Compare U.S. Congress, House, House Resolution 37, sec. 3(11), 93d Cong. (Washington, D.C.: GPO, 1973), with U.S. Congress, Senate, Senate Bill 1983, sec. 3(15), 93d Cong. (Washington, D.C.: GPO, 1973).

68. See Conference Report No. 93-740; see also statement of Representative Dingell reprinted in Committee on Environment and Public Works, *Legislative History*, 480.

69. See Committee on Environment and Public Works, *Legislative History*, 474.

70. Statement of Representative Dingell, reprinted in Committee on Environment and Public Works, *Legislative History*, 479–480.

71. See Committee on Environment and Public Works, *Legislative History*, 483–485.

72. Coincidentally, three of these four representatives were not reelected in 1974. See *Biographical Directory of the U.S. Congress* at *http://bioguide.congress.gov/*. (visited 5 Dec. 1998).

73. Nixon, *Public Papers, 1973*, 1027–1028.

74. Steven Yaffee, *Prohibitive Policy: Implementing the Federal Endangered Species Act* (Cambridge, Mass.: MIT Press, 1982), 51.

75. Garrett, "Wildlife," 131.

76. "Saving the World's Wildlife," editorial, *Washington Post*, 19 Feb. 1973, A14.

77. See Samuel Hays, *Beauty, Health, and Permanence: Environmental Politics in the United States, 1955–1985* (New York: Cambridge Univ. Press, 1987), 57–58.

78. Nixon, *Public Papers, 1972*, 173.

79. The consideration and passage of the ESA proceeded the Saturday Night Massacre and the beginning of the fight over the Nixon tapes. Nixon resigned on August 8, 1974. See Stanley Kutler, *The Wars of Watergate: The Last Crisis of Richard Nixon* (New York: W. W. Norton, 1990), 383–442, 547–548.

80. See John Flippen, "The Nixon Administration, Timber, and the Call of the Wild," *Environmental History Review* 19 (1995): 37. Flippen argues that Nixon's commitment to the environment was insincere and opportunistic.

81. See statement of Maxwell Rich, executive vice president of the National Rifle Association, in Subcommittee on the Environment, *Endangered Species Act of 1973*, 123.

82. See statements of John Gottschalk, of the International Association of Games, Fish, and Conservation Commissioners, Lawrence Jahn, of the Wildlife Management Institute, and James Sharp, attorney for the Fur Conservation Institute, in Subcommittee on the Environment, *Endangered Species Act of 1973*, 106, 108, 119.

83. See generally U.S. Congress, House, Committee on Merchant Marine and Fisheries, Subcommittee on Fisheries and Wildlife Conservation and the Environment, *Endangered Species*, hearing, 93d Cong., 1st sess., 15, 26, 27 Mar. 1973 (Washington, D.C.: GPO, 1973).

84. "Protecting Endangered Species," editorial, *Washington Post*, 26 June 1973, A22.

85. See Yaffee, *Prohibitive Policy*, 50–51.

86. Garrett, "Wildlife," 131; see also Yaffee, *Prohibitive Policy*, 46.

87. See statement of Representative Dingell, reprinted in Committee on Environment and Public Works, *Legislative History*, 193–194.

88. See statement of Representative Dingell, reprinted in Committee on Environment and Public Works, *Legislative History*, 72–73.

89. Statement of Senator Tunney, reprinted in Committee on Environment and Public Works, *Legislative History*, 359.

90. Statement of Senator Stevens, reprinted in Committee on Environment and Public Works, *Legislative History*, 362.

91. See U.S. Congress, Senate, Conference Report No. 93-307, 93d Cong. (Washington, D.C.: GPO, 1973), 1.

92. See Rocky Barker, *Saving All the Parts: Reconciling Economics and the Endangered Species Act* (Washington, D.C.: Island Press, 1993); see also Yaffee, *Prohibitive Policy*, 54–56.

93. See statement of Representative Dingell, reprinted in Committee on Environment and Public Works, *Legislative History*, 72–73.

94. See statement of Representative Sullivan, reprinted in Committee on Environment and Public Works, *Legislative History*, 192.

95. Statement of Senator Roth, reprinted in Committee on Environment and Public Works, *Legislative History*, 407.

96. Statement of Sen. Williams, reprinted in Committee on Environment and Public Works, *Legislative History*, 374.

97. See U.S. Congress, Senate, Committee on Commerce, *Endangered Species Act of 1973* (Washington, D.C.: GPO, 1974), sec. 12.

98. See Smithsonian Institution, *Report on Endangered and Threatened Species of the United States* (Washington, D.C.: GPO, 1974).

99. See U.S. Congress, House, House Resolution 4758, 93d Cong. (Washington, D.C.: GPO, 1973); U.S. Congress, Senate, Senate Bill 1592, 93d Cong. (Washington, D.C.: GPO, 1973).

100. Nixon, *Public Papers, 1973*, 1027–1028.

101. "Protecting Endangered Species," editorial, *Washington Post*, 26 June 1973, A22.

102. See "The Dwindling Wolf Pack," editorial, *Washington Post*, 7 Aug. 1973, A18.

103. George Wilson, "Hill Vote Set on Bill to Save Animals from Extinction," *Washington Post*, 16 Sept. 1973, A2.

104. See Seater, "Letter to the Editor: Protection of Wildlife."

105. See Vinzenz Ziswiler, *Extinct and Vanishing Animals: A Biology of Extinction and Survival*, trans. Fred Bunnell and Pille Bunnell (New York: Springler-Verlag, 1967), 1.

106. See Wolfgang Ullrich, *Endangered Species*, trans. Erich Tylinek and Isabella Tylinek (New York: Hart, 1972).

107. See H. A. Goodwin and J. M. Goodwin, *List of Mammals Which Have Become Extinct or Are Possibly Extinct Since 1600* (Morges, Switzerland: International Union for the Conservation of Nature and Natural Resources, 1973).

108. See, for example, U.S. Congress, House, Report No. 93-412, 93d Cong. (Washington, D.C.: GPO, 1973), 1–2.

109. The language referred to in Section 7 of this Senate bill was the exact same language adopted in the ESA. Statement of Senator Tunney, reprinted in Committee on Environment and Public Works, *Legislative History*, 398–399.

110. See U.S. Congress, *National Environmental Policy Act of 1969*, 83 Stat. 852 (Washington, D.C.: GPO, 1969).

111. See *Tennessee Valley Authority v. Hill*, 437 U.S. 153 (1978).

112. See statement of Thomas Garrett, wildlife director of Friends of the Earth, *Endangered Species Act of 1973*, 80.

113. See Bryan Norton, "Biological Resources and Endangered Species," in *Protection of Global Biodiversity*, eds. Lakshman Guruswamy and Jeffrey McNeely (Durham, N.C.: Duke Univ. Press, 1998), 247, 250.

114. Norton, "Biological Resources and Endangered Species," 251.

115. See Norton, "Biological Resources and Endangered Species," 252–253.

116. See Norton, "Biological Resources and Endangered Species," 252–253.

117. Subcommittee on the Environment, *Endangered Species Act of 1973*, 114.

118. See National Research Council, *Science and the Endangered Species Act* (Washington, D.C.: National Academy Press, 1995), 55.

119. "Saving the World's Wildlife," editorial, *Washington Post*, 19 Feb. 1973, A14.

120. See "Protecting Endangered Species," editorial, *Washington Post*, 26 June 1973, A22.

121. See "President Signs Manpower Bill," *New York Times*, 29 Dec. 1973, 13.

122. See Austin Scott, "Nixon Signs Bill to Give States Manpower Funds," *Washington Post*, 29 Dec. 1973, A1.

123. See "President Signs Bill Reshaping Federal Manpower Programs," *Los Angeles Times*, 29 Dec. 1973, 1.

CHAPTER 3. THE FISH THAT STOPPED A DAM

1. During oversight hearings held in October 1975, most environmental organizations testifying complained of the slow rate at which the ESA was being implemented. See U.S. Congress, House, Committee on Merchant Marine and Fisheries, Subcommittee on Fisheries and Wildlife Conservation and the Environment, *Endangered Species Oversight*, hearing, 94th Cong., 1st sess., 1, 2, 6 Oct. 1975 (Washington, D.C.: GPO, 1976), 69, 108–109, 171–172.

2. See U.S. Department of Interior, Fish and Wildlife Service, "Box Score of Species Listings," *Endangered Species Technical Bulletin* 2 (February 1977): 4.

3. See 38 *Federal Register* 14678 (4 June 1973).

4. See Linda Charlton, "Wildlife Service Invoking Law to Protect Rare Sandhill Crane," *New York Times*, 4 July 1975, A16.

5. See U.S. Congress, Senate, Committee on Commerce, *Endangered Species Act of 1973* (Washington, D.C.: GPO, 1974), sec. 11(g).

6. Committee on Commerce, *Endangered Species Act of 1973*, sec. 7.

7. See *National Wildlife Federation v. Coleman*, 400 F.Supp. 705, 710 (S.D. Miss. 1975).

8. See *National Wildlife Federation v. Coleman*, 529 F.2d 359, 362 (5th Cir. 1976).

9. *National Wildlife Federation v. Coleman*, 529 F.2d at 373.

10. *National Wildlife Federation v. Coleman*, 529 F.2d at 373.

11. See *National Wildlife Federation v. Coleman*, 529 F.2d at 373–374.

12. See *National Wildlife Federation v. Coleman*, 529 F.2d at 375.

13. *National Wildlife Federation v. Coleman*, 529 F.2d at 371.

14. *National Wildlife Federation v. Coleman*, 529 F.2d at 371.

15. See *National Wildlife Federation v. Coleman*, 529 F.2d at 375.

16. See *National Wildlife Federation v. Coleman*, 529 F.2d at 371.

17. See U.S. Congress, Senate, Committee on Commerce, Subcommittee on Environment, *To Amend the Endangered Species Act of 1973*, hearing, 94th Cong., 2d sess., 6 May 1976 (Washington, D.C.: GPO, 1976).

18. See Subcommittee on Environment, *To Amend the Endangered Species Act of 1973*, 79–80.

19. See U.S. Congress, Senate, Committee on Environment and Public Works, *A Legislative History of the Endangered Species Act of 1973*, report prepared by the Congressional Research Service (Washington, D.C.: GPO, 1982), 490.

20. See U.S. Congress, Senate, Committee on Commerce, Subcommittee on the Environment, *An Act to Extend the Authorization for Appropriations to Carry Out the Endangered Species Act of 1973* (Washington, D.C.: GPO, 1976).

21. See Committee on Environment and Public Works, *A Legislative History of the Endangered Species Act of 1973*, 490–491.

22. See Gladwin Hill, "Waste of Resources Imperils Man, World Wildlife Conference Is Told," *New York Times*, 1 Dec. 1976, A18.

23. Bias in favor of charismatic megafauna was reflected in listing decisions, designations of critical habitat, and the development of recovery plans. See Fish and Wildlife Service, "Box Score of Species Listings," 8.

24. See David Etnier, *Proceedings of the Biological Society of Washington* 88 (January 1976): 469–488.

25. See *Environmental Defense Fund v. Tennessee Valley Authority*, 339 F.Supp. 806 (E.D. Tenn. 1972), affirmed by *Environmental Defense Fund v. Tennessee Valley Authority*, 468 F.2d 1164 (6th Cir. 1972).

26. See *Environmental Defense Fund v. Tennessee Valley Authority*, 371 F.Supp. 1004, 1014 (E.D. Tenn. 1973).

27. See *Environmental Defense Fund v. Tennessee Valley Authority*, 492 F.2d 466, 467 (6th Cir. 1974).

28. See Zygmunt Plater, telephone interview with author, 18 Nov. 1999.

29. See *Hill v. Tennessee Valley Authority*, 419 F.Supp. 753, 755 (E.D. Tenn. 1976).

30. See 40 *Federal Register* 47505–47506 (1975); see also 50 *Code of Federal Regulations*, sec. 17.11(I) (1976).

31. See 41 *Federal Register* 13926–13928 (1976); see also 50 *Code of Federal Regulations*, sec. 17.81 (1976); U.S. Department of Interior, Fish and Wildlife Service, "October Hearing Set on Snail Darter Injunction," *Endangered Species Technical Bulletin* 1 (September 1976): 2.

32. See Zygmunt Plater, telephone interview with author, 18 Nov. 1999.

33. Committee on Commerce, *Endangered Species Act of 1973*, sec. 7.

34. See Committee on Commerce, *Endangered Species Act of 1973*, sec. 9.

35. See *Hill v. Tennessee Valley Authority*, 419 F.Supp. at 755.

36. *Hill v. Tennessee Valley Authority*, 419 F.Supp. at 760.

37. See *Hill v. Tennessee Valley Authority*, 419 F.Supp. at 762.

38. See *Hill v. Tennessee Valley Authority*, 549 F.2d 1064, 1066 (6th Cir. 1977).

39. *Hill v. Tennessee Valley Authority*, 549 F.2d at 1071.

40. *Hill v. Tennessee Valley Authority*, 549 F.2d at 1072.

41. See *Hill v. Tennessee Valley Authority*, 549 F.2d at 1075.

42. U.S. Department of Interior, Fish and Wildlife Service, "Section 7: Formal Consultation Steps Are Set Forth," *Endangered Species Technical Bulletin* 2 (February 1977): 1, 6.

43. See U.S. Department of Interior, Fish and Wildlife Service, "Section 7: Final Rules Set for Interagency Consultation," *Endangered Species Technical Bulletin* 3 (January 1978): 1, 6.

44. See U.S. Department of Interior, Fish and Wildlife Service, "Changes in ES Law Proposed," *Endangered Species Technical Bulletin* 2 (May 1977): 1–2.

45. See U.S. Congress, Senate, Committee on Environment and Public Works, Subcommittee on Resource Protection, *Endangered Species Act Oversight*, hearing, 95th Cong., 1st sess., 20–22, 28 July 1977 (Washington, D.C.: GPO, 1976), 4.

46. Subcommittee on Resource Protection, *Endangered Species Act Oversight*, 11.

47. See Subcommittee on Resource Protection, *Endangered Species Act Oversight*, 2.

48. See Subcommittee on Resource Protection, *Endangered Species Act Oversight*, 74–75.

49. Subcommittee on Resource Protection, *Endangered Species Act Oversight*, 80.

50. See Subcommittee on Resource Protection, *Endangered Species Act Oversight*, 366.

51. See Subcommittee on Resource Protection, *Endangered Species Act Oversight*, 241–242. Not all of the residents in the community near Tellico Dam, however, supported the project. Alfred Davis, a property owner along the Little Tennessee River, opposed the dam because it would result in the inundation of thirty-five acres of his land (222–223). Jean Ritchey, another local resident, also opposed the completion of the dam for similar reasons (224–225). They both claimed to represent other landowners in the region.

52. See Subcommittee on Resource Protection, *Endangered Species Act Oversight*, 268–275.

53. See Subcommittee on Resource Protection, *Endangered Species Act Oversight*, 339, 342, 345, 413, 549, 562, 793.

54. See Subcommittee on Resource Protection, *Endangered Species Act Oversight*, 519–526, 537–538, 541, 576–583.

55. See Comptroller General of the United States, General Accounting Office, *The Tennessee Valley Authority's Tellico Dam Project—Costs, Alternatives, and Benefits*, report to Congress (Washington, D.C.: GAO, 1977), iv.

56. Committee on Environment and Public Works, *A Legislative History of the Endangered Species Act of 1973*, 635.

57. Committee on Environment and Public Works, *A Legislative History of the Endangered Species Act of 1973*, 636.

58. Committee on Environment and Public Works, *A Legislative History of the Endangered Species Act of 1973*, 637.

59. See U.S. Congress, Senate, Committee on Environment and Public Works, *An Act to Authorize Appropriations for Fiscal Years 1978, 1979, and 1980 and to Carry Out State Cooperative Programs under the Endangered Species Act of 1973* (Washington, D.C.: GPO, 1978).

60. See U.S. Congress, House, Committee on Merchant Marine and Fisheries, Subcommittee on Fisheries and Wildlife Conservation and the Environment, House Resolution 10883, *A Bill to Authorize Appropriations to Carry Out the Endangered Species Act of 1973 during Fiscal Years 1979, 1980, and 1981*, 95th Cong., 2d sess. (Washington, D.C.: GPO, 1978).

61. See U.S. Congress, House, Committee on Merchant Marine and Fisheries, Subcommittee on Fisheries and Wildlife Conservation and the Environment, *Endangered Species Act Authorization*, hearing, 95th Cong., 2d sess., 15 Feb. 1978 (Washington, D.C.: GPO, 1978), 1.

62. See U.S. Congress, Senate, Committee on Environment and Public Works, Subcommittee on Resource Protection, Senate Resolution 2899, *A Bill to Amend the Endangered Species Act of 1973*, 95th Cong., 2d sess. (Washington, D.C.: GPO, 1978).

63. See U.S. Congress, Senate, Committee on Environment and Public Works, Subcommittee on Resource Protection, *Amending the Endangered Species Act of 1973*, hearing, 95th Cong., 2d sess., 13–14 Apr. 1978 (Washington, D.C.: GPO, 1978), 18–19.

64. Subcommittee on Resource Protection, *Amending the Endangered Species Act of 1973*, 18.

65. See Subcommittee on Resource Protection, *Amending the Endangered Species Act of 1973*, 18–19.

66. Subcommittee on Resource Protection, *Amending the Endangered Species Act of 1973*, 77.

67. See Subcommittee on Resource Protection, *Amending the Endangered Species Act of 1973*, 73, 78, 82, 404.

68. Subcommittee on Resource Protection, *Amending the Endangered Species Act of 1973*, 65.

69. Subcommittee on Resource Protection, *Amending the Endangered Species Act of 1973*, 223.

70. See, for example, U.S. Department of Interior, Fish and Wildlife Service, "Flexibility of ES Law Debated at Senate Hearings," *Endangered Species Technical Bulletin* 2 (August 1977): 1, 3.

71. See U.S. Department of Interior, Fish and Wildlife Service, "98 Snail Darters Lost in Accident," *Endangered Species Technical Bulletin* 2 (November 1977): 1–2.

72. See Charles Mohr, "Endangered Species Act Threatened," *New York Times*, 7 Apr. 1978, A11.

73. Charles Mohr, "Hearings Open on Amending the Endangered Species Act," *New York Times*, 14 Apr. 1978, A12.

74. Charles Mohr, "Bell Urges Court to Permit Dam to Open Despite Peril to Rare Fish," *New York Times*, 19 Apr. 1978, A19.

75. See U.S. Congress, House, Committee on Merchant Marine and Fisheries, Subcommittee on Fisheries and Wildlife Conservation and the Environment, *Endangered Species Oversight*, hearing, 95th Cong., 2d sess., 24, 25 May; 1, 15, 16, 20, 23, 28 June 1978 (Washington, D.C.: GPO, 1978).

76. See Subcommittee on Fisheries and Wildlife Conservation and the Environment, *Endangered Species Oversight* (1978), 54.

77. See Tennessee Valley Authority, Petition for a Writ of Certiorari, *Tennessee Valley Authority v. Hill*, 437 U.S. 153 (1978) (No. 76-1701).

78. See Brief for Respondents in Opposition to Petition for a Writ of Certiorari, *Tennessee Valley Authority v. Hill*, 437 U.S. 153 (1978) (No. 76-1701).

79. See Brief of Natural Resources Defense Council as Amicus Curiae in Opposition to Petition for a Writ of Certiorari, *Tennessee Valley Authority v. Hill*, 437 U.S. 153 (1978) (No. 76-1701).

80. See *Hill v. Tennessee Valley Authority*, 549 F.2d 1064 (6th Cir. 1977), certiorari granted, 434 U.S. 954 (14 Nov. 1977) (No. 76-1701).

81. See Brief for Petitioner, *Tennessee Valley Authority v. Hill*, 437 U.S. 153 (1978) (No. 76-1701), 19–21.

82. See Brief for Respondents, *Tennessee Valley Authority v. Hill*, 437 U.S. 153 (1978) (No. 76-1701), 4–9, 12–15.

83. See Reply Brief for Petitioner, *Tennessee Valley Authority v. Hill*, 437 U.S. 153 (1978) (No. 76-1701), 2, 4.

84. Reply Brief for Petitioner, 8.

85. See Reply Brief for Petitioner, 10–12.

86. See Brief of Southeastern Legal Foundation as Amicus Curiae, *Tennessee Valley Authority v. Hill*, 437 U.S. 153 (1978) (No. 76-1701), 2.

87. See Brief of Southeastern Legal Foundation as Amicus Curiae, 3.

88. See Brief of Southeastern Legal Foundation as Amicus Curiae, 1.

89. Brief of Monroe County, Town of Tellico Plains, Tennessee, Town of Madisonville, Tennessee, Town of Vonore, Tennessee, City of Sweetwater, Tennessee, the Little Tennessee River Port Authority, Monroe County Chamber of Commerce, and Tellico Area Services System, as Amicus Curiae on Behalf of Petitioners, *Tennessee Valley Authority v. Hill*, 437 U.S. 153 (1978) (No. 76-1701), 2.

90. See Brief of Monroe County, 2–7.

91. See Brief of the Pacific Legal Foundation, as Amicus Curiae on Behalf of Petitioners, *Tennessee Valley Authority v. Hill*, 437 U.S. 153 (1978) (No. 76-1701), 2–3.

92. Brief of the Environmental Defense Fund, the National Audubon Society, the National Wildlife Federation, the Natural Resources Defense Council, the Sierra Club, and the Defenders of Wildlife, as Amicus Curiae on Behalf of Respondents, *Tennessee Valley Authority v. Hill*, 437 U.S. 153 (1978) (No. 76-1701), 2.

93. Brief of the East Tennessee Valley Landowners' Association, as Amicus Curiae on Behalf of Respondents, *Tennessee Valley Authority v. Hill*, 437 U.S. 153 (1978) (No. 76-1701), 2.

94. Motion for Leave to File Brief of Amicus Curiae, Eastern Band of Cherokee Indians, in Support of Respondents, *Tennessee Valley Authority v. Hill*, 437 U.S. 153 (1978) (No. 76-1701), 1.

95. See Motion for Leave to File Brief of Amicus Curiae, Eastern Band of Cherokee Indians, 2–3.

96. See Brief of the Eastern Band of Cherokee Indians, as Amicus Curiae on Behalf of Respondents, *Tennessee Valley Authority v. Hill*, 437 U.S. 153 (1978) (No. 76-1701), 3.

97. See *Tennessee Valley Authority v. Hill*, 437 U.S. 153, 173 (1978).

98. See *Tennessee Valley Authority v. Hill*, 437 U.S. at 194.

99. *Tennessee Valley Authority v. Hill*, 437 U.S. at 173.

100. *Tennessee Valley Authority v. Hill*, 437 U.S. at 173.

101. *Tennessee Valley Authority v. Hill*, 437 U.S. at 173.

102. *Tennessee Valley Authority v. Hill*, 437 U.S. at 184.

103. *Tennessee Valley Authority v. Hill*, 437 U.S. at 178, 187.

104. *Tennessee Valley Authority v. Hill*, 437 U.S. at 175.

105. See *Tennessee Valley Authority v. Hill*, 437 U.S. at 183.

106. See *Tennessee Valley Authority v. Hill*, 437 U.S. at 190–191.

107. *Tennessee Valley Authority v. Hill*, 437 U.S. at 195–196.

108. *Tennessee Valley Authority v. Hill*, 437 U.S. at 196.

109. *Tennessee Valley Authority v. Hill*, 437 U.S. at 202.

110. See *Tennessee Valley Authority v. Hill*, 437 U.S. at 196.

111. See *Tennessee Valley Authority v. Hill*, 437 U.S. at 210.

112. See *Tennessee Valley Authority v. Hill*, 437 U.S. at 211.

113. See *Tennessee Valley Authority v. Hill*, 437 U.S. at 213.

114. Senator John Tunney (D-CA) was responding to another senator's question about whether Section 7 might stop the Army Corps of Engineers from building a road in Kentucky. Replied Tunney: "As I understand it after the consultation process took place . . . the Corps of Engineers, would not be prohibited from building the road if they deemed it necessary to do so. . . . they would have the final decision after consultation. . . . So, as I read the language, there has to be consultation. However, the Bureau of Public Roads or any other agency would have the final decision as to whether such a road should be built ESA" (Committee on Environment and Public Works, *A Legislative History of the Endangered Species Act of 1973*, 398–399).

115. See Committee on Commerce, *Endangered Species Act of 1973*, sec. 12.

116. U.S. Congress, House Committee on Merchant Marine and Fisheries, Subcommittee on Fisheries and Wildlife Conservation and the Environment, *Report on Endangered and Threatened Plant Species of the United States*, report prepared by the Smithsonian Institution (Washington, D.C.: GPO, 1975).

117. See U.S. Department of Interior, Fish and Wildlife Service, "Plant Regulations Issued, Clearing Way for Listing," *Endangered Species Technical Bulletin* 2 (July 1977): 1.

118. See New York Botanical Garden, *Extinction Is Forever: The Status of Threatened and Endangered Plants of the Americas and Their Significance in Ecosystems Today and in the Future*, ed. Ghillean T. Prance and Thomas S. Elias (Bronx, N.Y.: New York Botanical Garden, 1977); Meryl Miasek and Charles Long, *Endangered Plant Species of the World and Their Endangered Habitats: A Compilation of the Literature* (Bronx, N.Y.: New York Botanical Garden, 1978); World Wildlife Fund, *Endangered and Threatened Plants of the United States* (Washington, D.C.: Smithsonian Institution Press, 1978).

119. New York Botanical Garden, *Extinction Is Forever*, 3.

120. Clayton White, "Strategies for the Preservation of Rare Animals," *Great Basin Naturalist Memoirs: The Endangered Species; A Symposium* 3 (1979): 102.

121. Norman Myers, *The Sinking Ark: A New Look at the Problem of Disappearing Species* (Oxford: Pergamon Press, 1979), 38.

CHAPTER 4. DAMMED FISH

1. Warren Weaver, "High Court Bars Dam, Reprieving Rare Fish," *New York Times*, 16 June 1978, A1.

2. See U.S. Congress, Senate, Committee on Environment and Public Works, Subcommittee on Resource Protection, *A Bill to Amend the Endangered Species Act of 1973*, S. 2899, 95th Cong., 2d sess., 12 Apr. 1978 (Washington, D.C.: GPO, 1978).

3. See testimony of Lynn Greenwalt, director, Fish and Wildlife Service, Department of Interior, U.S. Congress, Senate, Committee on Environment and Public Works, Subcommittee on Resource Protection, *Amending the Endangered Species Act of 1973*, hearing, 95th Cong., 2d sess., 13, 14 Apr. 1978 (Washington, D.C.: GPO, 1978), 16.

4. See U.S. Congress, House, Committee on Merchant Marine and Fisheries, Subcommittee on Fisheries and Wildlife Conservation and the Environment, *Endangered Species Act Oversight*, hearing, 95th Cong., 2d sess., 24, 25 May; 1, 15–16, 20, 23, 28 June 1978 (Washington, D.C.: GPO, 1978), 565.

5. See Subcommittee on Fisheries and Wildlife Conservation and the Environment, *Endangered Species Act Oversight*, 628.

6. Subcommittee on Fisheries and Wildlife Conservation and the Environment, *Endangered Species Act Oversight*, 53.

7. U.S. Congress, House, Committee on Environment and Public Works, *Legislative History of the Endangered Species Act of 1973*, report prepared by the Congressional Research Service (Washington, D.C.: GPO, 1982), 797.

8. Committee on Environment and Public Works, *Legislative History*, 922.

9. See Committee on Environment and Public Works, *Legislative History*, 796.

10. Committee on Environment and Public Works, *Legislative History*, 637.

11. Committee on Environment and Public Works, *Legislative History*, 920.

12. Committee on Environment and Public Works, *Legislative History*, 976.

13. Gen. 1:26, 28.

14. Committee on Environment and Public Works, *Legislative History*, 1007.

15. See Committee on Environment and Public Works, *Legislative History*, 981.

16. Committee on Environment and Public Works, *Legislative History*, 1000.

17. Three senators did not vote. See Committee on Environment and Public Works, *Legislative History*, 1167–1168; see also Subcommittee on Resource Protection, *A Bill to Amend the Endangered Species Act of 1973*, S. 2899.

18. Thirty-four representatives did not vote at all. See Committee on Environment and Public Works, *Legislative History*, 895–898; see also U.S. Congress, House, Committee on Merchant Marine and Fisheries, Subcommittee on Fisheries and Wildlife Conservation and the Environment, House Resolution 14104, 95th Cong., 2d sess., 18 Sep. 1978 (Washington, D.C.: GPO, 1978).

19. Jimmy Carter, *Public Papers of the Presidents of the United States, 1978*, vol. 2 (Washington, D.C.: GPO, 1979), 2002.

20. See Samuel Hays, *Beauty, Health, and Permanence: Environmental Politics in the United States, 1955–1985* (New York: Cambridge University Press, 1987), 58–59.

21. See U.S. Congress, Senate, Committee on Environment and Public Works, Subcommittee on Resource Protection, *An Act to Amend the Endangered Species Act of 1973*, 95th Cong., 2d sess., 10 Nov. 1978 (Washington, D.C.: GPO, 1980), S. 2899, sec. 7(e), (h).

22. See Seth S. King, "U.S. Acts to Settle Dam-Wildlife Issue," *New York Times*, 26 Nov. 1978, A36.

23. See Carter, *Public Papers, 1978*, 2002.

24. See Subcommittee on Resource Protection, *An Act to Amend the Endangered Species Act of 1973*, sec. 11(l).

25. See Subcommittee on Resource Protection, *An Act to Amend the Endangered Species Act of 1973*, sec. 11(g).

26. See Cecil D. Andrus, secretary of the interior, letter to Thomas P. O'Neill Jr., Speaker of the U.S. House of Representatives, 23 July 1979, printed in Committee on Environment and Public Works, *Legislative History*, 1270–1271.

27. See testimony of Senator James McClure, vice chairman of the National Endangered Species Act Reform Coalition, U.S. Congress, Senate, Committee on Environment and Public Works, Subcommittee on Clean Air, Fisheries, and Wildlife, *Endangered Species Act Amendments of 1993*, hearing, 103d Cong., 2d sess., 15 June, 19 July, 29 Sep. 1994, pt. 2 (Washington, D.C.: GPO, 1994), 79. The ESC was first called the "God Committee" by officials within the Interior Department. See "Inside: The Interior Department Mussel's Fate May Rest with Panel," *Washington Post*, 27 Dec. 1985, A15. The origin of the term "God Squad" as applied to the ESC is unknown, but it was first used in newsprint in 1990. See Steve Duin, "We Hold These Truths to Be . . . ," *Portland Oregonian*, 12 Apr. 1990, D7.

28. See *Portland Audubon Society v. Endangered Species Committee*, 984 F.2d 1534 (9th Cir. 1993).

29. See Seth King, "Snail Darter and Whooping Crane Win the First Test of Species Act," *New York Times*, 24 Jan. 1979, A21.

30. Committee on Environment and Public Works, *Legislative History*, 1248.

31. Committee on Environment and Public Works, *Legislative History*, 1402–1403. Interestingly, Senator Chafee was not a member of Congress when it voted for the ESA in 1973.

32. U.S. Congress, Senate, Committee on Environment and Public Works, Subcommittee on Resource Protection, *Reauthorization of the Endangered Species Act of 1973*, hearing, 96th Cong., 1st sess., 3 Apr. 1979 (Washington, D.C.: GPO, 1979), 7.

33. "The Senator, the Darter and the Dam," editorial, *New York Times*, 8 May 1979, A22.

34. "The Senator, the Darter and the Dam," A22.

35. Charles Mohr, "Panel Blocks Baker Move to Revive Dam in Tennessee," *New York Times*, 10 May 1979, A18.

36. See Mohr, "Panel Blocks Baker Move to Revive Dam in Tennessee," A18.

37. See U.S. Congress, House, Committee on Appropriations, Subcommittee on Energy and Water Development, *Energy and Water Development Appropriations Act, 1980* (Washington, D.C.: GPO, 1980).

38. "Looking Down," *New York Times*, 20 June 1979, A22.

39. See Committee on Environment and Public Works, *Legislative History*, 1238–1242.

40. See Committee on Environment and Public Works, *Legislative History*, 1246.

41. See Committee on Environment and Public Works, *Legislative History*, 1258.

42. See Committee on Environment and Public Works, *Legislative History*, 1300.

43. See "Senate Votes to Finish Dam Halted by Snail Darter," *New York Times*, 11 Sept. 1979, A15.

44. "The Snail Darter Is Not the Problem," editorial, *New York Times*, 14 Sept. 1979, A24.

45. "The Snail Darter Is Not the Problem," A24.

46. See Jimmy Carter, *Public Papers of the Presidents of the United States, 1979*, vol. 2 (Washington, D.C.: GPO, 1980), 1995.

47. See Carter, *Public Papers, 1979*, 1760.

48. Zygmunt Plater, telephone interview with author, 18 Nov. 1999.

49. See "Gate Falls and Waters Rise As Tellico Dam is Finished," *New York Times*, 30 Nov. 1979, A20.

50. Anthony Lewis, "The Ultimate Corruption," *New York Times*, 17 Jan. 1980, A23.

51. See "Admiring the Doughty Darter," editorial, *Los Angeles Times*, 28 Mar. 1980, sec. 2, p. 6.

52. See "New Habitat of Snail Darter Found in Tennessee," *Los Angeles Times*, 8 Nov. 1980, sec. 1, p. 18.

53. See Bayard Webster, "More Snail Darters Found in Tennessee," *New York Times*, 8 Nov. 1980, A6.

54. See U.S. Department of Interior, Fish and Wildlife Service, "Snail Darter Discovered at a New Location," *Endangered Species Technical Bulletin* 5 (November/December 1980): 1.

55. See "Snail Darters Doing Better," *Washington Post*, 24 Feb. 1983, A5.

56. See U.S. Department of Interior, Fish and Wildlife Service, "Change Anticipated for Snail Darter Status," *Endangered Species Technical Bulletin* 8 (August 1983): 6–7.

57. See U.S. Department of Interior, Fish and Wildlife Service, "Snail Darter Reclassified," *Endangered Species Technical Bulletin* 9 (August 1984): 9.

58. See "Tiny Snail Darter Swims Off the Endangered List," *Washington Post*, 6 July 1984, A17.

59. "Those Ungrateful Little—!" editorial, *Los Angeles Times*, 24 Nov. 1980, sec. 2, p. 4.

60. Committee on Environment and Public Works, *Legislative History*, 1358.

61. See U.S. Congress, Senate, Committee on Environment and Public Works, *An Act to Extend the Authorization for Appropriations for the Endangered Species Act of 1973*, 1979 (Washington, D.C.: GPO, 1980). In May 1980, Congress approved appropriations to fund the federal-state cooperative programs without debate or consideration of other amendments. See U.S. Congress, House, Committee on Merchant Marine and Fisheries, *An Act to Authorize Appropriations under the Endangered Species Act of 1973 to Carry Out State Cooperative Programs*, 1980 (Washington, D.C.: GPO, 1980).

62. See Carter, *Public Papers, 1979*, 2288.

63. See Comptroller General, U.S. General Accounting Office, *Endangered Species—A Controversial Issue Needing Resolution* (Washington, D.C.: GPO, 1979), 11–20.

64. See Subcommittee on Resource Protection, *Amending the Endangered Species Act of 1973*, 85.

65. U.S. Congress, House, Committee on Merchant Marine and Fisheries, Subcommittee on Fisheries and Wildlife Conservation and the Environment, *Oversight Report on the Administration of the Endangered Species Act*, report, 96th Cong., 2d sess., 7 Apr. 1980 (Washington, D.C.: GPO, 1980), 1.

66. Subcommittee on Resource Protection, *An Act to Amend the Endangered Species Act of 1973*, sec. 11(4).

67. Ronald Reagan, quoted in William Graf, *Wilderness Preservation and the Sagebrush Rebellions* (Savage, Md.: Rowman and Littlefield, 1990), 231.

68. Hays, *Beauty, Health, and Permanence*, 59–60.

69. See the testimony of Patrick Parenteau, vice president of the National Wildlife Federation, U.S Congress, Senate, Committee on Environment and Public Works, Subcommittee on Environmental Pollution, *Endangered Species Act Oversight*, hearing, 97th Cong., 1st sess., 8, 10 Dec. 1981 (Washington, D.C.: GPO, 1982), 53.

70. See Mary Thornton, "How Interior Is Changing, From the Inside," *Washington Post*, 8 Jan. 1982, A21.

71. See "And Now the Timber Wolf," *Washington Post*, 20 Jan. 1982, A21.

72. "Endangered Species Live in Less Peril, Watt Tells Congress," *Washington Post*, 24 June 1983, A11.

73. Thornton, "How Interior Is Changing, From the Inside," A21.

74. "Florid over Flora," *Washington Post*, 8 Jan. 1982, A21.

75. See Steven Yaffee, *The Wisdom of the Spotted Owl: Policy Lessons for a New Century* (Washington, D.C.: Island Press, 1994), 73.

76. See *National Wildlife Federation v. Andrus*, 642 F.2d 589 (D.C. Cir. 1980).

77. See *Defenders of Wildlife v. Endangered Species Scientific Authority*, 659 F.2d 168 (D.C. Cir. 1981). This decision caused some to critique the court's substitution of its own scientific judgment for the administration's. See Gregory Chaimov and James Durr, "Defenders of Wildlife, Inc. v. Endangered Species Scientific Authority: The Court as Biologist," *Environmental Law* 12 (1982): 773.

78. See *Cabinet Mountains Wilderness v. Peterson*, 685 F.2d 678 (D.C. Cir. 1982).

79. U.S. Congress, Senate, Committee on Commerce, *Endangered Species Act of 1973* (Washington, D.C.: GPO, 1974), sec. 9(a)(1)(B). Section 4 allows the administration to extend this prohibition to species listed as threatened; sec. 4(d).

80. Committee on Commerce, *Endangered Species Act of 1973*, sec. 3(19).

81. U.S. Department of Interior, Fish and Wildlife Service, 50 *Code of Federal Regulations*, sec. 17.3(c) (1975).

82. See *Palila v. Hawaii Department of Land and Natural Resources*, 471 F.Supp. 985, 988 (D. Hawaii 1979).

83. See *Palila v. Hawaii Department of Land and Natural Resources*, 639 F.2d 495, 497 (9th Cir. 1981).

84. See "Clearing Up the Fine Points of 'Harm' to an Endangered Species," *Washington Post*, 8 June 1981, A3.

85. See "After 8 Years, Rule It a Victory for Environmentalists," *Washington Post*, 9 Nov. 1981, A13.

86. See Subcommittee on Environmental Pollution, *Endangered Species Act Oversight*, 79–81.

87. See Cass Peterson, "It's Open Season on Endangered Species Act," *Washington Post*, 8 Mar. 1982, A11.

88. See testimony of Michael Bean on behalf of the Environmental Defense Fund, World Wildlife Fund, National Audubon Society, Natural Resources Defense Council, Sierra Club, Wilderness Society, Friends of the Sea Otter, Center for Environmental Education, Fund for Animals, Defenders of Wildlife, Humane Society, Society for Animal Protective Legislation, International Primate Protection League, the Whale Center, Greenpeace, Friends of the Earth, and the Animal Protection Institute, U.S. Congress, House, Committee on Merchant Marine and Fisheries, Subcommittee on Fisheries and Wildlife Conservation and the Environment, *Endangered Species Act*, hearing, 97th Cong., 2d sess., 22 Feb., 8 Mar. 1982 (Washington, D.C.: GPO, 1982), 155–158.

89. Peterson, "It's Open Season on Endangered Species Act," A11.

90. See "Caution: Endangered Law," editorial, *Los Angeles Times*, 12 Mar. 1982, sec. 2, p. 10.

91. See Franklin McMillan, "Endangered Species Act," letter to the editor, *Los Angeles Times*, 4 Apr. 1982, sec. 5, p. 4.

92. James J. Kilpatrick, "Keep Protecting the Snail Darters," *Washington Post*, 23 Apr. 1982, A29.

93. Eleanor Randolph, "Man's Toll: Once-a-Day Extinctions," *Los Angeles Times*, 30 Dec. 1981, sec. 1, p. 1.

94. Randolph, "Man's Toll: Once-a-Day Extinctions," 16.

95. "What Gee Whiz Means," editorial, *Washington Post*, 7 June 1982, A14.

96. Colman McCarthy, "Endangered Species: The Gazelle-Goulash Theory," *Los Angeles Times*, 1 Apr. 1982, sec. 2, p. 7.

97. See Subcommittee on Fisheries and Wildlife Conservation and the Environment, *Endangered Species Act* (1982), 122.

98. Subcommittee on Fisheries and Wildlife Conservation and the Environment, *Endangered Species Act* (1982), 127.

99. See "House Approves Bill on Endangered Species," *Washington Post*, 9 June 1982, A21; see also "Senate Approves Endangered Species Act," *Washington Post*, 10 June 1982, A12.

100. "Wilds and the Public Will," *Los Angeles Times*, 15 June 1982, sec. 2, p. 6.

101. See U.S. Congress, House, Committee on Merchant Marine and Fisheries, Subcommittee on Fisheries and Wildlife Conservation and the Environment, *Endangered Species Act Amendments of 1982* (Washington, D.C.: GPO, 1982), sec. 10.

102. "Endangered-Species Rule Change Offered," *Washington Post*, 18 July 1983, A11.

103. See Margaret L. Sims, "When Will the Universe Notice?" *Washington Post*, 20 Feb. 1983, C6. Reported Sims, "Someday, it may be our turn. And as the last of our species comes to its lonely end, who will preside over that death?"

104. "On Behalf of a Unique Law," *Los Angeles Times*, 30 Dec. 1983, sec. 2, p. 4.

105. "The Legacy of James Watt," *Time Magazine*, 24 Oct. 1983, 25.

106. See Ronald Reagan, *Public Papers of the Presidents of the United States, 1983*, vol. 2 (Washington, D.C.: GPO, 1985), 1625.

107. See *http://www.fws.gov*.

108. See Michael Wines, "Official Bungling May Have Erased Rare Species," *Los Angeles Times*, 11 June 1984, sec. 1, p.1.

109. "Wildlife Review Pace Blasted," *Washington Post*, 29 May 1984, A5.

CHAPTER 5. SPOTTY WISDOM

1. Dale Russakoff, "Endangered Species Act Stemming the Trend," *Washington Post*, 1 Jan. 1984, A1.

2. See Russakoff, "Endangered Species Act Stemming the Trend," A1.

3. See R. J. Gutierrez, "An Overview of Recent Research on the Spotted Owl," in *Ecology and Management of the Spotted Owl in the Pacific Northwest*, U.S. Forest Service General Technical Report PNW-185 (Portland, Ore.: Pacific Northwest Forest and Range Experiment Station, 1985), 39–46.

4. Philip L. Lee, "History and Current Status of Spotted Owl *(Strix Occidentali)* Habitat Management in the Pacific Northwest Region, USDA, Forest Service," in *Ecology and Management of the Spotted Owl in the Pacific Northwest*, 5.

5. See Eric Forsman and Charles Meslow, "Old-Growth Forest Retention for Spotted Owls—How Much Do They Need?" in *Ecology and Management of the Spotted Owl in the Pacific Northwest*, 58.

6. See Mark Shaffer, "The Metapopulation and Species Conservation: The Special Case of the Spotted Owl," in *Ecology and Management of the Spotted Owl in the Pacific Northwest*, 96.

7. *Congressional Record*, 99th Cong., 1st sess., 7 Feb. 1985, vol. 131, E448-02; U.S. Congress, House, Committee on Merchant Marine and Fisheries, Subcom-

mittee on Fisheries and Wildlife Conservation and the Environment, *A Bill to Authorize Appropriations to Carry Out the Endangered Species Act of 1973*, H.R. 1027, 7 Feb. 1985 (Washington, D.C.: GPO, 1985).

8. *Congressional Record*, 99th Cong., 1st sess., 9 July 1985, vol. 131, S9203-02; U.S. Congress, Senate, Committee on Environment and Public Works, Subcommittee on Environmental Pollution, *A Bill to Authorize Appropriations to Carry out the Endangered Species Act of 1973*, S. 725, 20 Mar. 1985 (Washington, D.C.: GPO, 1985).

9. *Congressional Record*, 99th Cong., 1st sess., 29 July 1985, vol. 131, H6465-02.

10. See the testimonies of Robert Jantzen, director of FWS, and William Gordon, director of NMFS, U.S. Congress, House, Committee on Merchant Marine and Fisheries, Subcommittee on Fisheries and Wildlife Conservation and the Environment, *Endangered Species Act Reauthorization*, hearing, 99th Cong., 1st sess., 14 Mar. 1985 (Washington, D.C.: GPO, 1985), 14–15.

11. Testimony of Michael Bean on behalf of the Environmental Defense Fund, the Center for Environmental Education, the Defenders of Wildlife, the Humane Society, Greenpeace, the Natural Resources Defense Council, and the Society for Animal Protection Legislation, Subcommittee on Fisheries and Wildlife Conservation and the Environment, *Endangered Species Act Reauthorization* (1985), 37–38.

12. See Subcommittee on Fisheries and Wildlife Conservation and the Environment, *Endangered Species Act Reauthorization* (1985), 175, 176, 178, 182.

13. See Charles Lee Moriwaki, "Saving Spotted Owls to Cost 4,800 Jobs, Timber Groups Say," *Seattle Times*, 26 Aug. 1986, D1.

14. Moriwaki, "Saving Spotted Owls to Cost 4,800 Jobs, Timber Groups Say," D1.

15. See Charles Lee Moriwaki, "Forest Service Idea Criticized as Danger to Spotted Owl Habitat," *Seattle Times*, 30 Apr. 1987, C8.

16. See Moriwaki, "Forest Service Idea Criticized as Danger to Spotted Owl Habitat," C8.

17. See the statement of George Leonard, associate chief, U.S. Forest Service, U.S. Congress, House, Committee on Merchant Marine and Fisheries, Subcommittee on Fisheries and Wildlife Conservation and the Environment, *Endangered Species Act Reauthorization*, hearing, 100th Cong., 1st sess., 17 Mar. 1987 (Washington, D.C.: GPO, 1987), 41–42.

18. See the testimony of Michael Bean, representing fifteen major environmental organizations, U.S. Congress, Senate, Committee on Environment and Public Works, Subcommittee on Environmental Protection, *Reauthorization of the Endangered Species Act*, hearing, 100th Cong., 1st sess., 7 Apr. 1987 (Washington, D.C.: GPO, 1987), 12–14, 93–118.

19. See Subcommittee on Environmental Protection, *Reauthorization of the Endangered Species Act* (1987), 4.

20. See Guy Darst, "U.S. Faces Suit on Endangered Species: Interior Department Accused of Missing Deadlines on 17 Cases," *Washington Post*, 29 May 1987, A23.

21. See Kristen Jackson, "Petitions Seeking 'Endangered' Status for Spotted Owls," *Seattle Times*, 5 Aug. 1987, H2.

22. Cass Peterson and Philip Hilts, "Nation's Endangered Species Must Wait in Line for Protection," *Washington Post*, 8 Sep. 1987, A4.

23. See Peterson and Hilts, "Nation's Endangered Species Must Wait in Line for Protection," A4.

24. See *Congressional Record*, 100th Cong., 1st sess., 11 Dec. 1987, vol. 133, H11239-03.

25. See "Bill Would Reauthorize Endangered Species Act," *Congressional Quarterly Weekly Report*, 19 Dec. 1987, 3138.

26. See U.S. Department of Interior, Fish and Wildlife Service, "Service Decides Not to List Spotted Owl at This Time," *Endangered Species Technical Bulletin* 8 (January 1988): 3.

27. See Ronald Reagan, "Governmental Actions and Interference with Constitutionally Protected Property Rights," Executive Order No. 12630, 53 *Federal Register* 8859 (15 Mar. 1988).

28. See Kyung Song, "Groups Sue on Behalf of Spotted Owl," *Seattle Times*, 5 May 1988, H1.

29. *Congressional Record*, 100th Cong., 2d sess., 16 Feb. 1988, vol. 134, S741-01.

30. *Congressional Record*, 100th Cong., 2d sess., 16 Feb. 1988, vol. 134, S741-01.

31. See U.S. Congress, Senate, Committee on Environment and Public Works, Subcommittee on Environmental Pollution, *Endangered Species Act Amendments of 1988* (Washington, D.C.: GPO, 1988), sec. 1009.

32. See "'Compromise' on Spotted Owl," *Seattle Times*, 16 Aug. 1988, A13.

33. See *Christy v. Hodel*, 857 F.2d 1324 (9th Cir. 1988).

34. *Congressional Record*, 100th Cong., 2d sess., 27 Sep. 1988, vol. 134, H8249-02.

35. *Northern Spotted Owl (Strix Occidentalis Caurina) v. Hodel*, 716 F.Supp. 479, 483 (W.D. Wa. 1988).

36. *Northern Spotted Owl (Strix Occidentalis Caurina) v. Hodel*, at 481.

37. Bill Dietrich, "Judge Questions Spotted-Owl Decision," *Seattle Times*, 11 Nov. 1988, E1.

38. "Agency to Review Spotted-Owl Stance," *Seattle Times*, 20 Jan. 1989, E2.

39. See "Spotted-Owl Study Altered, GAO Says," *Seattle Times*, 21 Feb. 1989, C1.

40. "'Sanitizing' Spotted Owl Report Draws Fire," *Seattle Times*, 22 Feb. 1989, B3.

41. See "Spotted Owls to Get More Room," *Seattle Times*, 13 Dec. 1988, D2.

42. See U.S. Department of Interior, Fish and Wildlife Service, "Protection Proposed for the Northern Spotted Owl," *Endangered Species Technical Bulletin* 9 (July 1989): 1.

43. "Change of Mind on Spotted Owl: It's 'Threatened,'" *Seattle Times*, 25 Apr. 1989, C1.

44. "Old-Growth Controversy," editorial, *Seattle Times*, 2 May 1989, A10.

45. See T. R. Reid, "An American Success Story: Bald Eagle's Fortunes Soar," *Seattle Times*, 9 Mar. 1989, A3.

46. See "Spotted Owl Talks Sought," *Seattle Times*, 30 Apr. 1989, B4.

47. See "Fight for Spotted Owl Goes to Two Courts," *Seattle Times*, 9 Feb. 1989, F4.

48. See Bill Dietrich, "Judge Blocks Tree Harvest in 374,000 Acres," *Seattle Times*, 16 Mar. 1989, C11; see also "Spotted-Owl Advocates Win Another Timber Halt," *Seattle Times*, 6 Apr. 1989, C4; Jeff Barnard, "Timber Shortage Was Threat Before Spotted Owl Issue," *Seattle Times*, 4 June 1989, B2.

49. See "Appeal to Be Sought in Spotted-Owl Ruling," *Seattle Times*, 6 May 1989, A8.

50. See Jane Lehman, "Bird Battles May Raise Home Costs," *Washington Post*, 20 May 1989, F1.

51. See "Spotted Owl Talks Sought," *Seattle Times*, 30 Apr. 1989, B4.

52. See "Spotted-Owl Nesting Hampers Plan to Mine for Gold, Silver," *Seattle Times*, 6 Nov. 1988, D5.

53. See Jim Simon, "New Tactic in Old-Growth Fight," *Seattle Times*, 22 Aug. 1989, B1.

54. John Lancaster, "Spotted Owl Flies into Political Cross-Fire," *Washington Post*, 21 June 1989, A21.

55. "Summit Results in Proposal for Compromise," *Seattle Times*, 25 June 1989, B3.

56. John Lancaster, "Oregon Negotiations on Policy to Protect Spotted Owl Snag," *Washington Post*, 28 June 1989, A2.

57. See "Court Lifts Ban on Sale of BLM Old-Growth Trees," *Seattle Times*, 6 Sep. 1989, F2.

58. See "Senate OKs Bill on Old Growth," *Seattle Times*, 8 Oct. 1989, B2.

59. See the testimony of Jack Ward Thomas. U.S. Congress, Senate, Committee on Energy and Natural Resource, Subcommittee on Public Lands, National Parks, and Forests, *Report of the Interagency Scientific Committee to Address the Conservation of the Northern Spotted Owl*, hearing, 101st Cong., 2d sess., 23 May 1990 (Washington, D.C.: GPO, 1990), 29–31; see also Jay Mathews, "Scientists Urge Partial Logging Ban to Save Spotted Owl," *Washington Post*, 6 Apr. 1990, A16.

60. See Subcommittee on Public Lands, National Parks, and Forests, *Report of the Interagency Scientific Committee*, 27.

61. See Subcommittee on Public Lands, National Parks, and Forests, *Report of the Interagency Scientific Committee*, 49.

62. See David Schaefer, "Foley Walks Middle Ground on Issue of Spotted Owl," *Seattle Times*, 29 June 1990, B1.

63. See Subcommittee on Public Lands, National Parks, and Forests, *Report of the Interagency Scientific Committee*, 18.

64. See Subcommittee on Public Lands, National Parks, and Forests, *Report of the Interagency Scientific Committee*, 12.

65. Subcommittee on Public Lands, National Parks, and Forests, *Report of the Interagency Scientific Committee*, 2.

66. See "Maintaining a Species," editorial, *Seattle Times*, 30 Aug. 1990, A18.

67. David Hoffman, "Bush Straddles Northern Spotted Owl Controversy," *Washington Post*, 22 May 1990, A4.

68. James Kilpatrick, "Spotted-Owl Issue Has National Implications," *Seattle Times*, 10 June 1990, A22.

69. John Lancaster, "Lujan: Endangered Species Act 'Too Tough,' Needs Changes," *Washington Post*, 12 May 1990, A1.

70. See Lancaster, "Lujan: Endangered Species Act 'Too Tough,' Needs Changes," A1.

71. See *Congressional Record*, 101st Cong., 2d sess., 14 May 1990, vol. 136, H2269-01.

72. *Congressional Record*, 101st Cong., 2d sess., 6 Sep. 1990, vol. 136, E2747-01.

73. See Donella Meadows, "Preserving Biodiversity Is Protecting Life on Earth," *Los Angeles Times*, 13 May 1990, 4.

74. See *Congressional Record*, 101st Cong., 2d sess., 14 May 1990, vol. 136, S6183-02.

75. See David Schaefer, "Endangered Species: Hard Act to Follow," *Seattle Times*, 3 June 1990, B1.

76. See David Schaefer, "Timber Stand: Where Is Bush on the Spotted Owl?" *Washington Post*, 17 May 1990, B1.

77. Hoffman, "Bush Straddles Northern Spotted Owl Controversy," A4.

78. See James Kilpatrick, "Spotted-Owl Issue Has National Implications," *Seattle Times*, 10 June 1990, A22.

79. See U.S. Department of Interior, Fish and Wildlife Service, "Listing Action

Completed for Spotted Owl and Five Other Species," *Endangered Species Technical Bulletin* 15 (July 1990): 4.

80. See Fish and Wildlife Service, "Listing Action Completed for Spotted Owl and Five Other Species," 1.

81. David Schaefer and Sylvia Nogaki, "Threatened: Wildlife Agency Makes It Official on Spotted Owl," *Seattle Times*, 22 June 1990, A1.

82. See John Lancaster, "Northern Spotted Owl Is 'Threatened,'" *Washington Post*, 23 June 1990, A1.

83. See Fish and Wildlife Service, "Listing Action Completed for Spotted Owl and Five Other Species," 5.

84. Lancaster, "Northern Spotted Owl Is 'Threatened,'" A1; see also David Schaefer, "Foley Walks Middle Ground on Issue of Spotted Owl," *Seattle Times*, 29 June, 1990, B1.

85. See Schaefer and Nogaki, "Threatened: Wildlife Agency Makes It Official on Spotted Owl," A1.

86. Keith Ervin, Jim Simon, and David Schaefer, "The Spotted Owl: Threatened Species," *Seattle Times*, 23 June 1990, A1.

87. Paul Taylor, "Spotted Owl Creates Flap in Governor's Campaign," *Washington Post*, 6 July 1990, A6.

CHAPTER 6. GIVING A HOOT

1. U.S. Congress, House, Committee on Merchant Marine and Fisheries, Subcommittee on Fisheries and Wildlife Conservation and the Environment, *The Northern Spotted Owl and the Endangered Species Act*, hearing, 101st Cong., 2d sess., 18 July 1990 (Washington, D.C.: GPO, 1990), 1.

2. Subcommittee on Fisheries and Wildlife Conservation and the Environment, *The Northern Spotted Owl and the Endangered Species Act*, 3–4.

3. See U.S. Congress, House, Committee of Interior and Insular Affairs, Subcommittee on National Parks and Public Lands, *Protection of Ancient Forests and Northern Spotted Owl*, hearing, 101st Cong., 2d sess., 24 July 1990 (Washington, D.C.: GPO, 1990), 11, 34.

4. See Subcommittee on National Parks and Public Lands, *Protection of Ancient Forests and Northern Spotted Owl*, 17, 39.

5. See, for example, the testimony of James Blomquist of the Sierra Club, Subcommittee on National Parks and Public Lands, *Protection of Ancient Forests and Northern Spotted Owl*, 151–152.

6. See the testimony of Dale Robertson, chief of the U.S. Forest Service, Subcommittee on National Parks and Public Lands, *Protection of Ancient Forests and Northern Spotted Owl*, 87.

7. Dan Morgan, "Environmentalists Win 1, Lose 2 Votes in Senate," *Washington Post*, 24 Oct. 1990, A6.

8. See David Schaefer, "Effort to Speed Appeals of Spotted Owl Decision Fails," *Seattle Times*, 24 Oct. 1990, H1.

9. See Scott Sonner, "Politicians Standing Up for Beaten-Down Loggers," *Seattle Times*, 12 Aug. 1990, B7.

10. See Scott Sonner, "Spotted Owl Leads to U.S. Review of Public Land Policy," *Seattle Times*, 18 Jan. 1991, D9.

11. See "Living with the Spotted Owl," editorial, *Seattle Times*, 5 May 1991, A14.

12. See *Gifford Pinchot Alliance v. Butruille*, 742 F.Supp. 1077 (D. Or. 1990).

13. See Keith Ervin, "Loggers Turn the Tables," *Seattle Times*, 12 Oct. 1990, A1.

14. 16 U.S.C. Annotated Sec. 1533(a)(3).

15. See *Northern Spotted Owl v. Lujan*, 758 F.Supp. 621 (W.D. Wa. 1991).

16. See U.S. Department of Interior, Fish and Wildlife Service, "Critical Habitat Designation Proposed for the Northern Spotted Owl," *Endangered Species Technical Bulletin* 16 (June 1991): 3.

17. See "Feds' New Spotted-Owl Plan Hooted By All Sides," *Seattle Times*, 6 Aug. 1991, E1.

18. "Federal Plan to Reserve Land for Spotted Owl Draws Protest," *Seattle Times*, 18 Sep. 1991, B4.

19. *Seattle Audubon Society v. Evans*, 771 F.Supp. 1081, 1096 (W.D. Wa. 1991).

20. See *Seattle Audubon Society v. Evans*, 952 F.2d 297 (9th Cir. 1991).

21. See *Lane County Audubon Society v. Jamison*, 1991 WL 354885 (D. Or. 1991).

22. See *Lane County Audubon Society v. Jamison*, 958 F.2d 290 (9th Cir. 1992).

23. See Bill Dietrich, "Wholesale Lumber Costs Grow Quickly," *Seattle Times*, 31 May 1991, D8.

24. See *Sweet Home Chapter of Communities for a Greater Oregon v. Babbitt*, 806 F.Supp. 279 (D.D.C. 1992).

25. See Linda Shaw, "Bird Nailed to Tree Was a Spotted Owl," *Seattle Times*, 6 Aug. 1991, E1.

26. See "Agency Seeks Referee in Fight Over Spotted Owl," *Washington Post*, 12 Sep. 1991, A21.

27. See Tom Kenworthy, "Lujan to Assemble Panel to Study Spotted Owl-Timber Industry Issue," *Washington Post*, 2 Oct. 1991, A21.

28. Kenworthy, "Lujan to Assemble Panel to Study Spotted Owl-Timber Industry Issue," A21.

29. Tom Kenworthy, "'God Squad' to Ponder Spotted Owl," *Washington Post*, 21 Oct. 1991, A17.

30. "Panel Could Allow Logging Despite Peril to Spotted Owl," *Seattle Times*, 2 Oct. 1991, F1.

31. Kenworthy, "Lujan to Assemble Panel to Study Spotted Owl-Timber Industry Issue," A21.

32. See U.S. Congress, House, Committee on Agriculture, Subcommittee on Forests, Family Farms, and Energy, and Committee on Interior and Insular Affairs, Subcommittee on National Parks and Public Lands, *Review of the Report "Alternatives for Management of Late-Successional Forests of the Pacific Northwest" by the Scientific Panel of Late-Successional Forest Ecosystems*, joint hearing, 101st Cong., 2d sess., 18 July 1990 (Washington, D.C.: GPO, 1990), 4.

33. See Subcommittee on Forests, Family Farms, and Energy, *Review of the Report "Alternatives for Management of Late-Successional Forests of the Pacific Northwest,"* 8–9.

34. *Congressional Record*, 102d Cong., 1st sess., 26 Nov. 1991, vol. 137, E4125-02.

35. See "Biologists Say Spotted Owls Reproduce Only in Old Growth," *Seattle Times*, 25 Dec. 1991, A12.

36. See *Congressional Record*, 102d Cong., 1st sess., 26 Nov. 1991, vol. 137, S18539-02.

37. See *Congressional Record*, 102d Cong., 1st sess., 26 Nov. 1991, vol. 137, S18539-02.

38. See National Research Council, Board on Environmental Studies and Tox-

icology, Committee on Scientific Issues in the Endangered Species Act, *Science and the Endangered Species Act* (Washington, D.C.: National Academy Press, 1995), 3.

39. See "Recovering the Spotted Owl," editorial, *Seattle Times*, 15 Dec. 1991, A22.

40. Tom Kenworthy, "Lujan to Name Third Panel on Northern Spotted Owl," *Washington Post*, 19 Feb. 1992, A2.

41. See Kenworthy, "Lujan to Name Third Panel on Northern Spotted Owl," A2.

42. "Lujan's Stalling on Owl Plan No Help to Loggers," editorial, *Seattle Times*, 25 Feb. 1992, A6.

43. See Kenworthy, "Lujan to Name Third Panel on Northern Spotted Owl," A2.

44. U.S. Congress, House, Committee on Interior and Insular Affairs, Subcommittee on National Parks and Public Lands, *The Administration's Response to the Spotted Owl Crisis*, joint oversight hearing, 102d Cong., 2d sess., 24 Mar. 1992 (Washington, D.C.: GPO, 1992), 1.

45. Subcommittee on National Parks and Public Lands, *The Administration's Response to the Spotted Owl Crisis*, 1.

46. See Subcommittee on National Parks and Public Lands, *The Administration's Response to the Spotted Owl Crisis*, 1–2.

47. See Subcommittee on National Parks and Public Lands, *The Administration's Response to the Spotted Owl Crisis*, 16.

48. See Subcommittee on National Parks and Public Lands, *The Administration's Response to the Spotted Owl Crisis*, 16–17.

49. U.S. Congress, Senate, Committee on Environment and Public Works, Subcommittee on Environmental Protection, *Reauthorization of the Endangered Species Act*, hearing, 102d Cong., 2d sess., 10 Apr. 1992 (Washington, D.C.: GPO, 1992), 1.

50. See Subcommittee on Environmental Protection, *Reauthorization of the Endangered Species Act*, 5.

51. See Subcommittee on Environmental Protection, *Reauthorization of the Endangered Species Act*, 1992, 5–6.

52. *Congressional Record*, 102d Cong., 2d sess., 7 May 1992, vol. 138, H3025-01.

53. *Congressional Record*, 102d Cong., 2d sess., 5 May 1992, vol. 138, S6033-01.

54. See U.S. Congress, Senate, Committee on Environment and Public Works, Subcommittee on Environmental Protection, *Conservation of the Northern Spotted Owl*, hearing, 102d Cong., 2d sess., 13 May 1992 (Washington, D.C.: GPO, 1992), 1–2.

55. See Scott Sonner, "Bush Taken to Task Over Spotted Owl," *Seattle Times*, 24 Mar. 1992, B4; Scott Sonner, "Federal Official Defense Law Protecting the Spotted Owl," *Seattle Times*, 30 Apr. 1992, F4.

56. See Scott Sonner, "Economic Effects of Logging Bans Overemphasized, Say Two Reports," *Seattle Times*, 22 Mar. 1992, B3.

57. See U.S. Department of Interior, *Report of the Secretary of the Interior to the Endangered Species Committee: Related to the Application by the Bureau of Land Management for Exemption from the Requirements of Section 7(a)(2) of the Endangered Species Act* (Washington, D.C.: GPO, 1992).

58. See David Schaefer and Eric Pryne, "Bush Takes Offensive on Spotted-Owl Debate," *Seattle Times*, 14 May 1992, A1.

59. Schaefer and Pryne, "Bush Takes Offensive on Spotted-Owl Debate," A1.

60. See Schaefer and Pryne, "Bush Takes Offensive on Spotted-Owl Debate,"A1.

61. "Battling Over Old-Growth," editorial, *Seattle Times*, 18 May 1992, A6.

62. See U.S. General Accounting Office, "Endangered Species Act: Types and Numbers of Implementing Actions," *Reports and Testimony* 199 (1 June 1992).

63. See U.S. General Accounting Office, "Endangered Species Act: Factors Associated with Delayed Listing Decisions," *Reports and Testimony* 199 (1 Aug. 1992).

64. "Agriculture Chief Says Spotted Owl Is Doomed," *Seattle Times*, 15 July 1992, B2.

65. "Agriculture Chief Says Spotted Owl Is Doomed," *Seattle Times*, 15 July 1992, B2.

66. Ruth Marcus, "Endangered Species Act Must Change, Bush Says," *Washington Post*, 15 Sep. 1992, A8.

67. Marcus, "Endangered Species Act Must Change, Bush Says," A8.

68. Elliot Diringer, "Bush Leaving 'Green' Vote to Clinton," *San Francisco Chronicle*, 15 Sep. 1992, A2.

69. Marcus, "Endangered Species Act Must Change, Bush Says," A8.

70. *Congressional Record*, 102d Cong., 2d sess., 15 Sep. 1992, vol. 138, H8362-05.

71. See *Congressional Record*, 102d Cong., 2d sess., 15 Sep. 1992, vol. 138, H8362-05.

72. See Diringer, "Bush Leaving 'Green' Vote to Clinton," A2.

73. See "Lujan Leaves Spotted Owl Decision to Successor," *Washington Post*, 15 Jan. 1993, A10.

74. See *Portland Audubon Society v. Endangered Species Committee*, 984 F.2d 1534, 1550 (9th Cir. 1993).

75. See the report of the Scientific Analysis Team in Jack Ward Thomas et al., *Viability Assessments and Management Considerations for Species Associated with Late-Successional and Old-Growth Forests in the Pacific Northwest* (U.S. Forest Service, 1993).

76. Paul Richter, "Clinton Calls on Cabinet to Craft Forest-Jobs Plan," *Los Angeles Times*, 3 Apr. 1993, 1.

77. Richter, "Clinton Calls on Cabinet to Craft Forest-Jobs Plan," 1.

78. See Jim Pissot, "Timber Troubles: The Spotted Owl Is Not the Cause of the Northwest Forest Crisis," *Washington Post*, 2 Apr. 1993, A25.

79. See Eric D. Forsman et al., eds., *Demography of the Northern Spotted Owl* (Camarillo, Calif.: Cooper Ornithological Society, 1996), 1.

80. See Forest Ecosystem Management Assessment Team, *Forest Ecosystem Management: An Ecological, Economic, and Social Assessment* (Portland, Ore.: U.S. Depts. of Agriculture, Interior, and Commerce and the EPA, 1993), III-2.

81. See U.S. Forest Service et al., "Joint Draft Supplemental Environmental Impact Statement on Management of Habitat for Late-Successional and Old-Growth Forest Related Species Within the Range of the Northern Spotted Owl," 58 *Federal Register* 40444–40445 (28 July 1993).

82. See Roberta Ulrich and Don Hamilton, "Expected Forest Plan Draws NW Fire," *Portland Oregonian*, 29 June 1993, A9.

83. "Timber People Rip Clinton's Forest Plan," *Portland Oregonian*, 28 Sep. 1993, B5.

84. See Joan Laatz, "Clinton Plan Would Ease NW Logging Limits," *Portland Oregonian*, 11 Dec. 1993, A1.

85. Richter, "Clinton Calls on Cabinet to Craft Forest-Jobs Plan," 1.

86. William Clinton, *Public Papers of the Presidents of the United States, 1994,* vol. 1 (Washington, D.C.: GPO, 1994), 697.

87. *Seattle Audubon Society v. Lyons,* 871 F.Supp. 1291, 1300 (W.D. Wa. 1994); see also Eric Pryne, "Clinton Forest Plan Upheld," *Seattle Times,* 21 Dec. 1994, A1.

88. See *Seattle Audubon Society v. Moseley,* 80 F.3d 1401 (9th Cir. 1996).

89. U.S. Congress, House, Committee on Merchant Marine and Fisheries Resources, Subcommittee on Environment and Natural Resources, *The Endangered Species Act,* hearing, 103d Cong., 1st sess., 27 May 1993 (Washington, D.C.: GPO, 1993), 2.

90. See U.S. Congress, House, Committee on Merchant Marine and Fisheries, Subcommittee on Environment and Natural Resources, *Endangered Species Act Reauthorization—San Antonio,* hearing, 103d Cong., 1st sess., 6 July 1993 (Washington, D.C.: GPO, 1993); see also U.S. Congress, House, Committee on Merchant Marine and Fisheries, Subcommittee on Environment and Natural Resources, *Endangered Species Act Reauthorization—Marcos,* hearing, 103d Cong., 1st sess., 6 July 1993 (Washington, D.C.: GPO, 1993).

91. See U.S. Congress, House, Committee on Merchant Marine and Fisheries, Subcommittee on Environment and Natural Resources, *Endangered Species Act—Incentives to Encourage Conservation by Private Landowners,* hearing, 103d Cong., 1st sess., 13 Oct. 1993 (Washington, D.C.: GPO, 1994).

92. See "Forest Plan Sought before Endangered Act's Renewed," *Portland Oregonian,* 22 Sep. 1993, C2.

93. See opening statement of Senator Max Baucus (D-MT), U.S. Congress, Senate, Committee on Environment and Public Works, *Endangered Species Act Amendments of 1993,* hearing, 103d Cong., 2d sess., 23 July 1994 (Washington, D.C.: GPO, 1994), 1.

94. See Bruce Babbitt, "The Endangered Species Act and 'Taking': A Call for Innovation," *Environmental Law* 24 (1994): 361, 356.

95. *Congressional Record,* 104th Cong., 1st sess., 18 July 1995, vol. 141, E1455-06.

96. See Cindy Skrzycki, "Hill Republicans Promise a Regulatory Revolution," *Washington Post,* 4 Jan. 1995, A1.

97. See Tom Kenworthy, "House Passes Landowner Rights Bill," *Washington Post,* 4 Mar. 1995, A1.

98. See Bob Benenson, "Endangered Species Act Comes under the Gun," *Congressional Quarterly Weekly Report,* 18 Mar. 1995, 807.

99. See "House Panel's Bill Spares Parks, Limits Endangered Species Act," *Washington Post,* 16 June 1995, A11.

100. Opening statement of Dirk Kempthorne (R-ID), U.S. Congress, Senate, Committee on Environment and Public Works, Subcommittee on Drinking Water, Fisheries, and Wildlife, *Endangered Species Act: Review of Federal Agency Actions and Court Orders under Section 7 Provisions,* hearing, 104th Cong., 1st sess., 2 Mar. 1995 (Washington, D.C.: GPO, 1995), 2.

101. See U.S. Congress, House, Committee on Resources, Task Force on Endangered Species Act, *Endangered Species Act, Vancouver, Washington,* hearing, 104th Cong., 1st sess., 24 Apr. 1995 (Washington, D.C.: GPO, 1995); U.S. Congress, House, Committee on Resources, Task Force on Endangered Species Act, *Endangered Species Act, Stockton, California,* hearing, 104th Cong., 1st sess., 28 Apr. 1995 (Washington, D.C.: GPO, 1995); U.S. Congress, Senate, Committee on Environment and Public Works, Subcommittee on Drinking Water, Fisheries, and Wildlife, *Endangered Species Act Reauthorization,* field hearings, 104th Cong., 1st sess., 1, 3 June, 16 Aug. 1995 (Washington, D.C.: GPO, 1996).

102. See U.S. Congress, House, Committee on Resources, Task Force on Endangered Species Act, *Endangered Species Act: Washington, D.C.—Part I*, hearing, 104th Cong., 1st sess., 10 May 1995 (Washington, D.C.: GPO, 1995); U.S. Congress, House, Committee on Resources, Task Force on Endangered Species Act, *Endangered Species Act: Washington, D.C.—Part II*, hearing, 104th Cong., 1st sess., 10 May 1995 (Washington, D.C.: GPO, 1995); U.S. Congress, House, Committee on Resources, Task Force on Endangered Species Act, *Endangered Species Act: Washington, D.C.—Part III*, hearing, 104th Cong., 1st sess., 25 May 1995 (Washington, D.C.: GPO, 1995).

103. *Congressional Record*, 104th Cong., 1st sess., 10 May 1995, vol. 141, S6423-02.

104. See *Congressional Record*, 104th Cong., 1st sess., 10 May 1995, vol. 141, S6423-02; see also "Senators Introduce Restraints on Endangered Species Act," *Congressional Quarterly Weekly Report*, 18 May 1995, 1324.

105. See testimony of Secretary of the Interior Bruce Babbitt, U.S. Congress, Senate, Committee on Environment and Public Works, Subcommittee on Drinking Water, Fisheries, and Wildlife, *Moratorium on the Listing Provisions of the Endangered Species Act*, 104th Cong., 1st sess., 7 Mar. 1995 (Washington, D.C.: GPO, 1995), 26.

106. The author was the local resident who asked the question. See William Clinton, "Remarks at a Town Meeting in Billings," *Weekly Compilation of Presidential Documents* 31 (5 June 1995).

107. William Clinton, "Message to the House of Representatives Returning without Approval the Department of Interior and Related Agencies Appropriations Act," *Weekly Compilation of Presidential Documents* 31 (25 Dec. 1995).

108. See *Sweet Home Chapter of Communities for a Greater Oregon v. Babbitt*, 806 F.Supp. 285 (D. Or. 1992).

109. *Sweet Home Chapter of Communities for a Greater Oregon v. Babbitt*, 17 F.3d 1463, 1465 (D.C. Cir. 1994).

110. See *Palila v. Hawaii Department of Land and Natural Resources*, 852 F.2d 1106 (9th Cir. 1988); see also Natalie Angier, "Endangered Species Act in Danger," *San Francisco Chronicle*, 24 Nov. 1994, A17.

111. See Petitioner's Brief, *Babbitt v. Sweet Home Chapter of Communities for a Greater Oregon*, 515 U.S. 687 (1995), 1995 WL 89293 (Westlaw), 20.

112. See Respondent's Brief, *Babbitt v. Sweet Home Chapter of Communities for a Greater Oregon*, 515 U.S. 687 (1995), 1995 WL 130541 (Westlaw), 8.

113. See Reply Brief for the Petitioners, *Babbitt v. Sweet Home Chapter of Communities for a Greater Oregon*, 515 U.S. 687 (1995), 1995 WL 170170 (Westlaw).

114. See Oral Arguments, *Babbitt v. Sweet Home Chapter of Communities for a Greater Oregon*, 515 U.S. 687 (1995), 1995 WL 170170 (Westlaw).

115. See Joan Biskupic, "Justices Hear Key Case on Species Act," *Washington Post*, 18 Apr. 1995, A1.

116. See *Babbitt v. Sweet Home Chapter of Communities for a Greater Oregon*, 515 U.S. 687, 697 (1995).

117. See *Babbitt v. Sweet Home Chapter of Communities for a Greater Oregon*, 515 U.S. 687, 709 (1995).

118. Tom Kenworthy, "Justices Affirm Wide Power to Protect Wildlife Habitat," *Washington Post*, 30 June 1995, A1.

119. See "Endangered Species Act," *Congressional Quarterly Weekly Report*, 5 Sep. 1995, 2640.

120. Alex Barhum, "House GOP Turns Sights on Endangered Species Act," *San Francisco Chronicle*, 20 Sep. 1995, A8.

121. See "House Panel Votes to Restrict Endangered Species Act," *Congressional Quarterly Weekly Report*, 16 Oct. 1995, 3136.

122. D'Jamila Salem, "Campaign '96: Stronger Endangered Species Law Urged," *Los Angeles Times*, 1 Feb. 1996, 12.

123. Salem, "Campaign '96: Stronger Endangered Species Law Urged," 12.

124. Salem, "Campaign '96: Stronger Endangered Species Law Urged," 12.

125. Mark O'Keefe, "Religious Groups Reach Out, Embrace the Environment," *Portland Oregonian*, 3 Feb. 1996, A1.

126. Bill Broadway, "Tending God's Garden: Evangelical Group Embraces Environment," *Washington Post*, 17 Feb. 1996, C8.

127. O'Keefe, "Religious Groups Reach Out, Embrace the Environment," A1.

128. Broadway, "Tending God's Garden: Evangelical Group Embraces Environment," C8.

129. Broadway, "Tending God's Garden: Evangelical Group Embraces Environment," C8.

130. Ministry of God's Creation, *A Call to Defend God's Creation* (Washington, D.C.: Ministry of God's Creation, 1996), 2.

131. Ministry of God's Creation, *A Call to Defend God's Creation*, 4.

132. "House Minority Leader Richard Gephardt and Others Hold News Conference to Discuss Republican Record on Environmental Issues," verbatim transcript, 12 July 1996, Federal Document Clearinghouse, Westlaw Database, 1996 WL 392595.

133. "Congressional Democrats Hold Press Briefing Regarding the Republican Contract with America," verbatim transcript, 27 Sep. 1996, Federal Document Clearinghouse, Westlaw Database, 1996 WL 548952.

134. Bruce Babbitt, "Between the Flood and the Rainbow: Our Covenant to Protect the Whole of Creation," *Animal Law* 2 (1996): 5.

135. See Salem, "Campaign '96: Stronger Endangered Species Law Urged," 12.

136. Newt Gingrich, "Remarks on the Republican Environmental Agenda at a National Environmental Policy Institute Conference," verbatim transcript, 24 Apr. 1996, Federal Document Clearinghouse, Westlaw Database, 1996 WL 199457.

CONCLUSION

1. See Thomas Lovejoy, "Biodiversity: What Is It?" in *Biodiversity II: Understanding and Protecting Our Biological Resources*, ed. Marjorie L. Reaka-Kudla et al. (Washington, D.C.: Joseph Henry Press, 1997), 7.

2. See Edward Wilson, "Threats to Biodiversity," *Scientific America* (September 1989): 108.

3. See National Research Council, Board on Environmental Studies and Toxicology, Committee on Scientific Issues in the Endangered Species Act, *Science and the Endangered Species Act* (Washington, D.C.: National Academy Press, 1995), 5.

4. See Wilson, "Threats to Biodiversity," 108.

5. See National Research Council, *Science and the Endangered Species Act*, viii.

6. See National Research Council, *Science and the Endangered Species Act*, 27–29.

7. National Research Council, *Science and the Endangered Species Act*, 1.

8. See National Research Council, *Science and the Endangered Species Act*, 25.

9. See U.S. Fish and Wildlife Service, *Endangered Species Page* (visited 8 Nov. 2000) at *http://www.fws.gov.*

10. See F. Stuart Chapin et al., "Biotic Control over the Functioning of Ecosystems," 277 *Science* (1997): 500.

11. See *http://www.fws.gov.*

12. See Norman Myers, *A Wealth of Wild Species* (Boulder, Colo.: Westview Press, 1983), 106–107.

13. See Al Gore, *Earth in the Balance: Ecology and the Human Spirit* (New York: Plume, 1992), 139.

14. See, generally, Paul Ehrlich, *The Science of Ecology* (New York: Collier Macmillan Press, 1987).

15. Henry David Thoreau, *The Journal of Henry D. Thoreau*, ed. Bradford Torrey and Francis Allen (New York: Dover, 1962), 221.

16. See 16 U.S.C. § 1531(a)(3).

17. Gore, *Earth in the Balance*, 245.

18. National Research Council, *Science and the Endangered Species Act*, 1.

19. See U.S. Fish and Wildlife Service, *Endangered Species Page* (visited 20 Oct. 1998) at <*http://www.fws.gov/~r9endspp*>.

20. See Peter Kendall, "Eagle Soaring Off Threatened List," *Chicago Tribune*, 7 May 1998, 1.

21. See National Research Council, *Science and the Endangered Species Act*, 33.

22. See Jeffrey J. Rachlinski, "Noah by the Numbers: An Empirical Evaluation of the Endangered Species Act," *Cornell Law Review* 82 (1997): 383.

23. See *http://www.fws.gov.*

24. Jody Warrick, "Babbitt Sets Plan to Pare Endangered Species List," *Washington Post*, 6 May 1998, A3.

Index